Due Back			
2/12/16			

Cover illustration by Helen Milroy: *Dedicated to Mothers and Fathers*

First published in 2008 from a completed manuscript presented to
Australian Academic Press
32 Jeays Street
Bowen Hills Qld 4006
Australia
www.australianacademicpress.com.au

National Library of Australia cataloguing-in-publication entry:

> Infants of parents with mental illness : developmental,
> clinical, cultural and personal perspectives / editorsl
> Anne Sved Williams and Vicki Cowling.
>
> 1st ed.
>
> 9781921513039 (pbk.)
>
> Children of the mentally ill--Australia.
> Mentally ill--Australia.
>
> Cowling, Vicki
> Williams, Anne Sved
>
> 362.20854

Cover and text design by Andrea Rinarelli of Australian Academic Press, Brisbane.

This book is dedicated to our grandchildren, Ava and Tor, and Max, Sam and Chloe. Our profound hopes go with you that all the knowledge about infant mental health will enrich your lives.

Foreword

Second to one's own personal health, I truly believe that family is the most important aspect of a person's life. If you don't have good health yourself, you cannot be there for or assist your family. This book encapsulates the essence of these two very fundamental aspects of a person's life — health and family — and emphasises their importance for their wellbeing.

Depression and anxiety surrounding childbirth can have a profound impact on people from all walks of life and all cultures, justifying the importance of addressing perinatal mental health across Australia, involving both professionals and those directly affected. This book, *Infants of Parents with Mental Illness — Developmental, Clinical, Cultural and Personal Perspectives* addresses these disorders and other severe mental illnesses that may affect infant-parent relationships and infant development.

The book encompasses a wide range of insights and perspectives, both from clinical experts in the field and people who have lived through adverse experiences of one form or another in their lifetime. By integrating this range of information and experience, this resource assists us to learn and understand more about the impact that adverse life events may have on not only mother and infant, but the whole family, thus assisting practitioners in their work with infants and their parents.

In reading the chapters I acknowledge in particular the strength and courage of those who have shared their very personal experiences and perspectives. By doing so, they enable many of us to gain a deeper understanding of life's challenges and how they can impact on the mental health and wellbeing of families.

Another vital aspect of this book is its focus on the infant. A strong and healthy culture is one which values infants and their parents, and understands that meeting the physical and emotional needs of an infant sets that infant on a better pathway in life.

The book reminds us of the crucial importance of positive mental health surrounding a major life event, such as childbirth. Many of us — individuals, organisations and governments — are currently working to improve the detection, management and treatment of mental health problems at this time of life. This book is a strong contributor to addressing these issues and admirably complements the work undertaken by *beyondblue* to reform perinatal mental health throughout Australia.

The Hon Jeff Kennett
Chairman
beyondblue: the national depression initiative

Contents

Acknowledgments

—⁓—

Our sincere thanks go to each of the 24 authors who have contributed to this book. Some were invited to contribute when the book was just an idea, and have maintained their commitment to this publication for over four years.

All authors have met publication deadlines and requirements alongside other aspects of life such as work, birth of new family members, and death, and illness — including one author working on a chapter while in hospital.

A special acknowledgment is extended to those who have contributed as parents, partners, adult family members and grandparents. For some, this writing brings back painful aspects of the past and experiences that they may prefer to forget. Each person we approached responded to the invitation to contribute as they believe it will contribute to greater community understanding about people who have a mental illness. Our thanks to Amy, Nichole, Kevin, Jennifer, Paola, and to Sam's grandmother.

Thanks to Stephen May, Australian Academic Press, for his support in publishing this book, with the important information it contains, where others had declined our invitation to do so.

And our thanks to our families and friends for their support through each stage of the development of the book over the past 4 years.

Anne Sved Williams and Vicki Cowling

—⁓—

Increasing Knowledge, Increasing Hope for Infants?

Anne Sved Williams

‒‒‒

So much is known now about infants and their physical development. Science has contributed rich knowledge of the development of humans from prior to conception, as in vitro fertilisation has seen enormous progress in our understanding of the behaviour of sperm and ova. The time in the womb has shed some of its mystery as techniques such as ultrasound improve, and macroscopic and microscopic development in the first 3 years of life has been explored, investigated, documented and in many ways mastered.

During the last 100 years, survival of the human infant has improved dramatically. In 1901, the first year of Australia as a federated nation, more than 1 in 10 infants died before the age of 1 year and the infant mortality rate was 103.6 per 1000 live births (Hugo, 2001). The comparable figure in 1999, the last year of the century, was 5.3 and by 2007, even lower at 4.6 per 1000 live births.

The *New York Times* of August 6, 1906, noted that in the preceding week, 1653 children under the age of 5 years had died (from a total of 1804 deaths in New York). Dr Guilfoy of the Department of Health said that the improper feeding of infants was to blame. 'We have been trying to teach the mothers in the poorer sections of the city not to feed their infants meat and unripe fruit in the Summer. We have made considerable progress among the mothers . . . .'

The physical survival of children through their early years is therefore generally much better guaranteed in most 'Western' countries, with improvements in knowledge; for example, in sanitation, the treatment of infections, refrigeration, hygiene, immunisations, and perinatal care. Sadly, even in

Australia, this improvement is variable as, for example, examination of infant mortality in Aboriginal populations reveals. From 1999 to 2003, the mortality rate for Indigenous infants from three states (Western and South Australia, and Queensland) and the Northern Territory was 15 per 1000 live births for males and 12 per 1000 live births for females — three times the rate for non-Indigenous babies (Australian Institute of Health and Welfare, 2006). Infant mortality is a marker for many factors related to total population health: access to prenatal and postnatal health facilities and maternal education are clear contributors to better outcomes.

Thus even in a developed country such as Australia, physical health for infants is highly variable, despite the advances of science and technology. It has now become clear that for optimum emotional development, many additional variables begin to influence outcomes. Not only must physical development and health be adequate, but the presence of factors such as good-enough parenting, and the absence of others such as substance abuse and domestic violence, are now becoming better understood.

Science also continues to advance in this field, but the complexities involved make total understanding more challenging. In fact, it is clear that to maximise good emotional health as infants grow into adults, an understanding across many disciplines of science will provide a better guide. The corollary of this is that to intervene when circumstances are less than ideal will require both an understanding across disciplines and a rich web of working relationships across agencies. It is only in this way that better outcomes for infants may be achieved both physically and emotionally.

To best understand how to optimise emotional wellbeing for infants, we must understand:

- scientific knowledge through a wide spectrum of disciplines to understand how emotional development takes place
- what factors impinge on this emotional growth in the infant's world and how to assess problem development
- how best to work with families where infants are at risk. This is the substance of this book: to understand how to achieve improved outcomes for infants growing up in situations of risk, mainly focusing on parents' mental health, but also highlighting other related psychosocial circumstances that may impair parental functioning.

In this chapter, I provide a brief overview of the basic science and factors contributing to emotional health in all infants, mainly to guide the reading of those who may be less familiar with infant mental health. Excellent general accounts for working in infant mental health include Zeanah's (2005) comprehensive overview of the field and Mares, Newman, Warren and

Cornish (2005) have published a clear, basic text in this area. Stern (1995) and Sameroff, McDonough and Rosenblum (2004) provide expert accounts of parent–infant therapy.

Emotional Growth

An infant is born into a rich web of relationships, even when those people are notable by their absence. The infant can be considered to be at the centre of a large number of concentric rings, each of which, when functioning optimally, contribute to that infant's general wellbeing. If we assume that an infant is born healthy (not always the case, as will be seen in Chapter 3 about antenatal effects of maternal problems), then close to the infant at the core of the rings will be parents, with mother often the first ring and father surrounding next, close at hand. Extended family is the next logical ring, then neighbourhood, culture and country. There is interchange between these rings as they impinge and impact on one another.

Consider an infant born to loving parents who planned to have this child, and are both physically and emotionally well, with sufficient income to pay for all basic needs and more. The parents are, in turn, supported by a rich network of extended family who all live close at hand and show concern and interest in all infants born into this family. The local childcare and school are excellent; there is an abundance of good medical care, sporting facilities and supplies of food. The infant is physically healthy, belongs to the mainstream culture and is born at a time when the government of the day has produced policies to support paid parenting leave, a total of 3 years shared between the parents. Lucky child!

Now consider an infant conceived in a casual sexual encounter, born to a substance-abusing mother with greatly compromised home circumstances, including the disintegration of her family of origin. The infant's skin colour indicates that his parents are from different ethnic backgrounds. The infant's father is unknown, and is therefore not available to financially support his child. The government of the day has denied income support for parenting. The mother is homeless and her mental health is deteriorating each day. How can this infant survive to an adult life that will be emotionally healthy? It is well known that so many risk factors, as evident in this scenario, are likely to compromise health, and yet resilient children emerge from such situations and can do well. Nevertheless, one would prefer not to leave it to chance. Authors who have studied resilience in the face of adversity include Luthar (2003), Borkowski, Farris, Whitman, Carothers and Weed (2007) and Gordon (1996), building on the original contributions of Haggerty, Sherrod, Garmezy and Rutter (1996) and Anthony and Cohler (1987).

The Development of Emotionally Healthy Infants

The basis of emotional health for infants lies in the attachment relationship they develop with their main caregiver(s). John Bowlby developed his theory during the middle of the 20th century (Bowlby, 1979). Mary Ainsworth further developed this theory, recognising not only that there were secure and insecure modes of attachment, but that they could be reliably measured (Ainsworth, Blehar, Waters, & Wall, 1978). Karen's book (1998) provides an easy reading guide to these theories.

In brief, infants are 'hardwired' to ensure that their physical needs are met, with their cries and endearing mannerisms attracting the attention and care of those around them. They learn in the repetitive day-by-day and minute-by-minute interactions how each carer will respond, and whether the signals will be met sensitively by a person who is emotionally available (Biringen, 2004). The relationship that results with each frequent caregiver is the attachment relationship. The infant whose needs are met by the parent who is 'good-enough' (Winnicott, 1953) is more likely to develop a secure attachment. They will resonate with a profound knowledge that their physical and emotional needs will be met when needed so they can explore and master the world in a confident fashion. The Circle of Security program (Marvin et al., 2002) is a deceptively simple representation of this theory and many of the authors in this book use elements from their program.

Ainsworth originally described secure (depending on the sample, perhaps 65% of all infants) and anxious attachment, subdividing the latter into avoidant and ambivalent (sometimes known as resistant) attachment. Main and colleagues (1985) later described disorganised attachment, generally associated with parenting that is frightening but at times loving or comforting as well, a highly confusing state for an infant. Borderline personality disorders may both produce and result from this form of parenting and are further discussed in Chapter 17.

The style of relating to our principal caregivers in the early years of life tends to become the template for all other relationships throughout life, and remains as a measurable status within us. Hesse (1999) provides a clear account of the Adult Attachment Interview developed by Mary Main to measure adult attachment patterns which correspond, in part, to those developed in infancy. van Ijzendoorn (1992) showed that there is an intergenerational transfer of attachment relationships in nonclinical populations: secure parents will form secure attachment relationships with their offspring. Berlin, Ziv, Amaya-

Jackson and Greenberg (2005) have compiled a state-of-the-art text regarding attachment theory and its ramifications, including ways of intervening to optimise outcomes.

In the last 2 decades, Allan Schore (1994, 2001) has assembled work across many disciplines, including neurobiology, developmental neurochemistry, developmental psychology and psychiatry, and evolutionary biology, to propound mechanisms whereby securely attached infants have more optimal brain growth, particularly of the right cerebral hemisphere with its connections to the limbic system and autonomic nervous system. The concept of hard-wiring is used here too: the nerve cells are in place at birth but their rate of growth depends on the experiences encountered in the early years. Those parents who can sensitively tune into their infants and better provide them with relief from stress will help those infants' brain growth and the associated external signs: more exploration, enhanced learning, calmer behaviour and better coping mechanisms when anxious. This brilliant work has helped us to understand how more optimal parenting is associated with better outcomes for children. Shonkoff and Phillips (2000) have also collated a book that brings together the work of many scientists to give an understanding across disciplines regarding early childhood development. In addition, they move from scientific understanding to recommendations about policies and practices that may make a positive difference to small children's development. Gerhardt (2004) has provided an easy-to-read account of scientific findings on attachment and brain development.

Many other contributions are important in understanding good development. Fonagy and colleagues (1991) introduced the concept of reflective functioning — a person's ability to understand behaviour by relating it to underlying mental functioning. When a parent can reflect on the infant's experience, and understand the state of mind of the other, a rich interconnection develops, which allows the infant to learn over time how to interpret the actions of others as meaningful. Authors such as Slade (2005) describe the central importance of maternal reflective functioning in attachment relationships.

Thus infants raised in homes by parents who reflect on their infants and use this knowledge to meet their physical and emotional needs well enough, are likely to move into childhood with security of attachment, an ability to explore the world well and an understanding of their relationships with others and how to work with them.

Flory (2005), Siegel and Hartzell (2003), and Schmidt Neven (1996), among others, have written clear and easy-to-read accounts of parenting that focus on an understanding of how best to meet children's emotional needs and enhance their attachment relationships.

Problems in Parenting

There are many circumstances in which parenting is likely to be compromised, with the potential for less than optimal outcomes for the infant. Mental illness alone has the potential to impact greatly on parenting and this has been summarised previously (Sved Williams, 2004). In brief, the range of outcomes for infants of mothers with severe or enduring illnesses is highly variable, but schizophrenia particularly is likely to cause problems. Many symptoms of mental illness make good parenting difficult. Irritability or decrease in energy, for instance, associated with bipolar mood disorder or depression will interfere with family functioning. In addition, treatments can also disrupt parenting — heavy sedation will clearly impact on a parent's ability to 'be there' for their child, often particularly at night. All of these issues can also impair the parents' confidence in their ability to manage the tasks at hand, although it must be clearly stated that many mentally ill parents can parent well.

Many other risk factors that impact on optimal outcomes have been identified, and attempts made to quantify and understand them. The combination of mental illness with other psychosocial factors appears to be particularly problematic. Sameroff (1998), after analysis of previous data, followed a group of infants for 20 years, each of whom had a mother with mental illness. Nine other factors were identified for study (Table 1) and Sameroff found that these factors tend to be additive, with rapidly worsening outcomes particularly when more than four are present.

However, in addition to those factors under scrutiny in this longitudinal study, many other issues can cause the undermining of the family and community stability that helps infants to thrive. Some of these are explored in this book. These include:

Table 1

Risk Factors Followed By Sameroff (1998)

- maternal mental illness
- high maternal anxiety
- rigidity of parental attitudes and beliefs about child's development
- few observed positive parent–child interactions
- head of household in unskilled occupation
- minimal maternal education
- disadvantaged minority group
- single parenthood
- stressful life events
- large family size.

- the effects on Aboriginal families when their culture has been destroyed by European invasion (Chapter 12)
- refugee status, which generally severs extended family and 'village' support (Chapter 13)
- substance abuse, which often creates chaos for infant and parents (Chapter 16).

When professionals become aware that an infant's normal emotional and physical development is significantly threatened by family problems, child protection agencies are likely to become involved, as Anne Mercovich describes in Chapter 5. A special issue of the *Infant Mental Health Journal* edited by Stafford and Zeanah (2008) provides another entry point to some of the complex forensic matters that arise in these circumstances, including efforts towards collaboration across diverse agencies and orientations.

Throughout this book, the authors examine the effects of adverse life circumstances on infant and family and, in most cases, also describe assessments and interventions. Several chapters have been written by people personally affected by mental illness, or mental illness of a family member. This provides in-depth and often poignant understanding from the perspective of living with the effects of such illnesses, which helps to expand our knowledge.

In the beginning of this chapter, the gains in physical health for infants during the last 100 years were described. While science has already helped to expand our knowledge during these same 100 years, perhaps particularly in the last four decades, the pace of change is significant. No doubt in 100 years from now, so much more will be known about the brain and attachment relationships and how to optimise them. For now, we hope this book is the state-of-the-art.

References

Ainsworth, M.D.S., Blehar, M.C., Waters, E., & Wall, S. (1978). *Patterns of attachment: A psychological study of the strange situation.* Hillsdale, NJ: Erlbaum.

Anthony, E.J. & B.J. Cohler (Eds.). (1987). *The invulnerable child.* New York: Guilford Press.

Australian Institute of Health and Welfare. (2007). Available at http://www.aihw.gov.au/indigenous/health/mortality.cfm

Berlin, L., Ziv, Y., Amaya-Jackson, L., & Greenberg M. (Eds.). (2005). *Enhancing early attachments: Theory, research, intervention and policy.* New York: Guilford Press.

Biringen, Z. (2004). *Raising a secure child: Creating an emotional connection between you and your child.* New York: Perigee Books.

Borkowski, J.G., Farris, J.R., Whitman, T.L., Carothers, S.S., & Weed, K. (2007). *Risk and resilience: Adolescent mothers and their children grow up.* Hillsdale, NJ: Lawrence Erlbaum.

Bowlby, J. (1979). *The making and breaking of affectional bonds.* London: Tavistock.

Flory, V. (2005). *Your child's emotional needs.* Sydney, Australia: Finch.

Fonagy, P., Steele, M., Steele, H., Moran, G.S., & Higgitt, A. (1991). The capacity for understanding mental states: The reflective self in parent and child and its significance for security of attachment. *Infant Mental Health Journal, 12,* 201–218.

Gerhardt, S. (2004). *Why love matters: How affection shapes a baby's brain.* New York: Brunner-Routledge.

Gordon, K. (1996). *Infant and toddler resilience: Knowledge, predictions, policy and practice.* Paper presented at Headstart Conference. Retrieved January 12, 2008, from http://www.eric.ed.gov/ERICDocs/data/ericdocs2sql/content_storage_01/0000019b/80/14/b9/59.pdf.

Haggerty, R., Sherrod, L., Garmezy, N., & Rutter, M. (Eds.). (1996). *Stress, risk, and resilience in children and adolescents: Processes, mechanisms, and interventions.* Cambridge: Cambridge University Press.

Hesse, E. (1999). Adult Attachment Interview: Historical and current perspectives. In J. Cassidy & P.R. Shaver (Eds.), *Attachment theory, research and clinical applications.* New York: Guilford Press.

Hugo, G. (2001). *A century of population change in Australia. Year Book Australia, 2001.* Australian Bureau of Statistics. Retrieved January 12, 2008, from http://www.abs.gov.au/Ausstats

Karen, R. (1998). *Becoming attached: First relationships and how they shape our capacity to love.* Oxford: Oxford University Press.

Luthar, S.S. (2003). *Resilience and vulnerability: Adaptation in the context of childhood adversities.* Cambridge: Cambridge University Press.

Main, M., Kaplan, N., & Cassidy, J. (1985). Security in infancy, childhood and adulthood: A move to the level of representation. In I. Bretherton & E. Waters (Eds.), *Growing points in attachment theory and research: Monographs of the Society for Social Research in Child Development, 50* (1–2, Serial No. 209) 66–104.

Mares, S., Newman, L., Warren, B., & Cornish, K. (2005). *Clinical skills in infant mental health.* Melbourne, Australia: ACER Press.

Marvin, R., Cooper, G., Hoffman, K., & Powell, B. (2002). The Circle of Security Project: Attachment-based interventions with caregiver-preschool child dyads. *Attachment and Human Development, 4*(1), 107–124.

Sameroff, A. (1998). Environmental risk factors in infancy. *Pediatrics 102* (Suppl. Nov.), 1287–1292.

Sameroff, A., McDonough, S., & Rosenblum, K. (Eds.). (2004). *Treating parent–infant relationship problems: Strategies for intervention.* New York: Guilford Press.

Schmidt Neven, R. (1996). *Emotional milestones from birth to adulthood: A psychodynamic approach.* Melbourne, Australia: ACER Press.

Schore, A. (1994). *Affect regulation and the origin of the self: The neurobiology of emotional development.* Hillsdale, NJ: Erlbaum.

Schore, A. (2001). The effects of a secure attachment relationship on right brain development, affect regulation, and infant mental health. *Infant Mental Health Journal, 22,* 7–66.

Shonkoff, J., & Phillips, D. (Eds.). (2000). *From neurons to neighborhoods: The science of early childhood development.* Washington, DC: National Academy Press.

Siegel, D., & Hartzell, M. (2003). *Parenting from the inside out.* New York: Penguin Putnam.

Slade, A. (2005). Parental reflective functioning: An introduction. *Attachment & Human Development, 7,* 269–281.

Stafford, B., & Zeanah, C. (2008). *Infant Mental Health Journal, 29*(1), 1–75.

Stern, D. (1995). *The motherhood constellation: A unified view of parent-infant psychotherapy.* New York: Basic Books.

Sved Williams, A.E. (2004). Infants of mothers with mental illness. In V. Cowling (Ed.), *Children of parents with mental illness: Personal and clinical perspectives* (pp. 17–40). Melbourne, Australia: ACER Press.

van Ijzendoorn, M. (1992). Intergenerational transmission of parenting: A review of studies in nonclinical populations. *Developmental Review, 12,* 76–99.

Winnicott, D. (1953). Transitional objects and transitional phenomena. *International Journal of Psychoanalysis, 34,* 89–97.

Zeanah, C. Jnr. (2005). *Handbook of Infant Mental Health* (2nd ed.). New York: Guilford Press.

In the Beginning...

9 Months and More

Amy*

*Amy and Skye are pseudonyms

—❦—

I was asked to write about my experience of parenting an infant from ages 0 to
3 years while living with a mental illness, what impact this had on the infant
and the interaction between me and my child. I feel that to be able to give these
issues the necessary credibility they deserve, I need to write about my experiences
during pregnancy, for I believe that they have direct impact on the postnatal issues
that I experienced.

—❦—

Pregnancy

My pregnancy came as a complete surprise. I was very underweight and just
recovering from a suicide attempt by overdosing on a stockpile of prescription
drugs. It was not a planned pregnancy, but definitely not an unwanted one.
To me it felt like a new lease on life — literally. It was the first time in my life
that I felt that I had a goal, an aim, a purpose in life. I cannot say that it was like
that for my partner. We had met only 3 months earlier in a psychiatric hospital
and the stress of becoming a father-to-be exacerbated his mood swings and
binge drinking. I could not rely on him for emotional, physical, practical or
financial support.

Reactions of Mental Health Professionals

It was with great excitement that I informed my case manager of my pregnancy. It would be safe to say that the news was not received with enthusiasm. She promptly picked the phone up and informed me that she was booking me in for a termination of pregnancy at the first available appointment. I was at first flabbergasted. There was no discussion about it. She said that it was her duty of care to make sure that I terminate the pregnancy. I did not handle this well at all and became very cross and agitated. I yelled at her that she could not force me to have an abortion. Her reply to that was that she would have me committed as an involuntary patient and then I would not have a say in the matter. At that point in time I did not know what my legal rights where. I told her that I would rather kill myself than have a termination and I ran out of the clinic in tears.

I walked the streets for some time to try to clear my mind and take stock of the situation. When I did return home, there were three members of the crisis assessment team waiting for me. I wanted to run away for fear that they were there to take me away to hospital and strip me of my personal right to decide what happened with my own body and my life. However, I physically could not run any longer. They reassured me that they were not there to take me away, just to make sure that I was okay and safe. They offered me some Valium™, which I didn't take for I was unsure how it would affect the foetus. They asked me if I could guarantee my safety. I told them that I was not suicidal — far from it — I was just disillusioned by my case manager and bone tired, as you can only get in the first trimester of pregnancy.

They came back the next morning to see how I was going and to tell me that I had an appointment with my psychiatrist that afternoon. I was fearful of going to the clinic as I did not wish to see my case manager. They told me that it was within my rights to ask for a change of case manager.

When I arrived at my appointment my doctor suggested that I think of having a termination as a responsible option. I told him that it was not an option and that it was better if we discussed other options. We discussed the medication I was taking at that time and it was decided that I talk about this with the psychiatrist from the Mother–Baby Unit (MBU), as she specialised in this area.

I was allocated to a new case manager who was very proactive in supporting me throughout the pregnancy. She linked me in to the MBU in the area as well as to the Mother's Support Program (MSP), an outreach program for mothers with a mental illness.

I had regular appointments with the psychiatrist from the MBU. It was decided that I would come off all my medication except the antidepressants, as the other medications I was taking had not been tested on pregnant women. I didn't want to take any risks and, after much deliberation, I decided to come off my antidepressant as well. In hindsight that was not a good idea. It made things even harder, and I didn't have the emotional buffer that an antidepressant gives you, and having them on board during the postnatal period may have helped me.

Towards the end of my second trimester my partner and I moved into a lovely little flat, made available by the Mother's Support Program. I should have been elated that I had a place to call my own and to welcome my child into, but it seemed to heighten my feelings of isolation, loneliness and sadness. Cognitively, I knew that I was meant to be feeling excited and preparing for the arrival of my child, but in reality I felt lethargic and down most days. I slept most of the time, the house went unkempt most of the time, and so did I.

My doctors suggested that I return to taking antidepressants, but I would not have a bar of it. I didn't want anything having a detrimental effect on the baby. I wasn't thinking clearly and this was having a negative impact on the whole situation. So there were many unsettling factors even before I had given birth:

- I had no emotional or social supports.
- My relationship with the father of my unborn child was unstable.
- My financial situation was questionable.
- Although I had housing for the next 6 months, where I would go after that was playing greatly on my mind.
- I felt that the health professionals around me doubted my ability to be a good mother, and that made me question myself as well. However, being linked into the MBU was a very positive aspect. It enabled me to be hospitalised when I needed to be, with the minimum of difficulty.

Looking back on my pregnancy I'd say that I was depressed the majority of the 9 months. All these things had a great impact on my state of mind and my ability to cope as a new parent, when the time came.

Welcome to This World

I had wanted to give birth in the Birthing Unit. I wanted the least amount of intervention needed, while still being in the security of the hospital. All the antenatal classes were geared towards a birth in the unit. So when Skye* was in foetal distress at the beginning of labour, I went to the normal labour ward. I was not prepared for this. Bright lights, beeping of machines and monitors, people rushing all over the place — in short, a labour ward. Nothing like my idea of the idyllic birthing suite I had looked forward to, with its quiet, calming music and spa bath and dimming lights. I was unprepared for this.

The doctors needed to monitor Skye's heartbeat and wanted to put a clip onto her scalp. I did not want the first thing she felt to be nonhuman so they put a monitor around my stomach, which restricted my movements. Ultimately, she was around the wrong way so she was delivered by forceps and the doctors took her straight away to suction out the meconium she may have swallowed.

The lioness within me emerged — a primal urge ripped through me. My partner was holding Skye but I would have killed to get to her if he had not handed her to me. There was nothing wrong with my motherly instincts, they were as intact as they could possibly be. I held her close to me. She gave a few little bleating cries as she rooted around for my nipple, then she settled in for a long, long, well-deserved drink.

One has the way that you want to bring your child into the world in mind, and when the experience doesn't meet your expectation there is a feeling of loss, grief disappointment and guilt. This is especially so if the labour and birthing process has been a negative one. That is how I felt after my birthing experience. I felt robbed of the ideal way I wanted to welcome my child into the world. I also felt guilty that I had somehow contributed to pain inflicted on Skye as she was pulled from the birthing canal by cold hard forceps. She had bruise marks around her ears and temples for a good week after the birth. I didn't tell anyone how I felt for fear that they may deem these thoughts as irrational or an over-exaggeration; however, for me they where real and true and very intense.

I was sent home within 24 hours of giving birth. I was sore and tired and my milk hadn't properly come through yet. Skye's constant suckling began to be painful as my already tender nipples began to crack with the suction of her lips.

I was demand feeding at first because that was the only way I knew. A nurse from the hospital came out to visit for the first 3 days after coming home. She tried to show me how to sit while breastfeeding, and how to hold Skye's head so it wouldn't put pressure on my nipples. Feeding time was torture and just Skye's cry was enough to make my nipples sore. I would sit there all tensed up waiting for the searing pain to go through me as Skye latched on with her surprisingly strong suction. I was too tired to eat or drink properly and this made things worse as my milk didn't flow freely. I'm sure being so tense and anxious didn't help either. My breasts became engorged, as hard as rocks and hot to the touch.

I began resenting feeding Skye, and then I began to resent her. I felt so guilty that I could feel this way and tried to quash those emotions, to no avail. We spent most of our waking hours crying. Skye was constantly fitful and agitated and things were going from bad to terrible. I couldn't put Skye down for even a second. I began having suicidal/homicidal thoughts.

My partner came home from work and found me in a dark room holding Skye on my lap, sobbing. Skye was crying too. We had our first-week check-up so he took us back to the hospital. By that time I had a raging fever brought on by the developing mastitis. Looking back on the situation, it was becoming physically unwell that saved both of us in the long run. I was treated in the maternity ward for the mastitis. While I was there I was assessed by the psychiatrist of the MBU who diagnosed me with postnatal depression.

Mother–Baby Unit

When I was well enough, I was admitted to the MBU and here I was able to convalesce in an environment with routine and structure to the days.

Demand feeding was a thing of the past as they taught me that routine was also important for infants. It was difficult at first, but with the patient persistence of the nurses in the unit, I mastered the art of breastfeeding. Feeding time changed from dread to delight as I spent the time returning the gaze of my daughter's dark eyes, totally in awe of her.

I had begun to take antidepressants and was feeling better within myself. Skye cried less and became more settled. She began responding to my voice and my presence, by turning her head, and later her body, towards me. My anxiety and depression had impacted on Skye's wellbeing and our interactions — she was restless, fitful and inconsolable. As I got better these behaviours slowly disappeared and were replaced with a mainly content, happy baby.

A masseuse came in twice a week and we had baby massage groups. These groups were very laid back and informal. I could feel Skye reacting positively to my touch and enjoying the close attention. (Ten years on she still regularly asks for a back rub!) It also helped being around other mothers who were also struggling. We shared our joys and sorrows and helped each other out with our babies.

At the MBU I was given the opportunity to get better and to concentrate on the most important thing, my daughter. Well, actually, no — one thing I learned there was to 'be selfish'. That word no longer had negative connotations. I had to learn to look after number 1 — me, if I was to be able to look after Skye in the way she needed, and deserved. In total I was in the MBU for 3½ months.

My stay in the unit was positive in most ways; however, I felt they failed to see the bigger picture. I had identified my relationship difficulty as an aspect of life that I wanted to focus on. What we needed was couple's counselling, and if the MBU could not provide that then I felt that they needed to refer us on to a therapist who would be able to work with us. This was not done.

While I was in hospital, a lovely lady moved in to the flat across the way from us and we became fast friends. Having the support of this woman and being a support for her, was invaluable. We were part of each other's life in almost every way. My parents and I started reconnecting after years of being estranged from one another. I started to feel happy about myself and Skye responded in kind. She developed and grew into a happy, bubbly baby; a smile was never far from her face. Then we had to move.

We moved to the outer suburbs and everything was so different out there. I had left all my mental health supports. I had left my best friend and moved away from my parents. I began to feel very alone and anxious again. Dark ruminating thoughts were never far from my mind and I began to self-harm again. I had been suffering from posttraumatic stress disorder for a long time and this seemed to flare up. I was jumpy and easily startled by the smallest noise or by someone walking behind me. Skye seemed to pick up on this and her behaviour began to change. She started waking at all hours of the night demanding to be fed. I was so tired that I gave into her and let her fall asleep with me in bed as she suckled.

My mental state began to deteriorate. One night I went for a long walk. I was overwrought and sleep deprived. I didn't feel safe and was frightened that I would do something to myself that I would regret. As a last resort, I ended up going to the emergency ward of the nearest hospital. All the beds were taken up so they put me in the suture room but this was not a good move, considering I had just told the nurse that I was having self-harming thoughts. As usual the ward was busy and understaffed; I hid under the bed with a stitch cutter and did myself a fair bit of harm. The first thing the staff members knew about this was when my partner turned up with my daughter in his arms. She cried and reached out for me. I didn't want her to see me in the state I was in, I didn't want to frighten or traumatise her, but I also wanted to go and comfort her. I was caught between her need to be comforted by her mother and the knowledge that it was not the right thing to do at that time, given the condition I was in. My partner left with Skye crying and struggling in his arms.

Forced Weaning

I became very unwell and was hospitalised when Skye was 15 months old. I was still breastfeeding and supplementing Skye's diet with solids. The psychiatric hospital had no idea how to deal with a lactating woman, in fact they didn't even acknowledge it as something that needed to be considered — a classic case of treating the illness and not looking at the consumer as a whole being. Due to accumulation of milk I developed a very bad case of mastitis and my breasts where engorged with unexpressed milk. I couldn't even wear a top as the touch of cloth on my nipples was so painful it felt like needles being pricked into them. I tried to explain the situation to one of the nurses but I was too mentally unwell to be able to articulate this clearly to any of the staff. I took my top off for some reprieve from the pain. The staff became quite agitated and cross and one female nurse tried to forcefully put a top on me. In my pain and confusion I struck out, trying to keep her away from me. The next thing I knew was that I was surrounded by staff members. They bent my arms painfully behind my back and half dragged, half carried me to the high dependency unit. I was frightened, disoriented, confused and in pain. I tried to get out of their clutches but to no avail. They injected me with a sedative and left me to sleep it off in seclusion. I developed a very high fever and only when a doctor came to check me out, as is necessary with people in seclusion, did he detect that there was something wrong beyond my state of mental health. I spent the next couple of days in a medical ward where they used an electric pump to express the milk from my engorged, painful breasts and put me on a course of intravenous antibiotics.

I don't recall having contact with Skye during the critical part of my illness. When I was let out on day leave I spent it with Skye at a friend's place. Skye snuggled up to me and asked to have a feed; I hugged her close to me and told her that I no longer had any milk for her. She looked confused and nuzzled up to me and asked me again. I said, 'Darling, I have run out of milk, but there is milk in the fridge. Would you like me to get you some?' I could see her mind working this piece of information over. She patted me gently on both breasts and then said, quite matter-of-factly, 'Oh, okay,' and we went of to get her first drink of cow's milk.

This was not how I intended to wean Skye from my bosom and although she was quite accepting of the situation when I initially told her, over the next months she longed for the comfort and sustenance of a breast feed. She became quite clingy and when she used to have her meals, morning and evenings, she would still nuzzle into me for a feed.

I strongly believe that if the hospital was better educated regarding the patient as a whole this could have been avoided, and I would have been able to wean Skye gently and in her own time. Instead, we both had to deal with the trauma of her being torn from my bosom so suddenly and we were both grieving for this loss. It was an added stressor to our relationship that had just gone through a separation and we were trying to find our feet again. Feeding times were always Skye and Mum time and now that that was gone I needed to find something else that would give us that quiet, quality, bonding time.

Hospital Visits

In the periods that I was unwell and in hospital, Skye's father would usually look after her for a couple of days and then take her to my parents to be looked after. When Skye came to visit me in hospital the first thing she wanted to know was where was my bed, where were the toilets and the shower, where did I eat, and drink my coffee. She needed to know these concrete things and I think it put her mind at ease and reassured her that I was in a safe place and was being looked after. I think it also allowed her to envisage where I may be when she was away from me and thinking of me.

Having Skye visit me in psychiatric wards was always a contentious issue and, depending on which hospital (or which head nurse for that matter!), the rules differed. Some hospitals had no issues with her visiting, but I was always concerned at how other patient's behaviours may affect her — especially if there was a crisis, or just loud or unpredictable patients. Some let her visit me in my room, while other hospitals had 'no visitors in rooms' policy. Others wouldn't allow her to come into the ward because of the concerns of how it may affect her, which caused a difficulty if I wasn't allowed off the ward.

The best situation by far was a hospital that had a designated family room away from the noise and hustle and bustle of the ward. It was set up with kids' toys, books crayons and even a CD player; it had a warm colourful rug and bean bags to sit on. There was a window in the door where a nurse could look in without disturbing my time with my daughter. I have been in seven different hospitals over the last 12-year period and only one of them was set up in this way.

Returning Home

It is always difficult to return home and reacclimatise to a regular routine when you have been out of it, even for a short time. It is perhaps even harder coming home from hospital and having to go directly back into parenting, with all that entails. It makes it even more difficult if you are on your own. It was not only me who was out of routine, but my child as well. I found that the first few weeks after returning home where the most difficult as Skye was always very clingy, demanding and insecure. She needed to work out the boundaries again and was constantly testing them.

I came home from the hospital environment where I had only myself to think about and where all my needs were met. I had no domestic responsibilities and had 24-hour support in a safe environment. I returned home to a situation where I had total responsibility for not only myself but for my infant daughter as well. Compounding this was the sedating effects of psychotropic drugs that had been prescribed for me. Inevitably, my drugs are changed most times that I am hospitalised and my body is still getting used to them when I am sent home.

On one occasion when I was just home from hospital I had a lady from a local government service come to give me in-home support and help me and Skye readjust to all that is entailed in looking after an infant and running a home. She was only there for a couple of hours each day for a week, but made things a bit easier for me. At times I have asked for this service to be made available to me, but aside for that one time I never received this support. I feel in-home support for parents just home from hospital should be a service that is more readily available. If social workers or occupational therapists on the ward would identify this need and put in a referral before the client was discharged it would be easier on all parties involved.

My Ways of Managing to be a Responsive Mother

It goes without saying that being an attentive, on-the-ball, all-guns-blazing mother, when you can barely lift your head off the pillow, is next to impossible. I had to think of ways to be responsive to Skye and make sure her needs were being met.

I would take my night medication early, after I put Skye to bed at night, to lessen the residual sedative and hangover effect it had the morning after. It was very important to do this as I wanted to be able to respond to her when she woke in the morning. I had also worked out how to divide the medications up during the day and not take the full dose at night because I didn't want to have to respond to an emergency, or to have Skye call for me at night and I couldn't respond. (This had happened a few times and had left Skye very distressed.)

In the morning, I would change her nappy and put the kettle on. Sometimes I would fall asleep while waiting for it to boil and it was a good thing that it had a persistent, growing-ever-louder whistle! We would both have our morning drinks in bed and I would take my morning medication. Skye would bring books for me to read to her. Lucky for me she was at that age where she wanted the same book read to her over and over again, hence I knew it off by heart and was able to almost 'sleep read' to her. As my medications kicked in I'd try to stay awake but would more often than not snooze off and on while Skye looked at books, played or just had morning snuggles. Not all mornings were like this, and on days when she wanted to get up and at it I had to put extra effort into interacting with her. In the times I was not sedated I put together a box of activities to do with Skye for when I was sedated. In the box were crayons, stamps and ink pad, glue stick, cut-out pictures from magazines, stickers, pieces of fabric, buttons and lots more things to spark her interest. We would sit in the lounge and create art pieces that Picasso would envy! Yes, I would drift in and out of consciousness a bit, but still I was there with Skye doing activities and interacting with her and keeping her happy.

I am ashamed to say so, but the truth be told, I was an 'ABC for kids' mum, and when Skye wasn't interested in furthering her artistic career, I would turn the television on, curl up with her on her little fold-out Bananas-in-Pyjamas couch, and drift off while she was being entertained by plasticine Pingus and Teletubbies with terrible speech deficits.

Skye was enrolled in home-based childcare, which was a godsend for me. Her childcare mum was incredibly understanding, patient and very loving. I had full confidence that Skye was in good hands when she was there. On days where I was struggling more than usual, I would bring Skye still in her pyjamas and M would get her dressed. Skye loved being there, interacting with the other children, playing with the diverse range of toys M had. Sometimes I'd stay for a while to be able to be with Skye, but not have to worry about having full responsibility for her, and we could just enjoy each other's company. When I got home I'd take the rest of my medication for the day and go back to sleep for a few hours.

After I picked Skye up from childcare, we would go to the local park. It was always a lot easier to look after her when we were outside than trying to entertain her inside. She loved the swing and I would sit her on my lap, facing me, with her legs dangling on either side behind me, she'd snuggle into me and we'd swing like that for quite some time (we called it 'the spider'). This enabled me to have close contact with her without having to tax myself in any way.

Self-Doubts

Looking back on those times I know I was doing the best I could, and Skye didn't go without. But, at the time, I felt that I wasn't meeting her needs and I had great self-doubt about my abilities as a mother. I felt that I was not contributing to life in any way, shape or form. I was always tired and lethargic, and when I wasn't feeling sedated that meant it was time to take my next dose of medication. I began to feel that Skye would be better off without me. I knew I loved her and there were fleeting moments in the days when I felt that love, but mostly I felt a numbing nothingness or a profound sense of being lost without purpose or direction. I felt that there was no reason to live life if this is how it was going to be. I became more and more morose and disillusioned about myself and life, and my ability to parent Skye in all the best ways she deserved. This led to me feeling that Skye would be better off without me. I truly believed this and went about planning how to end my life, with the least amount of impact to Skye's welfare.

I saved up my medication for some time and when I felt that I had enough I drove out to the forest at night. My last recollections were of swallowing the tablets with liberal amounts of alcohol. I walked to the waterfall; the moon was full and the forest was magical. I recall climbing down the slope on the side of the bridge to the water. I felt calm and at peace and sure that this was the right decision. That is all I recollect until I awoke in hospital a week latter. There was no reason that I should have survived as it was well after midnight when I went down to the water. The chances of anyone being there were negligible. I was told later that two girls had been out walking when their attention was drawn to my car because the hazard lights were on. They found me slumped in the car unconscious and called an ambulance.

When I was medically well enough, I was moved to the psychiatric ward. I was still very angry at my attempted suicide being thwarted and it was obvious I wasn't meant to die yet. This angered me more and made me feel resentful to all around me and the universe at large. I felt that everything and everyone was out to make things difficult for me and I couldn't even do a simple thing, like kill myself. My moods oscillated between self-pity, self-hatred, feeling out of control, panicky and flighty, to just lying on my bed curled up in the foetal position, disassociating and not acknowledging anyone.

It was during one of those times that I was lying in my bed quite distant from everything, that Skye cuddled up to me in bed. I don't know who brought her into the room, as in this particular hospital visitors weren't allowed in patient's rooms. Skye didn't say anything to me and I didn't talk either. We fell asleep, I don't know how long for, but in this time a magical transformation transpired. I awoke and looked down at her peaceful sleeping face. I felt my heart warm and grow and soften toward her. A strong passionate feeling to nurture and protect her came over me; a feeling of love so strong that it brought tears to my eyes and I began to cry. I cried in fear for what the future may hold. I cried for myself in self-pity, and in anger for the bad things people had done to me, and the unfairness that I had experienced in life. I cried in pain for the struggles of the past. I cried with guilt for what I had put other people through. I cried in realisation of how final death is. I cried for the love I felt for my daughter. But most of all I cried with relief and gratitude that I had been saved and given a second chance. I remembered the promise I had made to myself and my then unborn child — to be the best I could be for her.

Skye woke up and looked at me, 'Mummy, don't cry, it's okay, I love you.' I wrapped her in my arms and hugged her tight to me and reaffirmed my vow to her. I had always thought of myself as unworthy of being a mother to such a precious soul, but it dawned on me that day that if she had been entrusted into my care that I surely must be of some worth.

My Role in Professional Development

Through my connection with the MSP I had the opportunity, when Skye was about 5 months old, to speak to a group of child protection workers attending a professional development session about children of parents with mental illness.

Over the last 10 years I have given more talks and co-facilitated talks to child protection workers, and to other professionals who work in domestic violence, supported housing, and mental health services. These talks were part of professional education and training programs. It gives me a great sense of satisfaction that I can contribute to increasing workers' understanding about parenting with a mental illness by giving them my personal insight. It also pleases me to have had input into possible changes in attitudes and ways therapists interact and work with these clients.

Perinatal Anxiety and Depression

Issues, Outcomes and Interventions

Susan R. Priest and Bryanne Barnett

- - -

The transition to parenthood, especially with the first child, is stressful physiologically, psychologically and socially. As with all developmental stages, the opportunity exists to grow and mature, but there is always the attendant threat of things going wrong, with physical or psychological disability as temporary or permanent outcome. Psychologically resilient people will use the challenges of this transition to review and appropriately modify their coping strategies and their relationships with others, even if all does not go according to plan.

Contrary to previous thinking on this subject, pregnancy does not protect women against distress, mental illness or suicide. Depression and anxiety are prevalent in women of reproductive age and are therefore common during perinatal times. The problems can predate conception and then continue into pregnancy, or start 'de novo' at any time after conception, childbirth or through the postnatal period. Some women (and men) are more vulnerable because of prior adversity in childhood or subsequent abuse, neglect, trauma, separation, grief and loss, poverty, illness and obstetric complications including infertility (Matthey et al., 2004). For other expectant or new parents, anxiety and depression are already longstanding companions, and this important life event may precipitate further difficulties (Cohen et al., 2006).

Disturbances that do not meet full clinical criteria for mental illness can be associated with adverse outcomes, as can more severe forms of mental illness (Cohen & Nonacs, 2005). Significant anxiety and depression will be found in around 15% of women pre- and postnatally, with higher rates in disadvantaged populations (Bennett, Einarson, Taddio, Koren, & Einarson, 2004; Gavin et al., 2005). It has been reported that the risk of illness onset is raised two- or three-fold in the early weeks postpartum and the risk is higher if there is any previous history of mental illness in the woman or her family (Cox, Murray, & Chapman, 1993). This constitutes the time of greatest risk of psychiatric hospitalisation, with an increase of 16-fold or more in the risk of psychotic illness (Kendell, Chalmers, & Platz, 1987).

Anxiety and depression in the perinatal stage thus have profound importance because of their frequency, potential severity, and long-term problem outcomes for the woman, her infant and the family. Outcomes for mother, foetus, and infant will be influenced by the balance of risk and protective factors present in the individual case along with the availability, access, uptake and response to interventions. In this chapter, we will review these issues and consider routine assessment or screening, and potential interventions.

Routine Perinatal Mental Health Assessment

Evidence indicates that many women fail to identify themselves as depressed or to seek help (Murray, Woolgar, Murray, & Cooper, 2003). Sadly, not all health-care providers will identify their condition. As most women will access obstetric, midwifery, nursing or paediatric care during pregnancy or post-natally, an ideal opportunity exists to ensure that mental as well as physical health is optimised.

There has been considerable debate regarding the best method for routine assessment to ensure reliable identification of illness or subclinical problems and a number of self-report measures have been reviewed by Muzik et al. (2000). The Edinburgh Postnatal Depression Scale (EPDS; Cox, Holden, & Sagovsky, 1987) is the most widely used brief self-report measure of maternal distress and depressive symptomatology. It has also been validated for use ante-natally (Murray & Cox, 1990) and in men (Matthey, Barnett, Howie, & Kavanagh, 2003). It has been translated into a number of different languages and validated across a range of cultures (Cox & Holden, 2003). As the scale includes several anxiety-related items, it has recently been argued that it also identifies anxiety.

Formal clinical or structured diagnostic interviews for anxiety and depressive disorders exist, such as the Composite International Diagnostic Interview (CIDI; Robins et al., 1988), but these are not appropriate for routine, universal screening or assessment in everyday clinical settings. They are indicated at the next level (usually postreferral) when accurate psychiatric diagnosis is required.

Self-report measures such as the EPDS are not diagnostic tools. Studies of concurrent validity comparing EPDS scores with results on structured diagnostic interviews do show that there is an increased probability of clinical levels of depression if scores are significantly elevated (e.g., above 12 in English-speaking populations). Nevertheless, scores can also be raised on the EPDS due to transient stress, or grief reactions, as well as anxiety disorders and depression. For community screening purposes it is usually recommended that a lower threshold (over 9) be used to ensure problems are not missed. Further exploration and, if necessary, repeat administration, are recommended to establish the nature of the difficulties and whether further action or referral to a mental health professional is required (Austin & Priest, 2005). Scores over 20 indicate complex histories often involving multiple stressors, including prior traumatic experiences, and any score on item 10 (thoughts of self-harm) requires further assessment. Downloadable versions and many translations are available.

Some models for perinatal assessment also include questions about presence of psychosocial risk factors known to be associated with perinatal mood disorders and difficulties in coping with the adjustment to parenthood (ACOG, 1999). Examples include the Integrated Perinatal Care Program (Barnett, Glossop, Matthey & Stewart, 2005), the Antenatal Psychosocial Health Assessment Form (ALPHA; Carroll et al., 2005), the National Postnatal Depression Program in Australia (Buist et al., 2007), and the Psychosocial Risk Assessment Model (Priest, Austin, Barnett, & Buist, 2008). These can be used alongside symptom-based measures and have potential to identify women at psychological or social risk. Such approaches are not without their critics and further validation studies are needed before it can be established whether early identification reduces incidence or prevalence of perinatal disorders or parenting difficulties and increases uptake of relevant services (Armstrong & Small, 2007; Carroll et al., 2005).

Anxiety and Depression in Pregnancy

Incidence of Antenatal Depression and Anxiety

Studies reporting prevalence rates for antenatal distress and depression indicate that these are comparable with postnatal rates (Golding, Pembrey, & Jones, 2001). Relapse rates for women with a pre-pregnancy history of major depression are high. Cohen et al. (2006) reported a study of 201 women with recurrent major depression followed through pregnancy. Among these 68% relapsed after discontinuation of medication while 22% relapsed despite continuation of medication. Over 60% resumed medication later in their pregnancy. Among women who discontinue mood stabiliser medication for bipolar disorder, 50% will develop an episode in pregnancy (Viguera et al., 2000). Anxiety disorders in pregnancy are as common as depressive disorders and around 40% of women with anxiety disorder present in pregnancy go on to develop postnatal depression (Matthey et al., 2003).

Risks

Compromised maternal mental health poses direct and indirect risks for the foetus and infant. A woman experiencing distress may:

- not attend for appropriate obstetric care
- not monitor her own health and nutritional status appropriately
- be unable to sleep
- be reckless, self-harming or even suicidal
- resort to using cigarettes, alcohol and other drugs to relieve stress
- be the victim of violence from a stressed partner
- be less able to relate positively to her foetus and infant
- be less likely to breast-feed
- have other children who are affected and their distress may elicit hostility.

Effects on the Foetus

Recent research indicates that early patterns of infant social–emotional responses begin developing in utero in response to innate genetic influences and the biochemistry of the intrauterine environment, in addition to being affected by later social and environmental influences (Huizink, Mulder, & Buitelaar, 2004). The precise nature of the impact of stressors upon the foetus and infant will vary depending on the nature, severity, timing and persistence of the stressors and degree of innate resilience (Yehuda et al., 2005). Women who suffer from stress in pregnancy are more likely to smoke, or use drugs or alcohol to manage their stress. The physical effects of such substance use are well known, while evidence for adverse psychological outcomes for offspring of women who smoke in pregnancy has been recently reviewed by Button, Maughan and McGuffin (2007).

Alder, Fink, Bitzer, Hösli and Holzgreve (2007), in a review of the literature, suggest that higher levels of depression and anxiety symptoms contribute independently of other biomedical risk factors to adverse obstetric, foetal and neonatal outcomes. Those authors note that most studies referred to subclinical levels of symptomatology associated with obstetric complications, pregnancy symptoms, preterm labour and requirement for pain relief. In this context subclinical should not be considered to mean insignificant and it might well be concluded that outcomes associated with a clinically diagnosed disorder or illness may be even more problematic. In other studies, lower birth weights have been found among infants of depressed versus nondepressed mothers in Asian countries (Harpham, Huttly, DeSilva, & Abramsky, 2005; Patel, Rahman, Jacob, & Hughes, 2004).

The work of O'Connor, Heron, Golding, Beveridge and Glover (2002) indicates that elevated levels of maternal stress during pregnancy that are likely to be genetically and/or biochemically mediated contribute to adverse infant and young child behavioural outcomes. One of the mechanisms proposed to account for transfer of stress from the mother to the foetus involves the functioning of the hypothalamic pituitary adrenal axis (HPA), which regulates the neuroendocrine response to stress. Studies have demonstrated that excess activation during pregnancy may interfere with the development of the foetal HPA axis and can lead to a chronically heightened stress response throughout life, altered immune response, anxiety disorders, and possibly other forms of psychopathology (Huizink et al., 2004; Yehuda et al., 2005)

Postnatal Anxiety and Depression

Incidence

Postnatal mood disorders are commonly described as falling into three main categories: the 'blues', postnatal depression, and postpartum psychosis, with rates of 50–80%, 10–15%, and 0.2% respectively. A range of postnatal anxiety disorders have been described, including generalised anxiety, phobias, obsessive compulsive disorder and posttraumatic stress disorder (Brockington, Macdonald, & Wainscott, 2006a; Rogal et al, 2007). Comorbidity is common, with Brockington et al. (2006a) reporting that 27% of women diagnosed with postnatal depression had two or more comorbid disorders.

The 'Blues'

The 'blues', common enough to be regarded as probably normative, are medically significant only in drawing attention to the likelihood of actual illness ensuing if the symptoms persist or are severe (Henshaw, Foreman, & Cox, 2004).

Puerperal Psychoses

At the other end of the spectrum, postpartum psychosis (affective or schizo-affective) constitutes a psychiatric emergency. Illness is often florid, acute, with onset in the first three weeks postpartum if not prior to the birth, and carries a high risk for the survival of mother and infant. Others may have to assist with care of the infant, and breastfeeding is often difficult to sustain, so lithium, other mood stabilisers, antipsychotic medication and electroconvulsive therapy (ECT) can be used in the usual way. Hospital admission, preferably to a dedicated mother–baby unit, is often necessary (see Chapter 15). With postpartum psychosis a recurrence rate of 50% to 90% is expected with subsequent pregnancies, while some women will also experience episodes at nonpregnant times (Viguera, Cohen, Nonacs, & Baldessarina, 2005).

Postnatal Depression

Postpartum depression (PND), minor or major without psychotic symptoms, may have an insidious onset over the early weeks and months, with the usual features of depressive disorder recognisable if an effort is made to identify them — for example, low mood, anhedonia, inability to concentrate, forgetfulness, low energy, insomnia, loss of interest and appetite, and thoughts of death (self and others). Irritable mood may be a prominent feature. This constellation, allied with extreme fatigue and the additional responsibilities for a new baby, can create difficulties in all the woman's close relationships and in her capacity to care for her baby. Timely identification of any problems and appropriate intervention are thus critical to the wellbeing of the whole family.

Previous studies of women admitted to a residential unit to address persistent 'mothercraft' problems reported that some 40% scored above the threshold for likely major depressive disorder, and a more recent study (Phillips, Sharpe, & Matthey, 2007) confirmed that there are high levels of psychiatric morbidity (depressive and anxiety disorders with a high level of comorbidity) among such clients. The authors emphasised the need for multifaceted interventions to address psychological issues for both mother and infant. Women with depression are not a homogenous group and it is important to note that not all parents experiencing anxiety and depression show impaired parenting skills, and that not all suboptimal care-giving is linked with parental mental illness (Brockington, Aucamp, & Fraser, 2006b).

Effects of PND on Infants

Payne (2007) has recently summarised the effects of PND and notes that postpartum maternal depression is reported to have adverse consequences for infants and children, including impaired bonding and attachment, impaired emotional, speech, language, and cognitive development, with subsequent behavioural problems. Mitigating factors include availability of alternate caregivers, maternal attachment status and maternal resilience (McMahon, Barnett, Kowalenko, & Tennant, 2005).

Adaptive brain development, including buffering of stress responses, is promoted by secure attachment based around sharing of positive emotional states, regulation of arousal and attunement between mother and infant. Some parenting and attachment behaviours also appear to be programmed at a neurobehavioural level (Cozolino, 2006; Swain, Lorberbaum, Kose, & Strathearn, 2007; Tronick, 2007). Much of the evidence for the impact of postnatal disorders on infant behaviour has centred on exposures to maternal postnatal depression, rather than anxiety disorders or other forms of mental illness (Murray & Cooper, 1997; Weinberg & Tronick, 1998), although we know that these problems often coexist. The timing, severity and duration of the maternal depression will have bearing on the outcomes.

Mechanisms proposed to account for the adverse effects of maternal anxiety and depression upon infants and young children include altered patterns of care-giving and suboptimal parenting behaviours (Milgrom, Ericksen, McCarthy, & Gemmill, 2006; Moehler, Brunner, Wiebel, Reck, & Resch, 2006). Various studies have confirmed that maternal depression impacts on infant nutritional status and health (Harpham et al., 2005; Patel et al., 2004; Rahman, Iqbal, Bunn, Lovel, & Harrington, 2004). Henderson, Evans, Stratton, Priest and Hagan (2003) found that depressed mothers had significantly reduced rates of uptake and continuation of breastfeeding compared with non-depressed mothers.

Interventions

General Considerations

A broad range of interventions for perinatal anxiety and depression have been reported, including psychological approaches, medications and complementary therapies. Anticipation, quality health care and adequate social support underpin all other management strategies offered, along with precise diagnosis and targeted interventions. Research findings from intervention studies have been mixed, and the research is of variable methodological quality. As pathways leading to perinatal disorders are heterogeneous, it is clear that one type of treatment does not fit all situations. More research that identifies which methods work best in different contexts is urgently required (Dennis, 2005; Lumley, Austin, & Mitchell, 2004; Priest, Henderson, Evans, & Hagan, 2003; Rahman, 2007).

Accurate history-taking and diagnosis followed by collaborative treatment approaches will aid in the selection of treatments and improve outcomes. In general, however, nonmedication interventions of proven efficacy for anxiety and depression in general populations are likely to be a reasonable guide to treatments for pregnant and lactating women. Psychotherapy (such as cognitive–behavioural [CBT], interpersonal) should be considered and offered individually or in groups in combination with the addition of medication if necessary and appropriate. Interventions should include attention to the mother–infant and other close relationships for best results (Milgrom, Negri, Gemmill, McNeil, & Martin, 2005).

Community-based care, where mental health services are integrated into collaborative, multidisciplinary approaches offered in one setting, are being promoted to address perinatal mental health issues (Lyons-Ruth, Wolfe, & Lyubchik, 2000). Collaborative approaches to management ideally consider and understand the woman's context as well as her individual strengths and vulnerabilities. It is vital to appreciate her need to understand and remain informed about the broad array of treatment options for emotional distress and difficulties in coping. Continuity of care and carer is an important and fundamental aspect of provision of care.

When depression or anxiety disorders are diagnosed, treatment requires:

- weighing of the risks and benefits
- discussing the availability and cost of the various modes
- determining the acceptability to the woman, and ideally her partner, of what is accessible.

Nonmedication Treatments

Studies demonstrating benefits are varied and include increased social support and nursing care with nurse home-visiting among high-risk populations (Shaw, Levitt, Wong, & Kaczorowski, 2006).

Various types of psychotherapies provided for individuals or groups have been used with efficacy mainly with women with postnatal depression (Murray, Cooper, Wilson, & Romaniuk, 2003b), including:

- supportive methods (Holden, Sagovsky, & Cox, 1989)
- cognitive–behavioural approaches (Milgrom et al., 2005)
- interpersonal psychotherapy (IPT; O'Hara, Stuart, Gorman, & Wenzel, 2000)
- other psychodynamic approaches (Newman & Mares, 2007).

Studies showing promise but needing further research (Freeman, 2007) include:

- increased levels of exercise for mothers
- bright light therapy
- omega-3 fatty acid use
- massage for mothers and for infants.

Involvement of partners in care has proven beneficial in a number of studies and partners are often also in distress (see Ballard, Chapter 7; Fisher, Feekery, & Rowe-Murray, 2002; Matthey, Barnett, Kavanagh, & Howie, 2001). Research into men with depression indicates that they tend to underreport distress, and often have different symptom patterns and reactions from women. In men with depressed partners, rates of depression are increased, although timing of onset of symptoms is later. Matthey et al. (2003) found that one in ten men met criteria for caseness when their partners were affected and when a father was depressed the partner was 2 to 3 times more likely to be symptomatic.

Thus no one psychological treatment approach is preferred, and intervention is likely to be chosen on the basis of patient choice combined with therapist skill level and availability.

Medication

A number of general principles are relevant when considering the use of medications during pregnancy and postpartum for treatment of anxiety and depression and these have been summarised in Table 1. It is important to check what other remedies the woman may be prescribing for herself and to avoid polypharmacy. As always, it is important to explain the situation to the partner, promote good communication and enlist their aid, to the extent that this can be provided. Medications may be indicated in combination with other forms of

Table 1

General Principles in Use of Medication for Perinatal Anxiety and Depression

- Medication should be avoided where possible, especially during the first trimester; however alternative, nondrug treatments need to be considered where available and untreated anxiety and depression also pose risks.
  - All the risks from exposure to *either* medication *or* illness are not yet known.
  - All medication crosses the placenta and also appears in breast milk — to varying degrees
- Following consultation among health professionals and consultation with the woman and her partner, agreed, written, care plans should be drawn up and available to all concerned.
- If conception occurs unexpectedly, medication *should not* be withdrawn abruptly and medical guidance is indicated.
- If medication is used, an effective dose should be prescribed:
  - most antidepressants are also effective for anxiety
  - polypharmacy should be avoided, also bearing in mind that patients may be self-medicating
  - medication that has previously been effective in that patient should usually be first choice
- Careful monitoring is essential:
  - mood stabilising drugs require close obstetric monitoring and adequate folate supplementation
  - pharmacokinetics can change over the pregnancy and doses may need to be changed
  - similar principles apply when using atypical antipsychotic drugs
- With a history of previous severe postnatal anxiety disorder, depression or psychosis, plan for prophylaxis in late pregnancy or immediately post-partum:
  - exposure is generally higher through placental passage than through breast milk so medication used during pregnancy should be the one continued postpartum
  - the infant should be clinically monitored subsequently
- Neonatal adaptation problems are common, though rarely severe, in healthy infants of women on antidepressant medication:
  - since reduction or withdrawal of medication prior to delivery is not always possible or advisable, the infants should be closely monitored for 3 to 7 days postpartum
- Information changes rapidly in this field and up-to-date information must be obtained from relevant hospital helplines or websites such as www.motherrisk.org; www.otispregnancy.org

therapies, as outlined above, and sometimes in conjunction with ECT (Ramos, Oraichi, Rey, Blais, & Berard, 2007). Severe mental illness is best treated in a specialist inpatient mother–infant unit, but this is rarely available. With reliable, 24-hour family support, even severe illness can sometimes be treated at home.

Treatment selection is influenced by a range of considerations that must be carefully weighed, including severity of symptoms, past history of depression and effective treatments, family history of illness and response to treatments, likelihood of compliance, suicide risk, risks to the infant, parental concerns regarding medication, and the baby; as well as financial or time constraints. Since depression itself can have direct and indirect adverse effects upon the woman and foetus or baby, there is not a 'no risk' option.

Self-reports about ceasing or taking medication, dosages and associated self-prescribed drug use contribute to unreliability of information in this emotionally charged setting. For obvious reasons, rigorously controlled double-blind clinical trials of many interventions have not been conducted, although there is a considerable body of clinical evidence about merits and problems of specific medications when used in pregnancy or postnatally. Information concerning the safety of medication is altering rapidly and prescribers would be well advised to become familiar with reliable websites and always seek contemporaneous information.

In Pregnancy

Chambers, Moses-Kolko and Wisner (2007) provide a recent review of medication usage in pregnancy. With the caveats in the previous paragraph, reported adverse effects of antidepressants (tricyclics, selective serotonin reuptake inhibitors, mirtazapine) in pregnancy include higher rates of miscarriage and preterm birth, but not of major malformations. Nevertheless, some studies recommend avoiding paroxetine and doxepin (Oberlander, Warburton, Misri, Aghajanian, & Hertzman, 2006), and recent research reports small increases in birth defects with many selective serotonin reuptake inhibitors (SSRIs) (Alwan, Reefhuis, Rasmassen, Olney, & Friedman, 2007; Louik, Lin, Werler, Hernández-Diaz, & Mitchell, 2007). Some current views on SSRI usage in pregnancy have been recently summarised by Cohen (2006), who states that 'there are more reproductive safety data available for SSRIs than for many medicines women take during pregnancy' (p. 12). A 'serotonin syndrome' (toxicity) and a 'neonatal abstinence (withdrawal) syndrome' with symptoms such as jitteriness, sleep disturbance, dysregulation, respiratory distress, irritability, lethargy, myoclonus and tremors, have been reported; also an elevated risk for severe respiratory failure — persistent pulmonary hypertension — where SSRIs have been used during the third trimester.

Raised levels of anxiety are to be anticipated during pregnancy, a venture where the outcome can never be guaranteed. Benzodiazepines are problematic as a treatment for anxiety in women at any time in their lives, and may add further risks for the foetus and breastfed infant. It had been suggested that benzodiazepines should be avoided during the first trimester as they might be teratogenic (e.g., resulting in cleft palate), but this finding has not been supported by later studies. Short-acting single doses may be acceptable later in pregnancy, but not in addition to other psychotropic drugs. Neonatal sedation is likely, especially if these drugs are used intramuscularly or intravenously before birth. Various neonatal problems have been described and include: Floppy Baby Syndrome, Neonatal Withdrawal Syndrome, including respiratory depression, jitteriness, and seizures (Moses-Kolko et al., 2005).

Mood-stabilising medication, such as lithium or anticonvulsants, is problematic during pregnancy. Folate supplements and careful monitoring of mother and foetus will be required. Collaboration with a specialist team is recommended (see Chapter 15).

Postpartum

Psychotropic medication is often avoided by women and their medical practitioners during lactation, as well as during pregnancy. Payne (2007) notes that studies support the use of tricyclic antidepressants, sertraline, paroxetine, bupropion, venlafaxine, fluvoxamine, and omega-3 fatty acids in the treatment of postpartum depression where the mother is not breastfeeding, but that breastfeeding mandates caution with medication. Problems similar to the toxicity and withdrawal syndromes described immediately after the birth, including (rarely) seizures, have been reported in infants breastfed by mothers on SSRIs. Both perinatally and postnatally, it can be difficult to differentiate withdrawal from toxicity. Caution has been advised when considering fluoxetine and citalopram (in high dosage) during lactation (Eberhard-Gran, Eskild, & Opjordsmoen, 2006) although in general terms, very little psychotropic medication per body weight is transferred in breast milk.

Depressed or Anxious Babies

Although most clinicians are aware of the signs and symptoms that may occur in depressed adults, fewer are aware that children and infants also suffer from this problem. The signs and symptoms are fundamentally the same, but expressed in age-appropriate fashion. That is, on careful observation and enquiry, one can expect to note developmentally appropriate expression of low mood, anhedonia, subdued affect, misery, crying, irritability, low energy levels, apathy, and appetite, weight and sleeping problems. The baby will not be happy, playful, willing to engage, interested in the caregivers and environment, gaining weight, trying to communicate, settling contentedly into a routine.

Case Studies

A. Freda was a 28-year-old woman who sought antenatal care from her general practitioner (GP) when 16 weeks pregnant with her first baby. She was concerned about recurrence of the depression she suffered in her first year at university. At that time, after refusing medication for many months, Freda had finally recovered spontaneously, but she remembered how awful the experience was. Since conceiving, she had been reading about postnatal depression on various websites.

At consultation, it was clear that Freda was not currently depressed but apprehensive and wishing to do everything she could to avoid an episode occurring. Her EPDS total score was 7 and she scored 0 on question 10, indicating the absence of thoughts of self-harm. The GP discussed the various management possibilities with her and commended her wish to do all that she could to become more resilient. They agreed on a plan that included fortnightly monitoring visits to the GP, a careful exercise and dietary regime, with anticipatory arrangements about how the early weeks and months of parenting would be managed by the couple, and some self-help CBT from one of the websites.

After guidance about the difference between birthing classes and parenting classes, Freda decided to attend the latter with her partner. Should medication be required, this would be gradually introduced. The plan was designed to enhance her coping skills and confidence, while ensuring that any onset of depressive illness would be quickly treated. All went well and Freda, despite a shaky start after a difficult labour, settled into her new role satisfactorily, managing to breastfeed for six months before returning to part-time work.

B. Amelia was a 34-year-old woman, referred by the Child and Family Health Nurse (CFHN) to her GP at 4 weeks postpartum because of possible postnatal depression. She had an EPDS score of 15, with 0 on Question 10, and was having panic attacks during the afternoon and early morning on most days. She believed she had not recovered from 'the baby blues', was miserable, irritable and could not sleep, even when the baby did. She was terrified something was going to happen to the baby or her husband. Amelia had no appetite herself and had given up trying to breastfeed Ben, having decided she was never going to be a good mother.

This was Amelia's first baby and he was very much wanted. The couple had been trying to conceive for many years, including eight cycles of in-vitro fertilisation (IVF), and Benjamin was conceived to their surprise after they decided to have a break from the treatment. There was no clear personal history of mental illness, although Amelia had always been an anxious, conscientious person — like her own mother, who suffered several episodes of depression and was finally treated successfully with medication. Amelia was dismayed to think she might be repeating her mother's history — remembering well what it had been like in the house when her mother became agitated or subsequently retired to bed, seemingly for weeks on end.

Information about anxiety, depression and the vicissitudes of mothering were offered to the couple and antidepressant medication was recommended. As Amelia did not wish to try and resume breastfeeding, she was willing to take the medication (sertraline). Her husband was very supportive once he knew not only why he had suddenly become the target for her irritability and misery, but also how he could help in practical ways. Amelia responded well to her antidepressant medication and attended a group for depressed new mothers, finding it very helpful and making some long-term friends into the bargain. When she had recovered from her depressive episode, Amelia was referred by the GP to a psychologist for a course of CBT, aimed at providing her with more adaptive strategies to deal with her chronic anxiety.

Meanwhile the CFHN had been visiting to provide information about infant development and enhance the mother–infant interaction. The nurse noted that Amelia's anxiety tended to make her oscillate between intrusiveness and avoidance, responding more to her own anxiety than to her infant's cues. Her infant was noted to avoid eye contact with his mother. After discussion with the GP, Amelia was referred to a mother–infant group run by a local clinical psychologist, where she learned to sit back, observe attentively and understand her infant and his communication (Cohen, Muir, & Lojkasek, 2003).

Conclusions

Always provide information and discuss options with the woman, and her partner whenever possible, especially where there is a history of mental illness.

* Understand relevant psychosocial risk factors that predispose women to difficulties in coping during the perinatal period in order to detect women at risk who may benefit from referral for additional supports.
* Anticipate difficulties, where possible, through careful history-taking and timely family planning.
* Offer biopsychosocial care and teamwork, link to relevant services, include psychiatric care where history indicates.
* Learn to use a simple self-report tool such as the Edinburgh Postnatal Depression Scale which can be downloaded from various websites (see below)
* Obtain information, support for the woman, her family, and for yourself, identifying available resources — professional and other. Websites such as: http://www.motherisk.org, http://www.otispregnancy.org, http://www.beyondblue.org.au, http://www.blackdoginstitute.org.au provide useful, up-to-date information in this dynamic field.

Useful websites

http://www.beyondblue.org.au
http://www.blackdoginstitute.org.au
http://www.motherisk.org
http://www.otispregnancy.org

References

ACOG. (1999). Psychosocial risk factors: Perinatal screening and intervention. *International Journal of Gynaecology and Obstetrics, 69,* 195–200.

Alder, J., Fink, N., Bitzer, J., Hösli, I., & Holzgreve, W. (2007). Depression and anxiety during pregnancy: A risk factor for obstetric, fetal and neonatal outcome? A critical review of the literature. *Journal of Maternal-Fetal & Neonatal Medicine, 20,* 189–209.

Alwan, S., Reefhuis, J., Rasmussen, S.A., Olney, R.S., & Friedman, J.M. (2007). Use of selective serotonin-reuptake inhibitors in pregnancy and the risk of birth defects. *The New England Journal of Medicine, 356*, 2684–2692.

Armstrong, S., & Small, R. (2007). Screening for postnatal depression: Not a simple task. *Australian and New Zealand Journal of Public Health, 31*, 57–61.

Austin, M-P., & Priest, S.R. (2005). Clinical issues in perinatal mental health: New developments in the detection and treatment of perinatal mood and anxiety disorders. *Acta Psychiatrica Scandinavica, 112*, 97–104.

Barnett, B., Glossop, P., Matthey, S., & Stewart, H. (2005). Screening in the context of integrated perinatal care. In C. Henshaw & S. Elliot (Eds.), *Screening for Perinatal Depression* (pp. 68–82). London: Jessica Kingsley.

Bennett, H.A., Einarson, A., Taddio, A., Koren, G., & Einarson, T.R. (2004). Prevalence of depression during pregnancy: Systematic review. *Obstetrics and Gynaecology, 103*, 698–709.

Brockington, I.F., Macdonald, E., Wainscott, G. (2006a). Anxiety, obsessions and morbid preoccupations in pregnancy and the puerperium. *Archives of Women's Mental Health, 9*(5), 253–63.

Brockington, I.F., Aucamp, H.M., & Fraser, C. (2006b). Severe disorders of the mother-infant relationship: Definitions and frequency. *Archives of Women's Mental Health, 9*, 243–251.

Buist, A., Ellwood, D., Brooks, J., Milgrom, J., Hayes, B., Sved-Williams, A., et al. (2007). National program for depression associated with childbirth: The Australian experience. *Best Practice and Research in Clinical Obstetrics and Gynaecology, 21*, 193–206.

Button, T.M., Maughan, B., & McGuffin, P. (2007). The relationship of maternal smoking to psychological problems in the offspring. *Early Human Development 83*, 727–732.

Carroll, J.C., Reid, A.J., Biringer, A., Midmer, D., Glazier, R.H., Wilson, L., et al. (2005). Effectiveness of the Antenatal Psychosocial Health Assessment (ALPHA) form in detecting psychosocial concerns: A randomised controlled trial. *Canadian Medical Association Journal, 173*, 253–259.

Chambers, C., Moses-Kolko, E., & Wisner, K.L. (2007). Antidepressant use in pregnancy, new concerns, old dilemmas. *Expert Review of Neurotherapeutics, 7*, 761–764.

Cohen, L.S. (2006). Weighing new evidence on SSRI use. *Ob/Gyn News, 41*, 8–12

Cohen, L.S., Altshuler, L.L., Harlow, B.L., Nonacs, R., Newport, D.J., Viguera, A.C., et al. (2006). Relapse of major depression during pregnancy in women who maintain or discontinue antidepressant treatment. *Journal of the American Medical Association, 295*(5), 499–507

Cohen, N.J., Muir, E., & Lojkasek, M. (2003). The first couple: Using *Watch, Wait and Wonder* to change troubled mother-infant relationships. In S.M. Johnson & V.E. Whiffen (Eds.), *Attachment processes in couple and family therapy* (pp. 215–233). New York: Guilford Press.

Cox, J., & Holden, J. (2003). *Perinatal mental health: A guide to the Edinburgh Postnatal Depression Scale (EPDS)*. London: Gaskell.

Cox, J.L., Holden, J.M., & Sagovsky, R. (1987). Detection of postnatal depression. Development of the 10 item Edinburgh Postnatal Depression Scale. *British Journal of Psychiatry, 150*, 782–6.

Cox, J.L., Murray, D., & Chapman, G. (1993). A controlled study of the onset, duration and prevalence of postnatal depression. *British Journal of Psychiatry, 163*, 27–31.

Cozolino, L. (2006). *The neuroscience of human relationships. Attachment and the developing social brain*. New York: W.W. Norton & Co.

Dennis, C-L. (2005). Psychosocial and psychological interventions for prevention of postnatal depression: Systematic review. *British Medical Journal, 331*, 15–23.

Eberhard-Gran, M., Eskild, A., & Opjordsmoen, S. (2006). Use of psychotropic medications in treating mood disorders during lactation: Practical recommendations. *CNS Drugs, 20*, 187–198.

Fisher, J.R.W., Feekery, C.J., & Rowe-Murray, H.J. (2002). Nature, severity and correlates of psychological distress in women admitted to a private mother-baby unit. *Journal of Paediatrics and Child Health, 38*, 140–145.

Freeman, M.P. (2007). Antenatal depression: Navigating the treatment dilemmas. *American Journal of Psychiatry, 16*, 8.

Gavin, N.I., Gaynes, B.N., Lohr, K.N., Meltzer-Brody, S., Gartlehner, G., & Swinson, T. (2005). Perinatal depression: A systematic review of prevalence and incidence. *Obstetrics and Gynecology, 106*, 1071–1083.

Golding, J., Pembrey, M., Jones, R., & ALSPAC Study team. (2001). ALSPAC-The Avon Longitudinal Study of Parents and Children. *Paediatric and Perinatal Epidemiology, 15*, 74–87.

Harpham, T., Huttly, S., DeSilva, M.J., & Abramsky, T. (2005). Maternal mental health and child nutritional status in four developing countries. *Journal of Epidemiology and Community Health, 59*, 1060–1064.

Henderson, J.J., Evans, S.F., Stratton, J.A., Priest, S.R., & Hagan, R. (2003). Impact of postnatal depression on breastfeeding duration. *Birth, 31*, 175–80.

Henshaw, C., Foreman, D., & Cox, J. (2004). Postnatal blues: A risk factor for postnatal depression. *Journal of Psychosomatic Obstetrics and Gynaecology, 25*, 267–272.

Holden, J.M., Sagovsky, R., & Cox, J. (1989). Counselling in a general practice setting: Controlled study of health visitor intervention in treatment of postnatal depression. *British Medical Journal, 298*, 223–226.

Huizink, A., Mulder, E., & Buitelaar, J. (2004). Prenatal stress and risk for psychopathology: Specific effects or induction of general susceptibility? *Psychological Bulletin, 130*, 115–142.

Kendell, R.E., Chalmers, J.C., & Platz, C. (1987). Epidemiology of puerperal psychoses. *British Journal of Psychiatry, 150*, 662–673.

Louik, C., Lin, A.E., Werler, M.M., Hernández-Diaz, S., & Mitchell, A.A. (2007). First-trimester use of selective serotonin-reuptake inhibitors and the risk of birth defects. *The New England Journal of Medicine, 356*, 2675–2683.

Lumley, J., Austin, M-P., & Mitchell, C. (2004). Intervening to reduce depression after birth: A systematic review of the randomized trials. *International Journal of Technology and Assessment in Health Care, 20*, 128–44.

Lyons-Ruth, K., Wolfe, R., & Lyubchik, A. (2000). Depression and the parenting of young children: Making the case for early preventive mental health services. *Harvard Review of Psychiatry, 8*, 148–153.

Matthey, S., Barnett, B., Kavanagh, D.J., & Howie, P. (2001). Validation of the Edinburgh Postnatal Depression Scale for men and comparison of item endorsement with their partners. *Journal of Affective Disorders, 64*(2), 175–84.

Matthey, S., Barnett, B., Howie, P., & Kavanagh, D.J. (2003). Diagnosing postpartum depression in mothers and fathers: Whatever happened to anxiety? *Journal of Affective Disorders, 74*(2), 139–147.

Matthey, S., Phillips, J., White, T., Glossop, P., Hopper, U., Panasetis, P., et al. (2004). Routine psychosocial assessment of women in the antenatal period: Frequency of risk factors and implications for clinical services. *Archives of Women's Mental Health, 7*(4), 223–9.

McMahon, C.A., Barnett, B., Kowalenko, N., & Tennant, C. (2005). Psychological factors associated with persistent postnatal depression, past and current relationships, defense styles and the mediating role of insecure attachment style. *Journal of Affective Disorders, 84*(1), 15–24.

Milgrom, J., Ericksen, J., McCarthy, R., & Gemmill, A.W. (2006). Stressful impact of depression on early mother–infant relations. *Stress and Health, 22*, 107–112.

Milgrom, J., Negri, L.M., Gemmill, A.W., McNeil, M., & Martin, P.R. (2005). A randomised controlled trial of psychological interventions for postnatal depression. *British Journal of Clinical Psychology, 44*(4), 529–542.

Moehler, E., Brunner, R., Wiebel, A., Reck, C., & Resch, F. (2006). Maternal depressive symptoms in the postnatal period are associated with long-term impairment of the mother–child bonding. *Archives of Women's Mental Health, 9*(5), 273–278.

Moses-Kolko, E.L., Bogen, D., Perel, J., Bregar, A., Uhl, K., Levin, B., et al. (2005). Neonatal signs after late in-utero exposure to serotonin reuptake inhibitors: Literature review and implications for clinical applications. *Journal of the American Medical Association, 293*(19), 2372–83.

Murray, L., & Cooper, P.J. (Eds). (1997). *Postpartum depression and child development.* New York: Guilford Press.

Murray, L., Woolgar, M., Murray, J., & Cooper, P. (2003). Self-exclusion from health care in women at high risk for postpartum depression. *Journal of Public Health Medicine, 25*(2):131–7.

Murray, L., Cooper, P.J., Wilson, A., & Romaniuk, H. (2003b). Controlled trial of the short and long term effect of psychological treatment of postpartum depression II:

Impact on the mother–child relationship and child outcomes. *British Journal of Psychiatry, 182*, 420–427

Murray, L., & Cox, J.L. (1990). Screening for depression during pregnancy with the Edinburgh Depression Scale (EDS). *Journal of Reproductive Health and Infant Psychology, 8*, 99–107.

Muzik, M., Klier, C.M., Rosenblum, K.L., Holzinger, A., Umek, W., & Katschnig, H. (2000). Are commonly used self-report inventories suitable for screening postpartum depression and anxiety disorders? *Acta Psychiatrica Scandinavica, 102*, 71–73.

Newman, L., & Mares, S. (2007). Recent advances in the theories of and interventions for attachment disorders. *Current Opinion in Psychiatry, 20*, 343–349.

Oberlander, T.F., Warburton, W., Misri, S., Aghajanian, J., & Hertzman, C. (2006). Neonatal outcomes after prenatal exposure to selective serotonin reuptake inhibitor antidepressants and maternal depression using population-based linked health data. *Archives of General Psychiatry, 63*, 898–906.

O'Connor, T.G., Heron, J., Golding, J., Beveridge, M., & Glover, V. (2002). Maternal antenatal anxiety and children's behavioural/emotional problems at 4 years: Report from the Avon Longitudinal Study of Parents and Children. *The British Journal of Psychiatry, 180*, 502–508.

O'Hara, M.W., Stuart, S., Gorman, L.L., & Wenzel, A. (2000). Efficacy of interpersonal psychotherapy for postpartum depression. *Archives of General Psychiatry, 57*, 1039–1045.

Patel, V., Rahman, A., Jacob, K.S., & Hughes, M. (2004). Effect of maternal health on infant growth in low income countries: New evidence from South Asia. *British Medical Journal, 328*, 820–823.

Payne, J.L. (2007). Antidepressant use in the postpartum period: Practical considerations. *American Journal of Psychiatry, 164*, 1329–1332.

Phillips, J., Sharpe, L., & Matthey, S. (2007). Rates of depressive and anxiety disorders in a residential mother–infant unit for unsettled infants. *Australian and New Zealand Journal of Psychiatry, 41*, 836–842.

Priest, S.R., Austin, M-P., Barnett, B.B., & Buist, A. (2008). *A Psychosocial Risk Assessment Model (PRAM) for use with pregnant and postpartum women in primary care settings.* Manuscript submitted for publication.

Priest, S.R., Henderson, J., Evans, S.F., & Hagan, R. (2003). Stress debriefing after childbirth: A randomised controlled trial. *Medical Journal of Australia, 178*, 542–545.

Rahman, A. (2007). Challenges and opportunities in developing a psychological intervention for perinatal depression in rural Pakistan—a multi-method study. *Archives of Women's Mental Health, 10*, 211–219.

Rahman, A., Iqbal, Z., Bunn, J., Lovel, H., & Harrington, R. (2004). Impact of maternal depression on infant nutritional status and illness: A cohort study. *Archives of General Psychiatry, 61*, 946–952.

Ramos, E., Oraichi, D., Rey, E., Blais, L., & Berard, A. (2007). Prevalence and predictors of antidepressant use in a cohort of pregnant women. *BJOG, 114*, 1055–1064.

Robins, L.N., Wing, J.K., Wittchen, H-U., Helzer, J.E., Babor, T.F., Burke, J., et al. (1988). The Composite International Diagnostic Interview. *Archives of General Psychiatry, 45,* 1069–1077.

Rogal, S.S., Poschman, K., Belanger, K., Howell, H., Smith, M., Medina, J., et al. (2007). Effects of posttraumatic stress disorder on pregnancy outcomes. *Journal of Affective Disorders, 102*(1–3), 137–143.

Shaw, E., Levitt, C., Wong, S., & Kaczorowski, J. (2006). Systematic review of the literature on postpartum care: Effectiveness of postpartum support to improve maternal parenting, mental health, quality of life, and physical health. *Birth, 33,* 210–220.

Swain, J.E., Lorberbaum, J.P., Kose, S., & Strathearn, L. (2007). Brain basis of early parent-infant interactions: psychology, physiology, and in-vivo functional neuro-imaging studies. *Journal of Child Psychology and Psychiatry, 48*(3/4), 262–287.

Tronick, E. (2007). *The neurobehavioural and social–emotional development of infants and children.* New York: W.W. Norton & Company.

Viguera, A., Cohen, L.S., Nonacs, R.M., & Baldessarini, R.J.. (2005). Management of bipolar disorder during pregnancy and the postpartum period. In L.S. Cohen & R.M. Nonacs, *Mood and anxiety disorders during pregnancy and postpartum (Review of Psychiatry,* Vol. 24, p. 57). Arlington, VA: American Psychiatric Publishing.

Viguera, A., Nonacs, R., Cohen, L.S., Tondo, L., Murray, A., & Baldessarini, R.J. (2000). Risk of recurrence of bipolar disorder in pregnant and nonpregnant women after discontinuing lithium maintenance. *American Journal of Psychiatry, 157,* 179–184.

Weinberg, M.K., & Tronick, E.Z. (1998). The impact of maternal psychiatric illness on infant development. *Journal of Clinical Psychiatry, 59*(Suppl. 2), 53–61.

Yehuda, R., Engel, S.M., Brand, S.R., Seckl, J., Marcus, S.M. & Berkowitz, G.S. (2005). Transgenerational effects of posttraumatic stress disorders in babies of mothers exposed to the World Trade Center attacks during pregnancy. *Journal of Clinical Endocrinology and Metabolism, 90,* 4115–4118.

Assessing the Situation

More Than a Question of Safety

Assessing Attachment Disorganisation and Protective Capacity in High-Risk Parent–Infant Dyads

Jennifer E. McIntosh

⌐⌐

Infants are born into a multitude of differing life circumstances. Not all parents are able to provide a safe, nurturing environment to appropriately ensure that the infant survives into adult life to become an autonomous and capable individual. As science advances, factors that ensure an infant reaches optimal adult development have become more apparent, with emotional care taking its place alongside adequate nutrition and physical safety. Complex life issues, including substance abuse, compromised parenting histories full of trauma, mental illness, poverty, lack of support, and domestic violence, can combine to make the psychological task of parenting a difficult one. When minimum parenting cannot be guaranteed, child protection authorities must intervene to safeguard the infant's wellbeing. Thus begins a complex path for the infant through out-of-home care and a sociolegal maze where the child's rights to healthy development may clash with the perceived right of birth parents to parent. This chapter explores debates around differing 'rights' and offers a perspective on assessment that ensures adequate consideration of the developmental needs of infants in decision-making processes regarding their future care. The framework advocated employs evidence-based approaches in the early assessment of high-risk infants, aiming to assist and truncate the 'adjudication' process through in-depth understanding of the traumatised attachment relationship, its historical underpinnings and its psychological trajectories for parent and child. In particular, such an assessment aims to delineate, from an evidence base, the capacity of the attachment and care-giving relationship to recover a sufficient level of organisation, within a time frame that is developmentally useful to the young child.

An Attachment-Based Redefinition of 'Rights': The Proposition

After many years of intensive practice review and research, new child protection legislation in the state of Victoria allows for earlier permanency planning for children in high-risk contexts, in some cases within 1 year of removal from their birth parent. Such birth parents are likely to have a range of issues already outlined — including substance abuse, domestic violence, mental illness and compromised parenting — some of which can potentially change with motivation and appropriate therapy. Some therefore protest planned legislation changes, suggesting that such legislation may not give parents sufficient time to redress their difficulties before a child is permanently placed away from them. Some have suggested that these laws could create a second generation of 'stolen children' in Australia, evoking the tragic history of Aboriginal children wrongfully removed from their parents in the early 20th century.

The potential for 'wrongful denial' of parental rights in child protection matters is real. Yet so too is the potential for 'wrongful denial' of secure base relationships for young children who face lengthy, well-intended but ultimately unsuccessful 'experimentation' with case plans, including multiple transitions in and out of birth family care. It can be argued that such tensions can be held and thought about productively, through reasoned, evidence-based consideration of what constitutes a 'good enough protective, organised attachment platform' in a caregiver, and what nature of damage to that person can and cannot respond in a timely way to treatment. Using the framework of Ainsworth, Blehar, Waters and Wall (1978) and Main and Solomon (1990), 'good enough' parenting would be sufficient to provide organised rather than disorganised attachment security — more of this later.

Existing legislation in Australia, as in most Western countries, has historically been structured around the biological parent's right to care for her/his child above the child's right to have a continuous nurturing relationship. Historically, as Willemsen and Marcel (1995) document, the permanent psychological importance of attachment in infancy was not recognised, and the effects of incoherent care experiences were presumed to be temporary or reversible.

In a system founded upon the rights of birth parents, high risk was defined as the child's risk of being removed from their birth family. From an attachment perspective, high risk may, with equal validity, be redefined as the risk of not being removed from a birth parent who cannot provide safety and the risk of not being allowed to form nurturing attachments outside of that family.

In the current child protection system, high-risk children, by either definition of risk, spend their formative years under multiple traumas. Initial, profound damage to their attachment with an overwhelmed or overwhelming birth parent is often confounded by removal to multiple foster placements, with periodic and at times ill-founded home release experiments. Throughout this journey, while these infants 'wait' for their birth parents to recover or to acquire capacity to safely parent them, the comfortable use of a continuous, reliable attachment figure as a base for exploring their world and their experience is denied them.

Do we have a biological right to parent our own children? It has taken the sobering force of neurobiological evidence (Balbarnie, 2001, 2003; Cicchetti & Rogosch, 2001; Schore 2003a, 2003b; Siegel, 2001) to confirm the enduring neurological trauma done to a young child who is not permitted a responsive, intimate, protecting relationship with a caring adult. This implies an imperative for preference of attachment above biology in the developmental health of the young child. Given the facts of developmental traumatology, many now believe child protection legislation must enable children to have and to secure a meaningful, organised care-giving relationship.

From Ideology to Clinical Investigation

Given that these outcomes for infants exist side by side with sociopolitical tensions and ideologies around parental 'rights', the challenge is to identify the following:

- a perspective for rigorous clinical assessment that securely identifies infants for whom a nonbiological home is in their best interests. This will be the subject of the rest of this chapter.

- mechanisms for ensuring that an alternative home, usually a foster home, will provide safe, appropriate, nurturing care. Long-term and permanent foster carers in this light would also, optimally, participate in assessments of the nature described in this chapter, to determine capacity for promoting organised attachments, recovery from trauma and integration for dependent children in their care.

The perspective of this chapter sits uniquely at the intersection of attachment theory, neurobiological research and psychoanalytic practice. Research in attachment has removed a layer of speculation from complex parent–child risk assessments, providing a conceptual framework and tools for both assessment and the psychotherapeutic treatment of damaged care-giving capacity. Clinical research has confirmed that parents' states of mind with respect to their infants' attachment needs lie at the core of their capacity for protective, sensitive behaviour (George & Solomon, 1999; Grienenberger, Kelly, & Slade, 2005). Related research sets a new benchmark for clinical assessment of the architecture of protective, reflective states of mind and their openness to change as a vehicle for both assessment and treatment.

High-Risk Attachment Trauma — Determinants of the Disorganised Care-giving System

It is long established that infants develop unconscious strategies for dealing with or responding to patterns of care from their parents: their attachment status shows what lessons they have learned about care. The groundbreaking work of notable researchers such as George, Solomon, Fonagy, the Steeles, Target, Slade and Zeanah, among others, has identified 'parental reflective function' and associated 'sensitivity of attunement' to the infant as central to the structure of a parent's care-giving system, and therefore central to the shape of the quality of the child's attachment.

The cornerstone of parental reflection and security in attachment is the parent's capacity to take the infant's perspective. It is the clarity and accuracy of parents' reflection on their own internal states and ability to differentiate and process the infant's internal states that usher in the formation of attachment and of the self. Parental reflective function is 'a crucial human capacity that is intrinsic to affect regulation and productive social relationships' (Slade, 2005, p. 270). The parent with high reflective function is present to a full range of core parenting experiences, from joy through to ambivalence, guilt and anger. Theirs is a capacity to experience, hold and regulate emotion and, in turn, these parents are more likely to assist their infant toward sound emotional regulation and hence development.

As Marvin, Cooper, Hoffman and Powell (2002) describe, derailments of parental reflection and attunement are at the heart of disruption to a child's development. In the high-risk arena, the core of such derailment is the parent's own profound and unresolved attachment trauma (James, 1994). For good reason, this parent cannot differentiate the young child's internal states from her own, with a dire quality of ego distortion and defensive exclusion that permeates the becoming of the infant, heralding a dysregulated, disorganised inner state with respect to attachment.

Disorganised Attachment

The disorganised pattern originally explicated by Main and Solomon (1990), is characterised by an incoherent attachment strategy in the young child, accompanied by odd behaviours that make sense only if one understands that the infant is confused, overwhelmed or fearful with respect to their caregiver (Solomon & George, 1999). In response to very disturbed patterns of care, these children do not develop consistent ways of understanding or signalling their needs and feelings. Instead, a chaotic response ensues when their attachment systems are aroused, in a playing out of unthinkable and unknowable anxiety. The chaos runs deep. Physiologically, the cardiac and cortisol levels of disorganised children rise four to five times higher than those of secure base children during 'Strange Situation' assessments (Spangler & Grossman, 1999).

Disorganisation in young children occurs in the presence of the lowest level of parental reflectiveness (Fonagy & Target, 2005). Preoccupied and dismissive approaches to a care-giver's reflections about the infant generally herald in the infant a need to form organised, defensive processes. While problematic, these are often amenable to shift via attachment-based treatment. When considering the complexities of high-risk child protection matters, it is the disorganised attachment spectrum that accelerates developmental risk. In the absence of confounding developmental problems, a disorganised attachment in a young child is a reliable symptom of chronically disturbed and unprotective care-giving patterns in their parent (George & Solomon, 1999).

Research confirms the disorganised attachment relationship to be among the greatest developmental risks to the young child (De Bellis, 2001). This pattern is frequent in maltreated and clinic samples. De Bellis describes from the neurological perspective how 'severe trauma of interpersonal origins may override any genetic, constitutional, social or psychological resilience factors' (p. 543). Lyons-Ruth and Block (1996) find that 82% of disorganised infants are maltreated, in contrast to 14% from a general population sample of middle-income families. In the shift from attachment disorganisation to maladaptive controlling behaviours in later childhood, a pattern of poor mental health outcomes emerges (Jacobvitz & Hazen, 1999). Children who develop disorganised attachment are among the angriest children in the world, significantly more so than children exposed to trauma outside of their attachment relationships (Kochanska, 2001). It follows that these children, in the absence of a corrective organising attachment experience, move into their own care-giving with an unintegrated, helpless/hostile (Lyons-Ruth & Block, 1996) and dysregulated (George & Solomon, 1999) platform for parenting.

Main & Solomon (1990) were among the first to identify the presence of frightening or frightened behaviours by the caregiver in the genesis of disorganised attachment. Importantly, Lyons-Ruth and Spielman (2004) have added that disrupted affective communication and failures to adequately engage and structure the infant are equally critical. Two subgroups of disorganised care-giving have emerged through the Lyons-Ruth laboratory: 'hostile/ self-referential regarding attachment', and 'helpless/fearful regarding attachment'. Both hostile and helpless profiles reflect 'alternative expressions of a single unbalanced controlling–controlled relationship prototype' experienced in the parent's own attachment history' (p. 325).

Further research has demonstrated both the subtle and profound ways in which the infant's mental self is undermined in the care of such a parent (Fonagy & Target, 2005). Fonagy, Gergely, Jurist and Target (2002) observe that in the case of chronically insensitive or misattuned parenting, a fault is created in the very construction of the infant's self. Here the baby's affects are repeatedly misrepresented by a chronically misattuned parent. Their view mirrors Bowlby's (1973) original clinical–developmental thinking. Fonagy and colleagues propose that the infant internalises the pattern of misrepresentation as a core part of himself, instead of internalising his own lived experience, which remains overwhelming and unrepresentable. Sharing his mind or his true experience with the parent becomes a dangerous task rather than a rich opportunity, and the child's inner life becomes unknowable, within a tapestry of profoundly unsafe psychological experiences. Frequently added to this are layers of attendant environmental trauma and neglect for caregiver and infant.

Implications for Assessment

Theory and research clearly delineate the territory of high risk from a developmental perspective. How is it identified in practice? How can determination reliably be made around whether a high-risk relationship may recover sufficiently to permit the infant adequate protective organisation and allow the restoration of parental rights?

Main, Kaplan and Cassidy (1985) highlighted a move to the level of representation in the measurement of attachment over 20 years ago in the research arena. Only recently have clinicians followed suit, and then not systematically. Assessments of reunification of infants in high-risk situations are often conducted around variables that have little to do with the origin of the failure in the protective state of mind. More often, symptom or systems management is advised (e.g., attendance at anger management and parenting skills classes, obtaining housing and complying with urine screens). In high-risk reunification, it has not been standard procedure for parental assessment to look at the level of representation. Yet this is where evidence locates both the diagnosis and prognosis of the child's attachment relationships that are hallmarked by the experience of threatening care. Thus, high-risk clinical assessment using current research should, logically, cover a dimensional matrix, approaching the infant–caregiver relationship as a complex system of observable interactions and internal representations, whose origins and trajectories have been established empirically.

An Illustration of High-Risk Attachment Assessments

The author has spent some years building assessment practices around such a matrix, together with ways of containing and supporting the clinical capacity to see and to think clearly, on behalf of the high-risk infants and young children who attend the clinic.[1] In this framework, attachment risk assessments typically take up to eighteen hours to conduct, across two days.

Typically, the children referred to the clinic are in foster care, usually for lengthy periods of time, and a decision about their permanent care placement is pending. It is often at this point that a birth parent contests the case plan prepared by the state child protection authority, hoping for reunification with their child.

The referral question, on the surface is, 'Is it safe for the infant to go home?' In the infant's best interests, however, following Zeanah et al. (1999), the first endeavour is to transform the question such that it reads, 'What is it like to be this infant in this relationship with this caregiver, at this time?' Additional questions that underpin the assessment include: 'Does the parental care-giving relationship have capacity for the change that is needed by the infant, within a developmental timeframe useful to the infant?' 'What developmental consequence is forecast, should the relationship continue, unchanged?'

Particular attention is paid to links between the parent's care-taking behaviours and her representations about the infant's needs (George & Solomon, 1996), including the capacity to affectively attune to her infant: to discern and respond to the infant's nonverbal signals, to demonstrate protective thought and an ability to wonder about her infant's full experience. This involves assessment of a parent's attachment and care-giving narratives, building an understanding of the parent's organisation of defensive processes, against which to consider the observable qualities of the infant–caregiver interaction and developmental context. Importantly in this work, the infant's own emerging representations also need to be assessed. In this light, wherever possible, observation includes the infant's inferred use of the parental mind, and is contrasted by observations of her/his inferred use of a different mind, namely his/her responses to the foster parent.

Several research groups have established measures (Appendix A) that guide the clinical observation of reflective function and care-giving sensitivity in the parent, together with the young child's own representations of attachment. These frameworks are employed, in various combinations and adaptations, to create a clinical assessment battery. Many require specific training for intensive research use and formal accreditation, and their application to clinical reflection on the complex and important issues outlined here is appropriate.

Clinical Indices of Disorganised Care-Giving and Attachment Systems

The key features of disorganised/traumatised attachment as they appear clinically on a number of these frameworks are as follows.

Disorganisation in Parent's Representations of Attachment History and Current Care-Giving Relationship

An abbreviated clinical administration of the Adult Attachment Interview (George, Kaplan, & Mais, 1985) typically helps to identify parents who, through necessity, used dissociation and identification to cope with profound attachment trauma in childhood, and who remain unresolved in their current state of mind with respect to attachment.

Lyons-Ruth and Spielman (2004) have identified particular defensive patterns in parents with low sensitivity in their care-giving. Helpless parents have adopted a lifelong hypervigilance to the moods of their own mothers at the expense of having their own attachment needs met, and experience great anxiety and fear in close emotional contact with their infant. Their coping strategies include dissociation. Hostile parents, in attempting to master unbearable vulnerability, deny feelings of fear and helplessness and identify with the hostile or controlling parent.

In bringing that history to bear on care-giving of her own child, history repeats, with distortion and impoverishment evident in narrative accounts about the child. The disorganising parent does not have an inquiring stance with regard to her infant. High-risk parents do not see their young children's core attachment experience, layered as it becomes with their own unconscious hostility and fear from unresolved attachment states of mind. Reflective function fails, profoundly. As Slade (2005) describes, these are parents who 'will not or cannot enter their child's experience as a means of understanding them, and who do not use their own internal experience as a guide for sensitive responsiveness' (p. 278). In clinical terms, they are highly defended and resort to primitive means of blocking out or distorting their child's internal life.

Following Bowlby, Carol George and Judith Solomon (2005) term these patterns of response 'segregated care-giving systems'. They propose that under normal circumstances, organised attachment in the child requires transformation of the parental self to become the person who is the 'stronger and wiser' individual (see Marvin, Cooper, Hoffman & Powell, 2002) in the attachment–care-giving relationship. The parent's attachment system (i.e., own attachment needs) should inform but not dominate the parent's commitment and ability to provide comfort and protection in response to the child's attachment signals. All caregiver defensive modalities should function to protect the caregiver from being overwhelmed. Organised modes of defensive exclusion, brought into play by interaction with a child, include deactivation and cognitive disconnection of attachment stimuli. Segregation functions to block experience and affect from conscious awareness (George & Solomon, 2005). This they term the most extreme and brittle form of defensive exclusion, associated with present or past attachment trauma in the parent's history. When this occurs, the parent's ability to respond to her child is overwhelmed by her own attachment fears and traumatic experiences. Parents become helpless, out of control, frightened, seek care from their children (i.e., role reversal), and often merge their traumatised self with their child. They also often become oblivious to, enraged by, or act cruelly toward their children. These dysregulated mental and behavioural states underlie failed protective capacity and place the child at high risk. Importantly, the child's own attachment system becomes dysregulated, with the underlying experience of self as abandoned and unprotected (Solomon & George, 1999). Parents with segregated care-giving systems have children who understand quickly that they must adopt behavioural strategies, however possible, to take charge of their own safety and survival and who risk becoming enraged, embittered, and precociously adultified over the course of development. These are the signs and symptoms of disorganised attachment.

Some of the features of segregation that predominate in our assessments of high-risk dyads (as identified in the parent's narrative on the Caregiver Interview of George and Solomon, 2005) include:

- denial or blocking of frightening realities/shutting down
- role reversed/merged view of their child

- abdication of care, psychologically abandoning
- parent expressing feelings of being hurt by their child
- parent is extremely controlling
- frightened/hypervigilant view of their child
- permits distress and fear in their child
- accounts contain graphic or bizarre detail.

Parents who rate higher in these domains are less likely to provide protective capacities, both psychological and environmental, for their infant, through their pervasively dysregulated care-giving.

The clinical features of disorganised attachments and segregated care-giving systems outlined above are illustrated in the following case example:

Case Illustration: Mother K and Jordan, Aged 2.4 Years[2]

At assessment, Jordan was living out of his mother's care, and had been since a severe, nonaccidental injury at 6 weeks. He had been in two foster care placements, the most recent for 16 months. The mother's contact with him was sporadic, although it was court ordered to occur weekly. The referral came from the child protection authority, whose officers were considering a Permanent Foster Care Order, with Mother K seeking reunification.

Responding to selected core questions from the Adult Attachment Interview, Mother K described her own parenting as emotionally scarring. As the scars do not appear to have healed, they are referred to as Unresolved:

> Mum: a battler, bloody hard as nails, scary, bossy. Is that five words?
> Interferes. She's got emphysema. Serves her right. There were a lot
> of us kids. Try not to have much to do with her now. She gave us
> what for. Guess we deserved it — bunch of ratbags. She ran us like
> the army. Still tries to ... It isn't right, what she does, I mean, what
> she did ... Does it affect me? Nup — who'd want to be like her? No
> way I'll treat my kids that way."
>
> Dad: a softy, bit of a loser really, drank himself away ... pretty
> pathetic ... He's dead ... Dad did stuff ... Mum gave us nothing.
> I'm not going to talk about it. You can't make me.

Mother's representations of care-giving make clear how her own unresolved attachment patterns impact dramatically on her views of her child and his current emotional needs, which she dismisses in derogatory terms, making her own unmet needs evident:

> **Could you tell me about a time you felt real joy in being Jordan's
> mother?**

Not really. It's not joy. When he's being cute … Nup. When he's asleep (sniggers). He doesn't need his foster mummy coddling him. She's made a nancy boy out of him. Have him wearing skirts soon she will.

Can you tell me about a time when you felt anger toward Jordan?

No. Nothing unusual … (laughs) … I don't get angry with him. I just put him in his room. Last contact visit he was screaming for the foster mum. Her fault. She let him be all clingy. And he wouldn't shut up, so I locked him in the room until he did shut up … took a while but he got the message that the tears weren't going to get him anywhere with me, and he won't be pulling that one again.

Disorganisation in the Care-Giving Response

The key feature here, seen on observation, is the maintenance of a frightened–frightening care-giving environment characteristic of disorganised attachment, embedded in a broader context of disrupted emotional communication. For example, the AMBIANCE scale (Bronfman, Parsons, & Lyons-Ruth 1993), identifies the following:

- parental withdrawal responses
- negative–intrusive responses
- role-confused responses
- disoriented responses
- affective communication errors

and specifically:

- delayed responsiveness or ignoring
- withdrawing and distancing
- cursory responsiveness
- directs infant away from self
- hesitation or tension at moments of heightened attachment
- little physical contact
- vacating parental role
- subtly fearful, submissive with regard to infant
- may show little overt negative affect.

On greeting his mother, Jordan smiled quickly, with eye contact and toddled quickly away from her to the toys in the room. She replied, 'Have you become a little girl Jordie, playing with toys?' Mother K .was encouraged to play with Jordan as she normally would. 'He usually plays alone' was her reply, as she sat stationary.

In the Clinical Problem Solving activities (Crowell and Feldman, 1988) simple games were done in a rote fashion, naming the cars and animals, but not extending it into a play sequence. There was some humour here, but generally the tone of the play was static.

The tea set that followed elicited taunting of Jordan by Mother K. She said 'all the food's gone', snatching food from him and the two began clutching things away from each other. Mother K encouraged Jordan's attacks on her, and rather than trying to contain him in any way, further antagonised him. When Jordan offered a pretend egg to his mother, she said, 'No Mummy don't want an egg'. Jordan became exasperated at this point, snatching the egg and yelling in a distressed fashion, 'Go 'way!' to his mother. She replied 'Make me'.

The doctor's kit had been Jordan's favourite activity in two previous observations with his foster mother. Mother K pulled all the items from the kit one by one and used them in a manner that was threatening or frightening. Jordan tried at first to correct her and to steer her toward the type of play that he had enjoyed with both his carer and myself, but Mother K persisted in jabbing, pinching and prodding him with the implements, telling him 'you are afraid of needles' as she put the needle to his arm. In retaliation, Jordan began to use the equipment on her in the same way. Her comments were 'I hope you never grow up to be a doctor … you've gone psycho'. At my request, the session was ended. Jordan, with a desperate quality, packed up the kit and yelled 'no' at his mother. Jordan took himself to the other side of the room and recovered somewhat with quiet solitary play. He nodded when I commented that this sort of play wasn't what he had been wanting. He asked for his foster mother.

Disorganisation in the Infant's Attachment System

Main and Solomon (1990) identified the following key indices of infant behaviour associated with emergent disorganised attachment, typically assessed through the Strange Situation:

- contradictory behaviours — simultaneous and sequentially displayed
- poorly directed cues
- anomalous postures and mistimed movements
- freezing, stilling
- apprehension
- disoriented wandering, confusion, rapid changes in affect.

Jordan's separation from Mother K was characterised by mutual lack of acknowledgment. When she left the room, he became animated and sought to play with the animal farm with the clinician. On reunion, Jordan's mother entered loudly, saying 'What you up to?' as she looked out of the window.

Jordan moved next to the clinician, looked up, down, up and finally locked his gaze on the farmyard. Mother sat silently over the play scene. Jordan did not resume play.

Separation–reunion observations with his carer showed a markedly different pattern, with Jordan's active use of her as a secure base, and a rhythmicity of gaze and proximity seeking. He protested when she left, and on return, experienced her as an interested and soothing presence.

Disorganisation in the Young Child's Representations of Attachment

For the child beyond the preschool years, there are a number of tools to facilitate an in-depth enquiry into the attachment state of mind. Frameworks useful to the assessment process described here include the Children's Attachment Interview (Target, Fonagy, & Shmueli-Goetz, 2003) and the Story Stem Battery (Hodges, Steele, Hillman, & Henderson, 2003).

Using these frameworks, the core features associated with disorganised attachment status that we typically identify in the clinic include:

- emotional rigidity
- incoherent anger and high levels of control
- distortion of their own attachment needs
- unresolved attachment conflicts
- themes of child being endangered, with unaware or absent parent.

Clinical Implications

If the revolving door of assessment and home release experimentation is to be avoided on behalf of the young child in out-of-home care, the assessment process must be thorough, comprehensive and forward-looking, beyond diagnosis to an informed view of prognosis. It must extend toward treatment, sidestepping a purely forensic intent, to include active exploration by the clinician of the parent's ability to use support for reflection. Can repair be made?

As these assessment frameworks identify pathology in the attachment and care-giving systems, they also point to treatment directions. For example, Steele and Baradon (2004), and Marvin et al. (2002) describe therapeutic processes based on a rigorous understanding of the representational space. Our work frequently identifies the need for an extended period of dyadic work to fully explore the potential for use of a therapeutic space. Here, the guided application of the therapist's own sense of organisation with respect to attachment is pivotal (Hughes, 2004).

In line with Balbarnie (2003), the attempt in extended therapeutic assessment is to locate the parent's ability to contemplate and articulate feelings, and to rebuild the preverbal foundations of attachment, so that dysregulation and abandonment are less prominent. The parent may then be able to redefine the infant's psychological environment so he/she can behaviourally access the parent and hopefully, in time, come to have more reliable mental access to the parent. These are the foundations of attachment treatment, also echoed in core therapeutic directions identified by Lyons-Ruth and Spielman (2004), as follows:

- establishing security in the therapeutic relationship
- creating room for openness to a wider range of affective experience
- differentiating attachment needs from other emotional communications from the baby
- developing new models of balancing the needs of self and baby.
- 'finding a third way' — a space that is neither hostile nor helpless.

The difficulty in the unresolved/traumatised caregiver, by definition, lies in their extremely limited and damaged capacity to engage in therapeutic relationships. While emerging treatment models such as the Circle of Security (Marvin et al., 2002) hold enormous promise, it must be acknowledged that there remains a group of parents for whom there has been 'too much' disorganisation in the care-giving system, who cannot be supported to achieve the change needed by their children. Here, the hostile/controlling subgroup of disorganisation in caregivers, or the high end of caregiver segregation, are frequently unresponsive to treatment. This was the case for Jordan. The hostile defensive exclusion that characterised Mother K's attachment and care-giving narratives and her psychological abandonment of her child were profound and deeply embedded. When occasional moments of vulnerability were approached during the assessment, she shut down repeatedly. Her anger permeated all attempts at supportive discussion and flooded the space with her son. Even if a level of engagement could be achieved, the nature of the change needed to ensure a protective mind would take many years, a time frame that Jordan could ill afford.

Conclusion

Returning to the beginning, this chapter supports legislative efforts to uphold the right of the child to early psychological security within an organised and continuous attachment relationship. In safeguarding the rights of both parent and infant, rigorous assessment-based evaluation of high-risk parent–child dyads early in the infant's out-of-home placement can identify either the potential for sufficient recovery of a protective state of mind in the parent with accompanying greater organisation in the infant's attachment experience, or the advisability of continuing appropriate out-of-home care. It is appropriate to identify and name the absence of a capacity to recover in a timely manner.

The attachment frameworks outlined here illustrate the level of precision that is available for application in clinical assessment of high-risk attachment relationships, particularly enabling a shift to the level of representation in assessment. With this kind of care, the high-risk parent and infant's experiences of attachment can be found, beneath acquired trauma, under layers of political and legal meaning, their availability to different minds observed, and recovery toward an organised attachment base begun for the infant, within or beyond the birth parent relationship.

Endnotes

1   Family Transitions, Carlton, Victoria
2   All identifying features of this case have been altered.

References

Aber, J., Slade, A., Berger, B., Bresgi, I., & Kaplan, M. (1985). *The Parent Development Interview*. Unpublished protocol, The City University of New York.

Ainsworth, M., Blehar, B., Waters, E., & Wall, S. (1978). *Patterns of attachment. A psychological study of the Strange Situation*. Hillsdale, NJ: Erlbaum.

Balbarnie, R. (2001). Circuits and circumstances: The neurobiological consequences of early relationship experiences and how they shape later behaviour. *Journal of Child Psychotherapy*, *27*, 237–255.

Balbarnie, R. (2003). The roominess of language: Mothers' descriptions of their infants and a discourse analysis approach to reflective function. *Journal of Child Psychotherapy, 29,* 393–413.

Biringen, Z. (2000). Emotional availability: Conceptualization and research findings. *American Journal of Orthopsychiatry, 70,* 104–114.

Biringen, Z. & Robinson, J. (1991). Emotional availability: A reconceptualization for research. *American Journal of Orthopsychiatry, 61,* 258–271.

Bohr, Y., Hudson Crain, R., & Holigrocki, R. J. (2005). *PCIA-II MAP treatment manual: Modifying attributions of parents intervention.* Unpublished manuscript, York University and the University of Indianapolis.

Bowlby, J. (1973). *Separation, anxiety and anger. Attachment and Loss Vol. II.* London: Hogarth Press.

Britner, P., Marvin, R., & Pianta, R. (2005) Development and preliminary validation of the caregiving behaviour system: Association with child attachment classification in the pre-school Strange Situation. *Attachment and Human Development, 7,* 83–102.

Bronfman, E., Parsons, E., & Lyons-Ruth, K. (1993). *Atypical maternal behaviour instrument for assessment and classification (ambience): Manual for coding disrupted affective communication, version 2.* Unpublished manuscript, Cambridge, MA: Harvard Medical School.

Cassidy, J., & Marvin, R.S. (1990). *Attachment organization in pre-school children: Guidelines for classification.* Unpublished scoring manual, Macarthur Working Group on Attachment, Seattle, WA.

Cicchetti, D., & Rogosch, F. (2001). The impact of child maltreatment and psychopathology on neuroendocrine functioning. *Development and Psychopathology, 13,* 783–804.

Crowell, J., & Feldman, S. (1988). The effects of mothers' internal working models of relationships and children's behavioural and developmental status on mother–child interaction. *Child Development, 59,* 1273–1285.

De Bellis, M. (2001). Developmental traumatology: The psychobiological development of maltreated children and its implications for research, treatment and policy. *Development and Psychopathology, 13,* 539–564.

Fonagy, P., Gergely, G., Jurist, E., & Target, M. (2002). *Affect regulation, mentalization and the development of the self.* New York: Other Press.

Fonagy, P., & Target, M. (2005). Bridging the transmission gap: An end to an important mystery of attachment research? *Attachment and Human Development, 7,* 333–343.

George, C., Kaplan, N., & Main, M. (1985). *The Adult Attachment Interview.* Unpublished manuscript, Berkeley, University of California.

George, C., & Solomon, J. (2005). *Internal working models of caregiving rating manual version 05.1.* Unpublished.

George, C., & Solomon, J. (1996). Representational models of relationships: Links between caregiving and representation. *Infant Mental Health Journal, 17,* 198–216.

George, C., & Solomon, J. (1999). Attachment and caregiving. In J. Osofsky & H. Fitzgerald (Eds.), *Handbook of attachment: Theory, research and clinical application* (pp. 649–670). New York: Guilford Press.

Grienenberger, J., Kelly, K., & Slade, A. (2005). Maternal reflective functioning, mother-infant affective communication, and infant attachment: Exploring the link between mental states and observed caregiving behaviour in the intergenerational transmission of attachment. *Attachment and Human Development, 7,* 299–311.

Hodges, J., Steele, M., Hillman, S., & Henderson, K. (2003). Mental representations and defenses in severely maltreated children: A story stem battery and rating system for clinical assessment and research applications. In R. Emde, D. Wolf, & D. Oppenheim, (Eds.), *Revealing the inner world of the child* (pp. 240–267). Chicago: University of Chicago Press.

Hodges, J., Steele, M., Hillman, S., Henderson, K., & Kaniuk, J. (2003). Changes in attachment representations over the first year of adoptive placement: Narratives of maltreated children. *Clinical Child Psychology and Psychiatry, 8,* 351–367.

Hughes, D. (2004). An attachment based treatment of maltreated children and young people. *Attachment and Human Development, 6,* 263–278.

Jacobvitz, D., & Hazen, N. (1999). Developmental pathways from infant disorganization to childhood peer relationships. In J. Solomon & C. George (Eds.), *Attachment disorganization* (pp. 127–159). New York: Guilford Press.

James, B. (1994). Human attachments and trauma. In B. James (Ed.), *Handbook for treatment of attachment-trauma problems in children* (pp. 1–17). New York: The Free Press.

Kochanska, G. (2001). Emotional development in children with different attachment histories: The first three years. *Child Development, 72,* 474–490.

Lyons-Ruth, K., & Block, D. (1996). The disturbed caregiving system: Relations among childhood trauma, maternal caregiving, and infant affect and attachment. *Infant Mental Health Journal, 17,* 257–275.

Lyons-Ruth, K., & Spielman, E. (2004). Disorganised infant attachment strategies and helpless-fearful profiles of parenting: Integrating attachment research with clinical intervention. *Infant Mental Health Journal, 25,* 318–335.

Main, M., Kaplan, N., & Cassidy, J. (1985). Security in infancy, childhood, and adulthood: A move to the level of representation. In I. Bretherton & E. Waters (Eds.), *Growing points in attachment theory and research. Monographs of the Society for Research in Child Development, 50,* (1–2, no. 209), 66–104.

Main, M., & Solomon, J. (1990). Procedures for identifying infants as disorganised/disoriented during the Ainsworth Strange Situation. In M.T. Greenberg, D. Cicchetti, & E. M. Cummings (Eds.). *Attachment in the pre-school years* (pp. 121–160). Chicago: University Press of Chicago.

Marvin, R., Cooper, G., Hoffman, K., & Powell, B. (2002). The Circle of Security project: Attachment based intervention with caregiver-pre-school child dyads. *Attachment and Human Development, 4,* 107–124.

Schore, A.N. (2003a). *Affect dysregulation and disorders of the self.* New York: W.W. Norton.

Schore, A.N. (2003b). *Affect regulation and repair of the self.* New York: W.W. Norton.

Siegel, D. (2001). Toward an interpersonal neurobiology of the developing mind: Attachment relationships, mindsight and neural integration. *Infant Mental Health Journal, 22*(1–2), 67–94.

Slade, A. (2005). Parental reflective functioning: An introduction. *Attachment and Human Development, 7,* 269–282.

Solomon, J., & George, C. (1999). The place of disorganization in attachment theory. In J. Solomon & C. George, (Eds.). *Attachment disorganization* (pp. 3–32). New York: Guilford Press.

Spangler, G., & Grossman, K. (1999). Individual and physiological correlates of attachment disorganization in infancy. In J. Solomon & C. George, (Eds.), *Attachment disorganization* (pp. 95–126). New York: Guilford Press.

Steele, M., & Baradon, T. (2004). Clinical use of the Adult Attachment Interview in parent-infant psychotherapy. *Infant Mental Health Journal, 25,* 284–299.

Target, M., Fonagy P., & Shmueli-Goetz, Y. (2003). Attachment representations in school-age children: The development of the child attachment interview (CAI). *Journal of Child Psychotherapy, 29,* 171–186.

Waters, E. (1987). *Attachment behavior Q-set* (Revision 3.0). Unpublished manuscript. Stony Brook, NY: SUNY, Department of Psychology.

Waters, E., & Deane, K. E. (1985). Defining and assessing individual differences in attachment relationships: Q-methodology and the organization of behavior in infancy and early childhood. In I. Bretherton & E. Waters (Eds.), Growing points in attachment theory and research. *Monographs of the Society for Research in Child Development, 50* (1–2, Serial No. 209), 41–65.

Willemsen, E., & Marcel, K. (1995). *Attachment 101 for Attorneys: Implications for infant placement decisions.* Retrieved February 2, 2008, from http://www.scu.edu/ethics/publications/other/lawreview/attachment101.html

Zeanah, C., Boris, N.W., Scott Heller, S., Hinshaw-Fuselier, S., Larrieu, J.A., Lewis, M., Palomino, R., Rovaris, M., & Valliere, J. (1999). Relationship assessment in infant mental health. *Infant Mental Health Journal, 18,* 182–197.

Appendix A

Frameworks for Assessing Reflective Function in Parents' Narratives Caregiver Interview (George & Solomon, 2005 version)

Parent Development Interview (Aber, Slade, Berger, Bresgi, & Kaplan, 1985)

Working Model of the Child Interview (Zeanah, Boris, Scott Hellier, Hinshaw-Fuselier, Larrieu, Lewis, Palomino, Rovaris, & Valliere, 1999)

The Adult Attachment Interview (George, Kaplan, & Main, 1989).

Frameworks for Assessing Sensitivity of Attunement and Contingent Infant Response: Strange Situation (Ainsworth, Blehar, Waters, & Wall, 1978; Cassidy & Marvin, 1990)

Caregiver Behaviour Classification System (Britner, Marvin, & Pianta, 2005)

Problem Solving Procedure (Crowell & Feldman, 1988)

AMBIANCE system (Bohr, Hudson Crain, & Holigrocki, 2005; Bronfman, Parsons, & Lyons-Ruth, 1993)

Emotional Availability Scales (Biringen, 2000; Biringen & Robinson, 1994).

Frameworks for Assessing Children's Attachment State of Mind Children's Attachment Interview (Target, Fonagy, & Shmueli-Goetz, 2003)

Attachment Q-set (version 3) (Waters, 1987; Waters & Dean, 1985)

Clinical Problem Solving Procedure (Crowell Procedure; Crowell & Feldman, 1988)

The Story Stem Battery (assessing dysregulated attachment representations; Hodges, Steele, Hillman, & Henderson, 2003; Hodges, Steele, Hillman, Henderson, & Kaniuk, 2003)

High-Risk Infant Assessments

The Child Protection Perspective

Anne Mercovich

———

Many parents with a range of mental illnesses parent successfully, without ever coming into contact with tertiary services or the welfare sector. However, of those children with whom the Department of Human Services (DHS) in the state of Victoria is involved and who are placed on orders through the Children's Court, mental illness of one or both parents was identified as a characteristic in 27% of cases for the period 2005–2006. This was an increase from 17% for the corresponding period of 1996–1997 (Department of Human Services, 2007a). This suggests that children and families coming into contact with the child protection system have increasingly complex needs and characteristics. Reports to child protection workers with mental illness as a parental feature can represent a range of concerns, from transient situational presentations, through acute episodes, to parents living with lifelong chronic illness diagnoses. Child protection practitioners may therefore provide a differential risk assessment and service response according to the presenting concerns and the corresponding risk posed to the infant.

In Victoria, the responsibility for child protection is held by the Department of Human Services (DHS). Child protection practitioners come into contact with the state's most vulnerable children, a significant proportion of whom are infants. In fact, for the financial year period 2005–2006, 19.7% of all cases of abuse or neglect substantiated by child protection services were infants aged less than 2 years (Department of Human Services, 2007a).

This chapter will consider the context surrounding statutory responses towards infants of parents with mental illness who come to be involved with child protection; the legislative mandate and recent changes to child protection legislation with the introduction of the *Children, Youth and Families Act 2005* (CYFA) which have prompted a reframing of service responses; and the practice issues that arise in a multifaceted service system.

Case Study 1: Child Wellbeing or a Need for Child Protection Intervention?

> A maternal and child health professional contacted the regional office of DHS to discuss her concerns in relation to the presentation of a first time mother of a 2-week-old infant. During her first home visit to the family, the mother tearfully described to the professional feeling overwhelmed at responding to her infant's needs, of his unsettled behaviour and that, on the previous evening during a period of his extended crying, she had thoughts of shaking him to stop the crying. The mother described the father as working extended hours and not assisting her sufficiently with the infant's care, and there was minimal other social support. The professional was concerned at the infant's poor weight gain since hospital discharge, that the mother appeared slow to respond to her son at the visit, and the disorganised state of the house. The contact was recorded under Child Protection legislation within the regional Intake Unit as a report for significant concern for the wellbeing of the child with a view to further assessment (Victorian Government *CYFA*, 2005, s.27).

Contacts of this nature to child protection authorities are not uncommon and, in a service context of shorter maternity hospital stays, parenting capacity and postpartum mental health adjustment issues may not become evident until parents are discharged and already at home with their infant, at times in an isolated setting and without extended family or service support.

The Maternal and Child Health (M&CH) service, funded and delivered through state and local government, has a longstanding history in Victoria, with a high participation rate, particularly in the first 12 months of an infant's life (Department of Human Services, 2007b). The service offers consultations and visits at key developmental stages; with a focus on both the mother and infant as an interrelated unit, it can provide a holistic approach to health and wellbeing. It remains a voluntary service, however, which a parent may elect not to accept, and thus there are some vulnerable families who may miss this valuable safety net. These families are perhaps more likely to come to the attention of child protection services.

Risk assessment is a significant primary function of child protection and forms the cornerstone of operational work. The presenting concerns identified by the professional in the above case study may or may not represent a risk of harm to the infant. The mother may be in the early phase of a potentially serious episode of postpartum depression, or simply expressing what could be considered to be normal frustration and adjustment to new parenthood, albeit along the spectrum. The risks to the infant could be serious if she acted upon her thoughts to shake her infant. The mother's capacity to respond to the infant's needs could also compromise his physical, emotional and psychological development. The child protection worker must work through these issues to form a risk assessment and, dependent on that assessment, may proceed in several different ways based on severity issues.

An appropriate risk assessment is of great importance to the health and wellbeing of such an infant. Young infant deaths are proportionately over-represented in deaths of children known to child protection authorities. During the period 1996 to 2005, 30% of deaths of children known to child protection authorities were for infants aged 6 months or less. Infants 0–3 years comprised 61% of all deaths of the same group (Victorian Child Death Review Committee, 2006a), making them the most represented age cluster and a potent indication of their risk and vulnerability to harm. Young infants with immature muscle and neurological development and with no capacity to self-protect, are highly vulnerable to shaking with outcomes of permanent brain injury or death in more serious incidents.

As a result, whether there is a direct role for child protection authorities is dependent upon the capacity to negotiate and secure a plan to secure the infant's safety, at least in the short term. This contact may be done directly by child protection practitioners or through the M&CHN professional. It is likely to involve contact with and further assessment of the infant's father, with a view to exploring the extended family and community network, and to clarify his awareness of the identified concerns and capacity to assume care or support the mother's care.

The work may involve further assessment of the mother's possible depression through liaison with existing treating practitioners or a referral to medical services, continued monitoring of the infant's wellbeing through M&CHN or other paediatric services, and possible referral to a family support service.

The Legislation

Victoria has seen significant changes to the welfare services sector with the introduction of the *Child, Youth and Family Act 2005* (Victorian Government, 2005). A key objective of this legislation has been to create an integrated child protection and family service system that provides improved supports to vulnerable children, young people and their families. The legislation also introduced a range of new reporting and referral arrangements, chief of which is the capacity to differentiate between reports for concerns for the wellbeing of a child or reports for a child in need of protection. Reports regarding concerns for child wellbeing can be made to child protection authorities or as a referral to ChildFIRST, which can facilitate connecting a family to a family support service.

In this case study, while gathering further relevant information, it was assessed that the mother's presentation was such that her infant was not at serious risk of harm. Contact with the infant's father ascertained that he was also struggling with being a new parent. It was clear he wanted to play a greater role with his infant and agreed to take some time off from work so that he could support the mother to care for the infant together. Sometimes referral to child protection authorities can be the catalyst for change. Within this family, contact with extended family members resulted in them understanding that the couple needed support in this early phase at home with a newborn. The ongoing involvement of child protection services was not going to be required, the report was classified as a Child Wellbeing report, a referral made with the parents' consent to ChildFIRST and the case closed. The service plan comprised ongoing M&CN support that included:

- parenting skills training
- a day-stay program for feeding and sleep settling support
- links to a new parents group.

Case Study 2: The Best Interests of the Child

A report was made to child protection authorities by police who were currently at a family home, the call having been made in relation to three young children. Police had attended the family home following a distressed call from one of the children who had arrived home from school to find the family home in a disorganised state, the family dog had been killed and there was blood throughout the house. Their mother was talking in a confused manner and the wall of the family home had been covered in writing. The youngest child, an 18-month-old infant, who had been home at the time, was lying in her cot, withdrawn and uncommunicative. The police had called the community mental health crisis team who were arranging for the mother to be admitted to hospital. Police were also contacting child protection services, as there was no-one apparent to care for the children. The family had been previously unknown to child protection authorities; however, there was some suggestion from the children that they had moved to Victoria from another state.

Contact with child protection services is often made in the context of a crisis, particularly a mental health crisis such as this. Police may attend an incident in which an adult is to be hospitalised and there is no-one to care for the children involved. In some circumstances, ad hoc arrangements are made for the children with neighbours, for example, so that police or medical staff can manage the adult's situation.

In this case, little was known about the family. As an emergency response was required, the report to child protection services was triaged rapidly, with an investigation team needing to respond urgently. The first step was an urgent check to ascertain whether the family history was known either in Victoria or interstate. Pattern and history with the service system is important and cannot be overlooked in informing future risk of harm. The investigation team attended the family home to make an assessment of the risk to the children, in this circumstance finding they were not able to speak to the mother due to her impaired mental health.

Child protection practitioners responding to situations of crisis often do so in circumstances of limited and confusing information. Clearly, cases of this nature present a significant challenge to child protection staff both in a professional and emotional sense. They are often young and with limited experience and must attend a family home where there has been violence. It is both professionally and emotionally challenging to not only attend to several children in varying states of distress but also simultaneously deal with a range of professionals including police, ambulance and medical and mental health staff.

The mother in this case study appeared to have experienced a psychotic episode of unknown cause and the police who arrived first had limited information. The mother told them that she had killed the family dog, at the urging instigation of 'messages' coming from her television. The role for child protection staff was to provide a response for children in need of protection as identified in s.162 of the *Child, Youth and Family Act 2005*. The dilemma facing workers was to gather relevant information sensitively, form a risk assessment and to secure the children's safety in a timely manner.

The Legislation

In a marked difference from earlier legislation, the *Child, Youth and Family Act 2005* provides guiding principles for practice for child protection as well as for the Children's Court. Of particular relevance are what are known as the 'Best Interests' principles, that the 'best interests of the child must always be paramount' and that 'intervention ... is limited to that necessary to secure the safety and wellbeing of the child' (Victorian Government, 2005, s.27).

Initial assessment of the mother in this case study suggested that her functioning was seriously impaired and that an involuntary stay in an acute mental health hospital placement was required. While the function of child protection workers is to secure the children's safety and wellbeing, seeking the consent of their mother in her impaired state in these circumstances was not possible, although it is generally desirable.

Rationale and Process for Undertaking Assessment

Child interviews and infant observation are an important aspect of child protection work and there is significant emphasis on childhood development and interviewing techniques in training and orientation programs. Depending on the age and functioning of the children involved, the worker would seek to interview the child. Given the circumstances of Case Study 2, this would be in the context of information gathering with an emphasis on reassurance and support for the children who have undergone a traumatic experience. While this would be done in as relaxed mode as possible, the worker is aware that the investigation may well lead to the case being presented to court. The evidence that he/she gathers must be accurate and reliable. In this respect, as well as in others, interviewing a child who has just experienced a traumatic event can be a significant challenge.

Dr Bruce Perry is a psychiatrist and researcher and an internationally recognised authority on childhood trauma and the neurobiology of brain development; his work has been instrumental in providing a framework for influencing practice and informing professionals working with children. A cornerstone of Perry's work is his view that the brain is sensitive to, and therefore shaped by, early childhood experiences from infancy and particularly during critical periods, and that this can then lead to 'enduring emotional, emotional, cognitive, social and physical problems' (Perry, 2006, p. 27).

Perry has described a range of behavioural responses that infants and children who have survived a traumatic event might display. These include withdrawn, depressed, impulsive, hypervigilant, hyperactive or dissociative behaviours or a loss of previous functioning (Perry, 2005). In infants whose communication is limited by their developmental stage, the task for the child protection practitioner is to try to understand the situation from the infant's perspective, and at times to advocate on behalf of the child, where there may be conflicting demands.

The infant is this case study may have been exposed to her mother's steadily deteriorating mental health and associated behaviours during the course of the day, when her siblings were out of the home at school or over an extended period. Her mother may not have been able to attend to her emotional and physical needs and her withdrawn presentation, lying in her cot, as noted by police may be indicative of a response to trauma. The challenge for child protection practitioners is to use their knowledge of child development and their observation skills to form an assessment of the child's situation and needs.

The High Risk Infant Initiative has been operating in Victorian child protection programs for the past 10 years and aims to provide a focus on infants, with specialist consultation and support from experienced practition-ers available to child protection staff as well as services for specialist parenting assessment and education. The use of Specialist Infant Protective Workers (SIPWS) to guide and mentor staff at critical case decision points is valuable and, in cases such as this, would be used to inform the risk assessment.

The overall goal of the High Risk Infant program is to improve outcomes and practice for infants in the child protection program. In circumstances such as the family in the case study, we can see that the needs of the infant could be placed secondary to other considerations. In responding to a clearly distressed older sibling with externalised behaviours, the protection worker needs to be able to interpret the infant's experience of the trauma. The quiet infant lying in her cot can belie a child who is extremely traumatised and has withdrawn as a means of coping with her experience. Perry (2005) discusses the dissociation technique of 'freeze and surrender' behaviour as a response to traumatic threat. Continued understanding and observation of an infant's behaviour after an experience of this nature requires close communication between the profes-sionals involved with the child, as well as carers.

Exploring a family genogram can be difficult, and this can be compounded in the situation of a sole parent, where the other parent or extended family might be unknown or the parent with custody might be reluctant to divulge information about other family members. The assistance of police in seeking information can be invaluable in these circumstances. It is not uncommon for a parent in times of crisis or impaired functioning to indicate that there are no extended family or friends to care for a child. The child may be placed in out-of-home care by the worker, only to discover, sometimes at the Children's Court the next day, a vibrant and supportive extended family who are willing to step in and assist, thereby rapidly diminishing the likelihood of ongoing child protection involvement.

In this case study, however, little information could be obtained about the children's father or extended family due to the children's age and their trauma experience. With their mother being taken to hospital, child protection staff were obliged to step in, to use the *Child, Youth and Family Act 2005* to go before the Children's Court and seek an order placing the children in an out-of-home care placement. Fortunately, a foster care home was found that enabled placement for all the children together.

The duration of child protection involvement can vary and, while the service can become involved with families in circumstances of crisis where long-term involvement looks likely, this can change significantly in a short space of time. As was seen in the first case study, where extended family involvement and support for the children could be rallied, there may not be a need for ongoing child protection involvement. In that situation, there can be withdrawal of applications made in the Children's Court or short-term orders while transitional support plans are made.

Furthermore, with appropriate treatment and care, the presentation of adults with acute episodes of mental health illness can be resolved, to the extent that they pose no risk to their children and can care for them adequately with support. This is achieved with a range of medication, in inpatient and community mental health support. The role for child protection is to maintain the focus on all the children, whose needs may at times be less prioritised by mental health staff with the parent's perceived 'best interests' in mind, or in worse case scenarios, the needs are not noticed at all. With an emphasis on case management and coordination, the child protection practitioner must liaise with professionals from other services to ensure a cohesive plan of support and services that can continue after child protection involvement is withdrawn.

Case Study 3: Short- or Long-term Care and Protection

Child protection services had been involved with a family of two children for several years. Their mother had experienced several serious psychotic episodes requiring hospitalisation, including one in which she had physically harmed one of the children. Her diagnosis suggested that she would experience long-term and chronic mental illness. During the early stages of child protection involvement, she was not compliant with a community treatment plan, refused services or accessed them intermittently, and frequently would not take her prescribed psychiatric medication. The children's father was unknown and they had been placed in out-of-home care on several occasions. The mother's prognosis for a return to good health was not considered to be positive and, in addition to her mental health difficulties, she had a history of significant substance abuse problems. In view of this situation, plans were being made to seek a permanent care placement for the children. In recent months, however, the mother's mental health appeared to have stabilised, she was now pregnant and advised protective workers that she was determined to have her next baby in her care.

The recent legislative changes under the CYFA 2005 allow reports to be made to child protection or ChildFIRST where there are significant concerns for an unborn child (Victorian Government, 2005). With an emphasis on early intervention, services have the capacity to provide advice, assistance to a child or family, or refer the family to a community agency such as a family support service. However, there is no capacity to intervene legally with an unborn child and any planning must be done with the knowledge and consent of the mother. It is likely that an unborn report would be made in the above circumstances.

In the commentary to the previous case study, I referred to the pattern and history of a parent's functioning needing to be considered in relation to the future prediction of risk of harm to the child. With two children already out of her care and a history of unstable mental illness, there are strong indicators of risk to a newborn being in parental care in these circumstances.

The Victorian Child Death Review Committee (VCDRC) is an independent multidisciplinary ministerial advisory body that reviews the deaths of children who are clients of the child protection service with a view to identifying issues of practice and policy. Sometimes, upon consideration of such reviews, the VCDRC recommends a group analysis of emerging themes. One such analysis reported during 2006 studied the cases of children who had died in the care of parents who had mental health and substance abuse issues. The study considered the interface between mental health, drug and alcohol, and child protection services and found that infants were highly represented in the subject group, accounting for 22 of the 25 cases analysed.

The report of the analysis noted several themes including:

- a greater likelihood of abuse where parents have a mental illness and are using a range of substances
- problems with treatment where one diagnosis overshadows another and can undermine treatment of either

- different, and at times competing, legislative frameworks under which services operate which may make no provision for the needs of children to be taken into account when treating adults (Victorian Child Death Review Committee, 2006).

In working with other services such as mental health and drug and alcohol services, the child protection practitioner can be faced with a dilemma where these services may advocate strongly for and have the adult as their focus. While child protection services may have a long history of involvement with a family and consider a range of risk factors to predict future harm, an adult-focused service may view the recent and current presentation of their client as being a fresh start. A new birth can be a catalyst for change in a parent and a great motivator to consistently seek help and support. At what point should the practitioner consider there to be no further capacity for change and how much does the past inform the future?

There are some circumstances in which child protection authorities remain involved with families with chronic mental illness over an extended time, with the children often being in out-of-home care on long-term orders from the Children's Court in order to provide stability for their care and development. Multiple reports and protective involvement can occur where parents have episodic acute presentations and in these situations children can end up in a range of different care arrangements. Child protection practitioners have long been familiar with what is referred to as the 'revolving door' of care that some children enter, as they move between home and placement.

The theme of stability is one that has been given greater prominence under the CYFA 2005. While the 'Best Interests' principles (Victorian Government, 2005) give support to the family as the fundamental group unit, identifies removal from family as a last resort, and promotes cultural and other identity, it also identifies cumulative patterns of harm having an impact on a child's safety and development. Most importantly, it articulates the possible harmful effect of delayed decision-making in disrupting stability. Jenn McIntosh articulates a similar view in Chapter 4 in this book.

The practice principles that arise from this legislative mandate focus on the harmful impact of multiple placements and the dangers of 'case drift'. Timely and well articulated decision-making in case planning becomes paramount, and it is important that child protection practitioners in their casework practice, in their case planning meetings, and in any reports, clearly identify the tasks and progress that a parent would need to achieve to ensure their child's safety in their care.

With infants, this becomes more critical as their developmental path is driven from birth with key tasks relating to bonding and attachment that must be achieved for healthy development to occur. The infant cannot 'wait' until such time as a parent can make sufficient progress. Under new practice guidelines, timeframes for stability planning have been established relating to the age of the child and, with infants under 2 years, stability planning needs to be considered where a child has been in out-of-home care for one or more periods totalling 12 months.

In approaching planning for the birth of an infant coming from a background of parental chronic mental ill health, there are a number of considerations. An assessment of the capacity for change and sustained health of the parent is paramount. While the case studies have focused on mothers of infants, clearly consideration of both parents is required. There are many circumstances in which a mother with an inconsistent pattern of serious mental illness can parent with the support of the father/partner, services and extended family. At times, the father can be the primary carer, with the mother playing a supportive role.

Specialist parent–infant assessment programs within acute settings play an important role in assessing parenting capacity and informing risk assessment. Where parents also have complex issues such as substance abuse, there may be a requirement to be drug-free to enter such programs, which can be a difficult requirement for some parents to achieve, particularly with chronic use and where there may be use of illicit substances for 'self-medication' purposes.

Demand for such programs is generally high, and this again can lead to delays and further disruption for the infant if a placement is required for the infant prior to the assessment. In these circumstances, the child protection practitioner must consider issues such as parental contact and access. Promoting good, healthy and meaningful contact between infant and parent where an infant is in out-of-home care, can be difficult. Issues such as infant routine and travel have to be woven into a plan that meets the needs of all involved.

There is significant impact for infants whose parents are affected by substance and alcohol abuse with mental illness, particularly those also taking medication. Factors that suppress the capacity of a parent to respond appropriately and in a timely manner to an infant, can compromise infant safety and development and can lead to serious outcomes, including death.

A parent such as the one in this case study is clearly facing a number of challenges to parenting, challenges that are likely to require the involvement of child protection staff on an extended basis with or without the child in parental care.

Towards a Stronger Future

The child protection system faces many challenges in meeting the expectation of optimal service delivery and successful outcomes for clients. These include increasing client complexity, demand management and a high level of public scrutiny. Practice has seen significant change over recent years, change which has been driven by legislation and operational reflection at a national and international level.

One of the most significant challenges is to recruit and retain a workforce able to undertake the demands of this emotional and publicly accountable work. Child protection practitioners need to have personal and professional skills, as well as specific training, for them to work effectively with clients and professionals in a range of settings, including the courts. The emotional impact of working with children and families in a statutory role cannot be underestimated, particularly with clients who have increasingly complex characteristics. Verbal and physical threats from clients towards staff, while not acceptable, are also not uncommon given the nature of the work. The hours can be long, the work demanding and confronting to one's experiences and values. A range of strategies are required.

Most frontline child protection practitioners start in the work as new graduates and, while they are drawn from various disciplines, most are social/welfare workers or are from a social science background. Generally, their studies have not focused on child protection; this means that they require targeted induction programs and ongoing training and support to do the work competently.

Regular supervision, both in a structured, scheduled format, and also available on an as needed basis, plays a critical role in formal case discussion and setting case direction, as well as providing emotional support and professional development. The use of 'live' supervision by senior staff to model and enhance skills is a useful tool and an adjunct to other forms of training and support in reducing 'burnout' and promoting staff retention.

The most positive outcomes for clients occur in the context of well-articulated risk frameworks that are understood by practitioners and clients alike; where practice alignments and conflicts can be robustly but respectfully, debated and considered; and where there is a responsive and well-integrated service system. Most importantly, practice needs to be delivered sensitively by well-trained practitioners who are suited to the role and well supported in their work. Child protection practitioners work in an emotionally charged environment, and while their actions and decisions affect their clients' lives at a most intimate level, they do so because the infants and children in their care are some of the most vulnerable in society and they want to make a difference to their worlds.

References

Department of Human Services. (2007a, November). *CASIS: Department of Human Services data in Child Protection Services. New ways of working in child protection* (Briefing and Feedback Session, p. 13). Melbourne, Australia: Author.

Department of Human Services. (2007b). *Maternal and child health services annual report 2005–2006.* Melbourne, Australia: Author.

Perry, B. (2005). *Neurodevelopmental impact of maltreatment: Support materials.* Paper presented at Working With Traumatised Children Forum, Melbourne, Australia.

Perry, B. (2006). Applying principles of neurodevelopment to clinical work with maltreated and traumatised children. In N.B. Webb (Ed.), *Working with traumatised youth in child welfare* (p. 27). New York: Guilford Press.

Victorian Child Death Review Committee. (2006). Tackling SIDS: A community responsibility. In *Child death analysis.* Melbourne, Australia: Office of Child Safety Commissioner.

Victorian Child Death Review Committee. (2006a). *Annual report of inquiries into deaths of children known to Child Protection 2006.* Melbourne, Australia: Office of Child Safety Commissioner.

Victorian Government. (2005). *Children, Youth and Families Act 2005.* Melbourne, Australia: Author.

SECTION

3

Fathers

CHAPTER

6

'... Get Yourself
Someone To Talk To'

Kevin Williams

⌒

Maureen and I have been married for 7 years and we have a 4-year-old boy, Gabrial, and a 1-year-old girl, Estelle. What do I write? What can I possibly say to someone else in this situation? I'd like to say that if you stick in there, that everything will be normal again one day — but I don't know that. I think things will get better — but you are both headed to a new place.

It's a bit hard to say where Maureen's depression came from. Probably lots of things combined. Maureen went through a tough time with both pregnancies. We were both apprehensive about having a child and there was a degree of uncertainty. We certainly didn't enjoy the pregnancy as much as we could have. I had no previous experience with babies and was not quite ready for father-hood. I really had no idea. With Gabrial, it was not a happy birth and there were complications. Maureen was in hospital for almost 2 weeks after the birth with retained product, blood clots and drug reactions — and Gabrial just cried all the time. He slept only if he was held and always cried when he was put down. We took it in turns to sleep on the couch and were struggling. We had minimal environmental support and neither of us had decent sleeps. I had a full-time job and wanted to give Maureen as much rest as I could, so I often took over care of Gabrial. But I wasn't there — I was so zonked I was just a walking zombie. Maureen's sister helped out a few times when we badly needed respite, but he was a difficult child. Maureen and Gabrial spent a period in Torrens House to assist with infant care and routines. We saw paediatricians and their wonderful advice was 'He'll grow out of it'. After we had barely survived months of Gabrial's crying, a naturopath gave Maureen a yogurt to eat and Gabrial was perfect within a few days! That really shook our faith in doctors.

It didn't help that during the first few months after Gabrial's birth, nurses tended to teach Maureen about infant care, but not me. They kept saying 'We'll teach mum and she can teach you'. But that put all the pressure on her to get it right. We were also apprehensive that the second pregnancy would be a repeat of the first. 'What if it wasn't an easy baby?'

Between having Gabrial and having Estelle, Maureen miscarried at 3 months, had her not-so-close father die, had to put down her went-there-everywhere-with-her-dog, and we moved house twice. Any psychiatrist will tell you that any one of those events is stressful — and we did them all over 3 years! During the first 6 months of Estelle's life, Maureen was in various hospitals for four of them trying to get Estelle to sleep properly!

Even during the 'better' times, Maureen still felt quite removed from the world — not being able to work, certainly bored each day, and not feeling that she had a purpose. I kept showing her what an amazing son and daughter we had, and that she was a great mother for bringing them up so well, but she never felt fulfilled. She told me that the connection she felt to our children was no stronger than she felt to other people's children. She was missing that fantastic 'mother' feeling that everyone was telling her she was supposed to have — and she felt guilty about that. She also felt (and still feels) that a lot of the children's problems were because of her. I guess I never really got into the babies either. For the first 12 months they're just lumps; after that they start to interact and respond to you. My lack of emotional involvement probably put more pressure on Maureen as well.

Before her depression, Maureen was so outgoing, independent and confident. But during the past few years, she's been a different person. She's often tired and drained, prone to sudden crying and timid; I'd even use the words needy and clingy. That's certainly tested me, because that's exactly the attributes I never wanted in a partner. Although it's harsh to say, but if I met her again tomorrow, I would never have gone out with her.

How do you devote yourself to a marriage like that? There have been times after heated discussions that I would have left Maureen had it not been for the kids. But I live in hope. Hope that this process will get at least some of her old self back, and that by going through this together we will come out even stronger.

I don't know how or when Maureen is going to get better. There's a strong chance she will never be the same. Whatever happens, it's going to take years. She has three appointments a week to see psychiatrists and I have no idea what they do. So far it seems they just try to make her cry — to make her feel and express whatever's going on in her head. I've tried to have them explain the process to me, but I'm not any wiser. It's not like on TV where they can just tell you 'you never let your grief out when your Dad remarried' and after a good cry you're fixed. It's really not like that. It's been a long hard road and the end is not in sight.

Luckily, I have a full-time job; I get to escape each day and be somewhat 'normal'. But Maureen does not, she's a stay-at-home mum. Her days are lonely, pointless and mundane. I've never quite understood it, but her sense of self-worth suddenly rests with me. I am the only person in her life who can tell her she's doing a good job, who can recognise when she's putting in effort and when she needs validation. Even that's hard. There were days when doing her hair constituted 'putting in effort' and if I didn't notice, well it'd be like kicking the winning goal and have no-one care. She'd be devastated and that'd usually lead to another fight about me not supporting her.

I can never pick what mood she's going to be in. There were times when I'd leave for work with Maureen holding a crying baby on the sofa and be in the same position when I return home in the evening. She would be in tears saying she hates her life, and I have to be strong enough to know that it's not my fault and strong enough to accept that I can't do much about it. All the things we used to do together, all the things I could do to cheer her up, just don't work anymore. I'm so lost.

That's hard for a guy to accept — that there's a problem with no solution. I used to think that Maureen was just 'feeling down' because she missed the things in her life that child-rearing took away. So the solution was simple — get them back! Do some part-time work, see your friends, enjoy your hobbies — just go and do those things you miss. But that's not it at all. Depression is this thing that just is. Perhaps it was triggered by a loss of her life and everything she enjoyed, but once triggered, getting those things back won't help. As a guy, this makes me feel pretty useless. When I sit on the couch with her crying and her telling me everything that she misses — there's nothing I can say to fix that, I just need to agree, hold her, and say … well I still don't know what to say — and it's been 3 years.

So what's my role as husband and father? I've certainly had to lift my game — do more around the house, do more with the kids, and just be there for her. It sounds so clichéd, but communication really is the key. Maureen is great in being able to help me through conversations. Quite often she'll apologise that what she's about to say makes no sense and it's 'not her' talking, then to launch into a highly emotional lecture about everything that's bugging her. And all I can do is listen.

I went through the first year absolutely bewildered at what she said. I defended myself, explained my actions and suggested things she could do for herself. Of course, all the problems seemed to have logical, easy solutions. But my words only made things worse. She already knew the logical solutions — but the conversation wasn't about anything logical — it was about expressing emotions. All she needed was to be listened to. She wasn't complaining about me or the world, she was just frustrated that she was frustrated! If she complained that I never picked up the dirty towels, what she was actually saying was that she felt pressure to keep the house clean and she didn't feel that she had the time. She would even acknowledge that it wasn't me putting pressure on her — she just felt 'someone' was. It took me a long time to work out how to talk 'girl' and it feels so pointless, but it works. I'd recommend ANY book that helps you talk with her, but essentially that's all you can do.

You will not be able to fix her! In a way, you almost need to ignore the depression. Remember it's there, but don't dwell on it. Accept that you may do or suggest something that was fine last week, but that it's completely wrong this week. Accept it. Yes, it makes no sense, but don't blame her — it's the depression. Our relationship has been extremely strained and tested but we are talking better now. Apart from caring for Gabrial and Estelle, we haven't done a lot together over the past 5 years. We need to work on common interests but are tentatively beginning to socialise.

Get yourself someone to talk to as well — someone to REALLY talk to. I didn't do this and I went about 2 years without talking to someone. By the end, I was so emotionally numb that I lost interest in my own hobbies and friends because, by blocking out the bad feelings, I also blocked out the fun feelings. I was probably depressed. I was a zombie most of the time. I didn't even talk to Maureen because I thought she had too much to deal with already. It wasn't until much later that I realised that she needed to see me cry as part of her own healing. She needed to hear my worries and concerns to know that hers were valid. While I thought I was being strong, I was actually alienating Maureen and just making things worse.

So what would I do differently with the next baby? Get support. Get friends and family to help. Not by taking over, not by removing the baby, but helping with everything else to make parent time with the babies better. I'd try my hardest to keep something fun in our lives, something to do together as a couple. We've got friends in a similar situation and the mum hasn't been away from their 18-month-old baby for more than 3 hours — ever. It's not healthy. Certainly enjoy your kids, but for their sake be your own person as well.

So, stick in there. Accept that you will never understand it. Know that it will take a long time and remember that she thinks it's strange as well. But she lives with it all every day and is probably scared that she'll never be herself again too.

Fathers

Bringing Them Into the Picture

Peter Ballard

When an infant's mother has a serious mental illness (SMI), the baby's father also enters a critical period. Not only is he coping with the transition to fatherhood, the presence of new life and the needs of any other children, but also to his partner's unwell state (Davey, Dziurawiec, & O'Brien-Malone, 2006). The family home will have been prepared for the new arrival, with both parents eagerly anticipating this new phase in their life. Serious mental illness is an unwelcome intruder. When a woman is overwhelmed by a major depression or other psychiatric illness in the perinatal period, the whole family needs support as everyone adjusts to the ravages of the condition. The infant's parents are the cornerstone of the family unit and the father must be resilient, positive and persevering during the course of the illness. However, along with his greatly increased sense of responsibility for his partner and dependent children, the secure base he has found in his partner will be fragile. In the absence of 'good enough' couple communication, solid social supports and an understanding of the nature of his partner's condition, many men are at a loss.

It is essential, therefore, that health professionals acknowledge the father's position, empathise with his experience and work at including him in the assessment and treatment process so that the woman's recovery is optimal. In addition, the development and maintenance of a healthy attachment between primary carers and infant must be nurtured through this critical period.

Father Consciousness

The nature of fatherhood underwent a radical change following the Industrial Revolution. Men began to be less domestically involved as they went out to work. They brought things home to the family rather than working within the domestic economy. 'Paterfamilias' gave way to 'homolaboriosus' (Pittman, 1993). Bolen (1989) refers to the emergence in Western culture of a new father archetype during the second half of the 20th century. Men, she suggests, have been evolving from distant 'Sky', or patriarchal, fathers to 'Earth', or nurturing, fathers. As a result, they are less authoritarian and more emotionally available to their children. They retain them in consciousness even when not present in the family home, perhaps echoing the primary maternal preoccupation that Winnicott noted in mothers (1956). This evolution has special significance when a contemporary man is caring for both a partner who is unwell and their children.

Infant's Arrival

Prior to the 1950s, the labour and delivery rooms were out of bounds for expectant fathers and parturition was viewed as the preserve of women and health professionals (Brockington, 1995). Men are now increasingly more likely to be present at childbirth, bond with their infant and be more involved from early infancy rather than waiting for the 'interesting stage' when they can play with their child. In the UK Millenium Cohort Study (Centre for Longitudinal Studies, 2005), over 80% of fathers interviewed had attended the birth. With the advent of paternity leave in some Western countries and an ethos of 'families first', there is more space for balance between work and domestic demands. In one survey, 32% of Australian employees had paid paternity leave, with an average of 2 weeks' leave per worker (Australian Government, 2005).

Dad's Pot Pourri

Fathers will be in a variety of social situations that have a bearing on infant care and management of the mother's illness. They include:
- **Teen dads:** Many already withdrawing from the partnership and perhaps also from parenting.

- *Away dads:* Due to work demands, men may have to spend lengthy periods far from the family home. In such cases, women will be relying heavily on other available supports.

- *Multi dads:* Women may have additional children with different biological fathers. It could be clarified whether or not she is in receipt of Child Support payments.

- *Blended dads:* Both partners may have children from previous relationships as well as their infant, 'yours, mine and ours'. Men living in stepfamilies have more than twice the rates of depression than men in more traditional families (Deater-Deckard, Pickering, Dunn, & Golding 1998).

- *Who is dad?* Paternity may be an issue and DNA technologies are increasingly used to challenge and explore (Gilding, 2004).

- *Dads non grata:* The relationship may be ambivalent, moribund or irretrievable. Family Court proceedings may be anticipated or already be in progress.

- *Good dads:* A welcome group! 'Let's clone this one' state the staff in the mother–baby unit.

- *Indigenous dads:* Cultural norms are generally very different for Aboriginal fathers, with long established patterns changing for some younger men (see Chapter 12).

- *Ethnic dads:* Cultural sensitivity is required, especially in relation to child-rearing practices and attitudes to mental illness.

- *Plus dads:* They can be overly keen to help their partner recover and tend to take over infant care, thus reducing mother's ability to optimise the security of her attachment to her infant.

- *Minus dads:* Encouragement is needed for men who are not sufficiently involved due to the perception of their role as father or response to partner's mental state.

- *Bad dads:* 'Intimate partner violence' has been positively associated with the number of times a woman has been admitted to psychiatric hospital and the number of symptoms related to psychiatric disability (McPherson, Delva, & Cranford, 2007). Health workers need to be alert to signs of domestic violence (DV) so that a woman can be counselled regarding her options. Collaboration with DV counsellors is recommended.

- *Mad dads:* When both parents are mentally unwell, there is an exponential increase in stress and fragmentation within the family unit.

Dad's Reaction to His Partner's Illness

Although he may present a mask of coping, a dad will often become overwhelmed and struggle when his partner has a SMI during the postnatal period. Male partners can have an impact on the coping process of women with a postpartum psychiatric disorder, either by having a positive attitude to managing the emotional stress or by exacerbating the situation with negative behaviour (Grube, 2005). The latter can include actively or passively undermining her efforts to cope with her SMI, such as not supporting her compliance with treatment (Nicholson, Sweeney, & Geller 1998). Attitudes may range from being committed to doing the 'hard yards and being in there for the long haul' to 'I thought I was strong but I'm really struggling' and 'I'm not sure if I want to stay around'.

His other responses may include:

- fear, confusion and anger
- sense of powerlessness and feeling overwhelmed
- lack of understanding of SMI
- adopting a 'snap out of it' attitude
- denial that she has a SMI — this can affect recovery time
- isolating himself
- being influenced by the stigma of SMI
- dreading that the woman he knows has changed irrevocably
- 'how long will it last?' worrying that she might never recover
- reluctance to see health professionals
- becoming depressed himself.

He will benefit from the support of a skilled professional in order to temper the above.

As well as trying to cope with his partner's illness a dad has to ensure that the infant's needs are met. As, according to Stern (1985), 'a sense of core self' is being formed during early infancy, it is vital that the baby has the presence of a sensitive and responsive father (Edhborg, Lundh, Seimyr, & Widstrom, 2003). When dads have a very positive influence on the baby from the earliest stages, it is likely to act as a buffer against the mother's depressive symptoms. Like most fathers, not only will he have to assist with night feeds and settling the baby, but also help substantially with a range of other infant care tasks. For most men, this presents a steep learning curve and he must work doubly hard for the duration of the illness. In addition, when the woman is hospitalised in a psychiatric ward or mother and baby unit, he may struggle as the sole adult at home and prefer to stay with a friend or relative, depending on whether he has older children. Some men also need assistance with the housework or finance management.

Factors influencing his coping ability include:

- inner resources — his resilience and ability to handle a crisis
- previous experience with infants
- family structure and availability of supports
- sleep pattern
- work pressures and capacity to modify hours
- finances and accommodation
- other psychosocial stressors.

Postnatal Depression (PND)

Sometimes a man does not recognise the symptoms of PND in his partner. When it does register that there is something amiss, he may just not 'get it'. He may dismiss her distress as being due solely to the effects of childbirth or fatigue and not see the bigger picture. Some dads view their partner's mental state in 'concrete' terms as they struggle to comprehend what is happening for her. He may question her coping ability by referring to his mother having managed her babies without suffering depression or needing assistance. 'My mother had six children which she brought up by herself with Dad away on work for months at a time and she managed.'

The study by Everingham et al. (2006) in relation to major depression postpartum used Goffman's (1997) concept of 'framing' that identifies the 'taken-for-granted sociocultural elements that give meaning to a situation' (p. 1746). He concluded that, while mothers tend to see their postnatal experience mainly within an 'identity' frame and how they saw the 'good mother', fathers see it through a physical hardship frame or in relation to the mother's individual personality.

Everingham further suggests that the most important form of support from her partner desired by a mother was being understood, and that his lack of understanding created distress for her. Fathers in her study felt they were expected to know what was happening for their partner and became frustrated that they were unable to 'fix it'. Kevin Williams' personal account (Chapter 6) strongly echoes this theme.

While major depression postpartum tends to have a relatively predictable recovery process both parents may, during the acute phase, be challenged to see light at the end of a dark tunnel as the process can be long and the symptoms disabling. Consequently, they will both derive support from being listened to, understood and reassured. Fathers will benefit greatly from guidance during this period of destabilisation of their family life. With the benefit of a well-considered treatment regime and sustained social supports, in time, most men can normally be reassured that their partner will return to a more optimal level of functioning.

Serious Mental Illness Other Than Major Depression

While there have been several studies relating to partner response to major depression postpartum, there is a paucity of literature referring to his response to other SMI in the postnatal period, such as puerperal psychosis, bipolar affective disorder or schizo-affective disorder. When their children are born, women who have a schizophrenic illness are less likely than non-mentally ill women to be living with a partner (Miller & Finnerty, 1996).

Over a 3-year period, less than half of the women (47%) admitted to Helen Mayo House with an SMI other than major depression, had a partner. This compared well with a study by Ritsher, Coursey, and Farrell (1997) who found that 48% of women in that diagnostic area had a partner. Women with schizophrenia are not as likely to have a current partner when their baby is born as those who are not seriously mentally ill and the infant is more likely to be raised by someone else (Miller & Finnerty, 1996).

In a mother and baby unit context, colleagues and I have observed dads handling these illnesses in a variety of ways. The rapid onset of puerperal psychosis in his partner, following his elation at being a new dad, can cause alarm for him — especially when he has not previously had an encounter with acute mental illness. His ability to remain objective will be tested when his partner has uncharacteristic behaviours and attitudes. Some men become very disconcerted when they are implicated in any paranoid or delusional thinking. When the mother becomes confused and disorganised, the dad must step into the breach in order to keep the family afloat. He will have to ensure that she receives urgent specialist medical treatment, including the probability of hospitalisation, and especially so if she makes references to harming herself, their infant or others. Keeping faith in the treatment environment, the efficacy of the medication of choice and that there will be a good recovery are ongoing requirements, sometimes hard to meet.

If a man knows of a pre-existing and treated condition, such as bipolar affective disorder, he may appreciate the potential for his partner to become unwell after the birth. Sometimes a woman, following confirmed pregnancy, will secretly cease taking prescribed medication for a chronic condition such as schizo-affective disorder, and then her postpartum relapse can take him by surprise. In these situations, resentment looms large and relationship issues must be addressed by the therapy team.

Paternal Depression

Postnatal stressors may combine with other pre-existing vulnerabilities and an infant's father may himself display symptoms of depression, anxiety or other psychiatric disorder. This will clearly have implications for managing the mother's condition. Recent studies have found a wide range of paternal depression rates, depending on the sample content and measures used. Soliday, McCluskey-Fawcett and O'Brien (1999) reported depressive symptoms in 25% of males during the postpartum period. In a Brazilian study, almost 12% of fathers scored above the selected threshold of 10, using the Beck Depression Inventory (Pinheiro et al., 2006), with moderate to severe depression being present in 4% of that sample. Condon, Boyce and Corkindale (2004) have followed a cohort of Australian men from pregnancy through to the end of the first postnatal year. While they found that adjustments during pregnancy are likely to cause the most distress, rates of depression for men — irrespective of their partner's mental health — are at least 4%.

Matthey, Barnett, Kavanagh and Howie (2001) suggested that the EPDS (Edinburgh Postnatal Depression Scale) 'is a reliable and valid measure of mood in fathers' (p. 175) and health professionals should complete it as routine with dads of new infants. Given that men tend to be less likely than women to express negative emotions, they suggested that a lower cut-off score of 5/6 is used when screening for anxiety and depression. In a later study, they recommended that the term 'postnatal mood disorder' (PMD) is a more accurate reflection of the postpartum adjustment difficulties in both parents (Matthey, Barnett, Howie, & Kavanagh, 2003). In a New Zealand study, men whose partners had PND tended to have more symptoms of depression, aggression, nonspecific psychological impairment and 'problem fatigue' than comparison group men (Roberts, Bushnell, Collings, & Purdie, 2006).

In light of the above, it is important that any discernible signs of mood disorder in the father are factored into the clinical assessment of the mother and that he is encouraged to seek professional help.

Enter the Professionals

Given complex family and social structures, accessing dads can often be a challenge because of psychosocial issues — such as domestic violence and its ramifications, employment commitments, the tyranny of distance and travel time, couple estrangement, and antipathy towards health professionals. Men may ask 'why do you want to see me?' partly inferring that this is women's business but also because of their apprehension about what is happening for their partner. It is not uncommon for a woman to say 'you won't get him to talk'. Although perseverance is often needed when encouraging a dad to express his view, many fathers will have a positive response when given the invitation, especially if there is some focus on their experience during the crisis. Developing rapport and building trust is of the essence. Good contact with the partner can also facilitate the obtaining of useful collateral history.

Mother and baby units for women with a serious mental illness tend to have a significant gender imbalance in their staff complement. It is important, therefore, that workers acknowledge how men can often feel intimidated in such a female environment and that their resulting insecurity may result in a distant or defensive presentation. Although not exclusively so, it can be useful for a father to have face-to-face contact with a male worker. When a father's forbearance is severely tested, it is important to help him understand how his partner's attitude to him can be illness-related. When the health professional adopts a nonjudgmental, accepting and compassionate attitude, a dad will have the opportunity to express some emotion in a containing environment.

On occasions, a father may normalise the mother's presentation and inappropriately challenge her thoughts and opinions. On occasions, some men resort to verbal abuse and try to physically control the unwell partner. When a father perceives the baby to be very vulnerable, he will usually endeavour to protect his child and, given the mother's compromised state, may seek help from others, including health or social services. He might fear that the baby will be removed into state care. Intervention by mental health professionals is needed before the situation deteriorates further. With support, some men take extended leave from work and may adopt the role of full-time carer and recipient of Social Security payments.

Coping Strategies for Dads

In general:

- ensuring that his partner consults with a general practitioner (GP) or psychiatrist as early as possible
- becoming involved in the assessment and treatment process
- obtaining information regarding the signs and symptoms of his partner's illness and its likely pathway
- having access to fact sheets on SMI written in plain English
- being open to guidance from other health professionals
- seeing himself as part of a team working on his partner's recovery
- supporting his partner to comply with treatment, especially when she has little or no insight into her illness
- taking very seriously any talk of suicide or of harming the infant. He needs to immediately consult a health professional to ensure a psychiatric assessment
- being constantly aware that her illness is markedly affecting her functioning
- reassuring his other children that this is not their fault
- scheduling times when infant and other children can be minded to give the mother respite
- using a childcare centre or family day care, when available
- entrusting his employer with information about what is happening for his partner
- looking after himself
- taking one day at a time.

In his attitude to his partner:

- asking her what he can do to help. It is good to be there for her
- avoiding criticism of her as she already has enough feelings of inadequacy and failure
- learning a better understanding of the illness to avoid adopting a 'pull up your socks' attitude to his partner who has major depression
- recognising that just listening to his partner can be helpful
- acknowledging the 'small steps' she takes
- reassuring her regarding her mothering capacity

- reassuring her that he is committed to both her and infant
- cuddling may be more acceptable than sexual intercourse for the mother at this time; even where a woman does not a have a serious mental illness couples will often take months to resume sexual intercourse, and for mentally ill women, this resumption may be even longer. Condon et al. (2004) found that, for most men, a return to prepregnancy levels of sexual activity did not occur by the end of the first year postpartum.
- scheduling meetings to discuss practicalities
- postponing major decisions and setting small goals only
- providing other adult support for mother, infant and any other young children each time he leaves the house if necessary, after discharge

And with his supports:

- accessing available supports and being helped to locate supplementary supports
- encouraging him to share his feelings with a friend or relative
- suggesting he accepts assistance that is offered such as home help, food in the freezer, gardening, transport to school etc.
- advocating on a father's behalf with an employer can be helpful especially in relation to time off
- helping him to access a men's support group
- encouraging him to retain his interests. High energy activities and sports are ideal.

Strategies for Those Working With Fathers

For many men, the partner is their sole confidante (George, 1996). When his partner is unavailable, a man can become very isolated, ruminative and some-times depressed. His contact with friends may be superficial and circumspect, especially given the social stigma of mental illness. Sometimes he invests heavily in work and may delay the daily homecoming. When a man's partner is debilitated, many men are highly challenged in the area of domestic organisa-tion. This is especially so when the woman normally does the lion's share of tasks in the home. He may need assistance from extended family or friends to keep the home fires burning at this time. Some fathers become overinvolved in their partner's recovery by being excessively present in the hospital environ-ment. In such cases it is suggested that clinicians advise them to 'hang back' to allow the woman some space in which to heal. This requires sensitive handling at a time when the family is very vulnerable; the infant's needs must be met, and the mother–infant attachment must be nurtured.

Prompt contact with a health professional can help attenuate the father's fear and uncertainty. It is essential that he has worker contact details plus an arranged follow-up after the first interaction. In these times of fuller employment, it may be necessary to make face-to-face contact with the man at his place of employment, a strategy that can help him to feel less alienated. Contact by phone, sometimes supplemented by an e-mail connection, can be useful options. Consideration could be given to facilitating groups for either couples or just dads. Morgan, Matthey, Barnett and Richardson (1997), who facilitated a group program for women with PND and their partners over eight weekly sessions, reported an increase in the women's self-esteem and a decrease in their distress. Davey, Dziurawiec and O'Brien-Malone (2006) found that, in a fathers-only program, there was a subjective decrease in both depression and stress, together with a feeling of increased social support. Potential inputs could include psychoeducation, sharing personal experiences, plus a range of coping strategies as listed earlier. Experience shows that men are often reluctant to attend therapy sessions, particularly groups, but once they become involved, they report experiencing great benefit.

Couple Issues

It has been suggested that the best predictor of postnatal marital adjustment is the level of relationship satisfaction in pregnancy (Wallace & Gottlib, 1990). Childbirth, however, can lead to an 'uncoupling', as the dyad becomes a triad (Raphael-Leff, 2001). There is no longer the freedom of the antenatal period and some couples have only a short courtship from which to draw a fuller knowledge of each other as they embark on parenthood (Pacey, 2004). Gottman and Notarius (2002) suggest there is a significant drop in the quality of couple relationships within the infant's first year that includes a decrease in conversation and sexual activity. This is supported by Condon, Boyce and Corkindale (2004) who found that, from the male viewpoint, there is a very significant deterioration in the couple relationship from pregnancy to 6 to 12 months postpartum. SMI in one partner places a further test on the relationship, and additionally, if both partners have a SMI, there is a manifold increase in stress and adversity. Joy within the relationship may be restricted, but it is vital that the couple maintain communication and reserve any available energy for maintaining some intimacy.

When there is relationship dysfunction, couple counselling can be useful. Although specialised counselling services are widely available, mother–baby unit staff can begin the process by identifying key issues and possible strategies for addressing them. In a randomised controlled trial of antidepressants versus couple therapy in the treatment of people with depression living with a critical partner, it was concluded that couple therapy is more acceptable than antidepressants and is at least as efficacious (Leff et al., 2000).

Psychoeducation of this sort can be a very useful starting point at times of great stress. In the mother–baby unit context, we have found it gainful to see partners individually and then as a couple especially in relation to psychoeducation and interpersonal communication. This contact also provides an opportunity to fully address the prevailing psychosocial issues. Couple maintenance needs to be attended to, given that it is often rated low in the couple's list of priorities during this period of high stress. Nonmaintenance can become entrenched within the relationship, especially as much of their available energy is spent on surviving the crisis. Couples present to Helen Mayo House (see Chapter 15) who have not had one child-free evening out together in the first year postpartum. Sustaining individual and mutual interests is encouraged. On occasions, it is appropriate and very useful to include dads in the emerging technique of mother–infant therapy. In such situations, they can play a significant part in the assessment and recovery process by developing new insights regarding triadic dynamics (Fivaz-Depeursinge & Favez, 2006).

In the absence of clear understanding regarding the ramifications of his partner's illness, plus marked ambivalence, a man may become abusive within the relationship to the point where the partnership is no longer viable. Such a pathway may necessitate Family Court proceedings and, at times, intervention by child protection agencies. Facilitating family meetings involving grandparents, in-laws and significant others can assist with clarifying issues, working towards a common understanding and assisting with the formulation of a supports package for the family.

Case Examples

Chris, Sue and Tania

Chris, the 32-year-old partner of Sue, aged 30, and first-time father of 5-month-old Tania, is employed in his family's butchery business. This couple, who live in an industrial area of the city, had emotionally unavailable parents and met when on holiday in Bali. During a child-free decade, they developed a co-dependant pattern of relating in the context of a carefree lifestyle until it was interrupted by a pregnancy about which both were ambivalent and underprepared. Some weeks postnatally, Sue began to become increasingly depressed and exhausted. In addition to finding it hard to respond positively to her daughter, Sue and Chris's relationship became highly conflictual to the point where they decided to separate. Although physically apart, Chris maintained contact with Sue, and his daily visits included assisting with childcare and housework. Until perinatal team intervention, their respective parents gave them minimal support and had only occasional contact with their grandchild.

When Sue became overwhelmed, she was admitted to a mother and baby unit. During her 5 weeks stay, Sue benefitted greatly from the unit milieu that included psychiatric assessment, medication, nursing assistance, cognitive–behavioural therapy and mother–infant therapy (including some triadic sessions). Although initially reluctant to be part of the treatment regime, Chris gradually responded in an increasingly positive way when the social worker reached out to him and he began to show more trust in unit staff. He disclosed that this was the first time he had ever spoken to an adult male regarding deeper issues. He gradually became open to psychoeducation and the suggestion of couple therapy.

Chris's parents separated in his early teens following which he experienced two foster care placements. During partner sessions, it became clear that there were fundamental communication issues that had never been addressed, including lack of relationship maintenance and an entrenched negative communication style, often leading to continuation of unresolved issues. Chris's injudicious use of family funds provided an additional stressor, and there was a negative response from his employer when staff advocated that his situation be sympathetically considered. Role-play provided a useful tool for illustrating positive ways of developing this couple's interaction. They responded well to homework tasks and started to risk bringing up issues with each other rather than fearing rejection.

A series of meetings involving Chris, Sue and her family provided a forum for developing understanding of the issues as well as reducing the tension between Chris and his in-laws. Chris responded positively to efforts to mobilise community supports, including Tania's attendance at childcare, for which the social worker successfully applied for Special Child Care Benefit, and an in-home family carer. During his home visits, Chris assisted with household tasks and repairs as well as infant care. Now that Sue is pregnant again, her mental health is being closely monitored by outreach staff and Chris, who has made an appointment with a psychologist to further address his own issues, is especially keen to bond with their new infant. A home help service will be provided when Sue is discharged from the maternity hospital and unit out-patient appointments will recommence during the higher risk post-natal period.

Ben, Denise and Ingrid

Ben was the 32-year-old partner of Denise, aged 26, and father of 10-week-old Ingrid. Ben and Denise knew each other for only a few months prior to Ingrid's conception. Ben, from a Lebanese back-ground, was manager and part-owner of a tyre-fitting centre located a few streets away from their recently mortgaged home in a small country town. Denise took unpaid maternity leave from her job as a dental receptionist, and during her pregnancy ceased taking the medication prescribed for her longstanding schizoaffective illness. She had a 16-year-old son from a previous relationship who has mainly lived with his widowed grandmother, Jeanette, because of his mother's frequent mental illness hospitalisations. Jeanette, a retired schoolteacher, reports having had great difficulty in handling Denise's illness over time. Although Denise's illness was relatively well contained until conception, her mental state deterio-rated during pregnancy.

When Denise became floridly psychotic she was admitted to the local hospital and later transferred to a metropolitan mother and baby unit. Staff contacted Child Protection Services because Denise reported thoughts of wanting to harm her baby. During a 2-month admission, Denise responded well to treatment and, with staff support, was able to increasingly manage Ingrid's care. Although, for logistical reasons, the unit social worker was unable to have face-to-face contact with Ben, he had several conversations with him, including one a few days after Denise's admission. It became clear that Ben was very apprehensive about his partner's condition, had no insight into her behaviour and had been previously unaware that she had a SMI. He found difficulty in accepting her psychotic pres-entation that included auditory hallucinations and her thoughts that he was the leader of a drug ring. When Ben managed to visit the unit, it became clear that he barely acknowledged information provided to him regarding schizoaffective disorder. Furthermore, he had a tendency to control her behaviour that, on occasions, developed into physical restraint. As a consequence, unit staff con-tacted domestic violence services.

Although Ben had a rather superficial response to the psycho-education provided and adopted a 'concrete' style of thinking, it was seen as vital to maintain contact with him during Denise's admission. He made periodic phone calls to the unit expressing his frustration and seeking guidance on how to handle his partner's thought patterns and behaviour when she was on home leave. Pressures on him included his work demands, attending to his 4-year-old son from a previous relationship, and travelling to and from the treatment setting. He also found it hard to respond to his parents' lack of understanding regarding their daughter-in-law's plight and their requests to see their grandchild, despite Denise's objection. When he eventually agreed to engage in a couple session it was observed that he had a controlling stance towards his partner and she readily deferred to him. He did become involved in discharge planning and, while he was initially reluctant for Denise to have available in-home supports, he agreed to her having contact with the mother–infant therapist as an outpatient. He became increasingly aware of the importance of his partner complying with medication and understood the rationale for the Community Treatment Order that had recently been invoked.

Denise recovered well despite an underlying psychotic illness. She is now assisted by the area community mental health team and attends a mother and baby support group.

Summary

Partners, it is clear, are often overlooked in the clinical situation (Downey & Coyne, 1990). Health professionals spend less time with men, and health services have been challenged regarding the 'mother-centred bias' in their programs (Fletcher, Matthey, & Marley, 2006). In this author's experience, prompt contact with a skilled professional can ease the father's angst. When a community mental health service is involved they need to have some contact with a male partner, when there is one, rather than exclusively with the female consumer. Contact with the partner also engenders a more comprehensive biopsychosocial appraisal.

It is absolutely essential, therefore, that the health professional acknowledges the father's role in recovery, as well as his efforts to ensure the safety and wellbeing of their infant. In many instances, he is battling to hold the family together. It is important that he is not regarded as peripheral to 'women's business' and that his situation and perspective are factored into overall clinical management. His experience of the crisis has to be acknowledged and his understanding of mental illness expanded. By nurturing some rapport with him, it can be ascertained how his beliefs, attitudes and mental state affect both his partner and, at times, the pathway of her illness. This, together with an appraisal of the relationship dynamics, will have positive implications for the infant–carer attachment and the baby's development.

The health professional needs to:

- Find out how the partner is coping
- Acknowledge his experience and perspective
- Tell him that his involvement is critical in the woman's recovery
- Help him to shore up his supports
- Educate him regarding partner's symptoms and the treatment process
- Refer to the couple relationship; it may need your attention
- Stay in touch with him until the woman's mental health is optimal.

Useful Contacts

Men's Line Australia — Phone 1300 789 978
The Engaging Fathers Project, Family Action Centre, University of Newcastle
http://www.newcastle.edu.au
http://www.postpartumdads.com
http://www.menstuff.org
http://www.fatherhood.org.au
http://www.fathersdirect.com
http://www.lonefathers.com.au

References

Australian Government. (2005). *Equal opportunity for women in the workplace survey 2004. Paid maternity leave. Results of the 2004 Annual EOWA survey of reporting organisations.* Canberra: Equal Opportunity for Women in the Workplace Agency. Retrieved January 18, 2008, from http://www.eowa.gov.au/Information_Centres_Resource_Centre.EOWA_Publications

Bolen, J.S. (1989). *Gods in everyman.* New York: Harper Perennial.

Brockington, J.F. (1995). *Motherhood and mental health.* New York: Oxford University Press

Centre for Longitudinal Studies. (2005). *Millenium cohort study.* London: Institute for Education.

Condon, J.T., Boyce, P., & Corkindale, C.J. (2004). The first-time fathers study: A prospective study of the mental health and wellbeing of men during the transition to parenthood. *Australian and New Zealand Journal of Psychiatry, 38,* 56–64.

Davey, S.J., Dziurawiec, S., & O'Brien-Malone, A. (2006). Men's voices: Postnatal depression from the perspective of male partners. *Qualitative Health Research, 16,* 206–220.

Deater-Deckard, K., Pickering, K., Dunn, J.F., & Golding, J. (1998). Family structure and depressive symptoms in men preceding and following the birth of a child. *American Journal of Psychiatry, 155,* 818–823.

Downey, G., & Coyne, J.C.(1990). Children of depressed parents: An integrative review. *Psychological Bulletin, 108,* 50–76.

Edhborg, M., Lundh,W., Seimyr, L., & Widstrom, A.M. (2003). The parent-child relationship in the context of maternal depressive mood. *Archives of Women's Mental Health, 6,* 211–216.

Everingham, C.R., Heading, G., & Connor, L. (2006). Couples' experiences of postnatal depression: A framing analysis of cultural identity, gender and communication. *Social Science and Medicine, 62,* 1745–1756.

Fletcher, R., Matthey, S., & Marley, C.G. (2006). Addressing depression and anxiety among new fathers. *Medical Journal of Australia, 185,* 461–463.

Fivaz-Depeursinge, E., & Favez, N. (2006). Exploring triangulation in infancy: Two contrasted cases. *Family Process, 45,* 3–18.

George, M. (1996). Postnatal depression, relationships and men. *Mental Health Nursing, 16,* 16–19.

Gilding, M. (2004). DNA paternity testing without the knowledge or consent of the mother. *Family Matters, 68* (Winter), 68–75.

Goffman, E. (1997). Frame Analysis. In C. Lemert, & A. Branaman (Eds.), *The Goffman reader* (pp. 167–192). Cambridge: Blackwell.

Gottman, J.M., & Notarius, C.J. (2002). Marital research in the 20th century and a research agenda for the 21st century. *Family Process, 41,* 159–197.

Grube, M. (2005). Inpatient treatment of women with postpartum psychiatric disorders: The role of the male partners. *Archives of Women's Mental Health, 8,* 163–170.

Leff, J., Vearnals, S., Brewin, C.R., Wolff, G., Alexander, B., Asen, E., Dayson, D., Jones, E., Chisholm, D., & Everitt, B. (2000). The London depression intervention trial. Randomised controlled trial of antidepressants v. couple therapy in the treatment and maintenance of people with depression living with a partner: Clinical outcome and costs. *British Journal of Psychiatry, 177,* 95–100.

McPherson, M.D., Delva, J., & Cranford, J.A. (2007). A longitudinal investigation of intimate partner violence among mothers with mental illness. *Psychiatric Services, 58,* 675–681.

Matthey, S., Barnett, B.E.W., Kavanagh, D.J., & Howie, P. (2001). Validation of the Edinburgh Postnatal Depression Scale for men, and comparison of item endorsement with their partners. *Journal of Affective Disorders, 64,* 175–184.

Matthey, S., Barnett, B.E.W., Howie, P., & Kavanagh, D.J. (2003). Diagnosing postpartum depression in mothers and fathers: Whatever happened to anxiety? *Journal of Affective Disorders, 74,* 139–147.

Miller, L., & Finnerty, M. (1996). Sexuality, pregnancy, and childrearing among women with schizophrenia spectrum disorders. *Psychiatric Services, 47,* 502–506.

Morgan, M., Matthey, S., Barnett, B.E.W., & Richardson, C. (1997). A group program for postnatally distressed women and their partners. *Journal of Advanced Nursing, 26,* 913–920.

Nicholson, J., Sweeney, E.M., & Geller, J.L. (1998). Focus on women with mental illness: Family relationships and the context of parenting. *Psychiatric Services, 49,* 643–649.

Pacey, S. (2004). Couples and the first baby: responding to new parents' sexual and relationship problems. *Sexual and Relationship Therapy, 19,* 223–245.

Pinheiro, R.T., Magalhaes, P.V.S., Horta, B.L., Pinheiro, K.A.T., da Silva, R.A., & Pinto, R.H. (2006). Is paternal postpartum depression associated with maternal postpartum depression? Population-based study in Brazil. *Acta Psychiatrica Scandinavica, 113,* 230–232.

Pittman, F. (1993). Fathers and sons: What it takes to be a man. *Psychology Today,* September, 52–54.

Raphael-Leff, J. (2001). *Pregnancy. The inside story.* London: Karnac.

Roberts, S.L., Bushnell, J.A., Collings, S.C., & Purdie, G.L. (2006). Psychological health of men with partners who have post-partum depression. *Australian and New Zealand Journal of Psychiatry, 40,* 704–711.

Ritsher, J.E.B., Coursey, R.D., & Farrell, E.W. (1997). A survey on issues in the lives of women with severe mental illness. *Psychiatric Services, 48,* 1273–1282.

Soliday, E., McCluskey-Fawcett, K., & O'Brien, M. (1999). Postpartum affect and depressive symptoms in mothers and fathers. *American Journal of Orthopsychiatry, 69,* 30–38.

Stern, D. (1985). *The interpersonal world of the infant: A view from psychoanalysis and developmental psychology.* New York: Basic Books.

Wallace, P.M., & Gotlib, I. (1990). Marital adjustment during the transition to parenthood: Stability and predictors of change. *Journal of Marriage and the Family, 52,* 1.

Winnicott, D. (1956). *Through paediatrics to psychoanlysis.* London: Hogarth.

Personal Perspectives

'... No Question'

*Jennifer**

*All names have been changed.

--- ---

I was on holiday in New South Wales in 2003 when I got a call from one of Margaret's friends asking me to get home as soon as possible. (Margaret is my youngest child and only daughter.) At the time, Margaret's former house-mate James, and my youngest son, John, were living with me, not far from Margaret's flat.

The boys tried to explain Margaret's behaviour to me, and it was exceedingly embarrassing for both of them. She claimed 'voodoo' people were attacking her and telling her that the boys were both evil; she was screaming this out for the whole neighbourhood to hear. The extent of her departure from reality included accusations that both James and John were 'psychically raping her'. When she confronted me the first time after I arrived home, she was so angry when I didn't believe her, she seized a hatchet and chased me around the back yard, until I went inside and called the police. This was the beginning of her treatment for psychotic episodes, as she went to the Royal Adelaide Hospital (RAH) and thence to a ward in the psychiatric hospital. She was eventually sent to a hostel.

After she was released from there, she rented a Housing Trust flat, where she met her husband. She fell pregnant, and they were married in March 2004. She seemed reasonably well during the pregnancy, and Jake arrived in October that year.

During this time she was on medication and looked after by a community mental health team. Although she still had delusions about voodoo, she seemed to be better most of the time. However, there were several episodes when she would phone me to come and help her, as she was 'being attacked'. Her husband was becoming less and less patient with her illness, and at the time I sympathised with him.

Jake was a good baby, and seemed to thrive. However, as I did not get on well with his father, I didn't spend as much time with him as I would have, in retrospect, had I been aware of the facts. These included his father's jealousy of Margaret's time taken up with Jake, his method of discipline (yelling and shutting him in his room), Margaret's lack of quality time with Jake (DVDs in preference to teaching toys), her lack of motivation to train him, and the haphazard way in which she fed him.

By this time only my eldest son, Rick, was living with me. When Margaret told us she was expecting a second child we were both worried, as we did not know how she could cope with two if the illness had not shown any further improvement. Shortly before Susanna was born, Jake's father hit him and then Margaret. As a result of this, I took Margaret to our local police station and Jake's father was picked up, charged, and bailed on condition that he did not go near any of us. At this time, the case has not been heard, due to continuous deferrals. The week following this event, Margaret went to hospital and Susanna was born in August 2007.

Jake came to stay with Rick and me while she was in hospital, and it became immediately apparent that he had many issues that would need to be addressed — including toilet training, weaning from bottle (he was still having three feeds per day), and weaning from jars of baby food. He had frequent disturbed nights, but was able to go to sleep again after much reassurance.

Margaret and Susanna went home after 6 days, and I stayed with her for the first 2 nights, with Jake back in his own bed. Observing that her leg was swollen, I insisted she get an appointment with her general practitioner (GP). We went the next day, and after radiology she was rushed back into hospital with a deep vein thrombosis (DVT). Jake came home with me again.

After about 10 days, I was called in by the hospital to have a meeting with people from various agencies, to discuss Margaret's inability to care for Susanna. At the time, I felt that with the underlying mental illness, the domestic violence, having a baby, DVT, and being separated from Jake, were all valid reasons for her to 'lose the plot'. She seemed to think that she was a danger to all the babies in the hospital, believing they were being attacked through her. This was her explanation for the babies' crying.

So Susanna came home with me at 14 days old and Margaret was sent to the RAH psychiatric ward while waiting for a bed in Helen Mayo House, the specialised mother–baby unit. Jake was still unsettled, and having his second home 'invaded' by the baby was a further challenge for him. In due course, a bed was found for Margaret and Susanna at Helen Mayo House (HMH), and Jake and

I went into the 'visiting' stage. By this time, he seemed quite settled into coming 'home' to my house, and not his own.

Unfortunately, Margaret was not able to respond to treatment in HMH or improve her care of Susanna and, on Jake's birthday, we brought the baby home again. At this stage, Margaret went back into another ward of the psychiatric hospital, where a drastic medication change was tried using clozapine, which is a very strong medication. It became apparent fairly soon that the drug was making a difference and, for the first time, her 'voices' were fading. When the staff thought she was ready, she went back to HMH with Susanna for another trial. Finally (and sadly on her own birthday) it was agreed that although the clozapine was working for her, it did not mean that she was in a position to care for the children. After a further meeting with agencies (mental health and child protection), both children were placed in my care.

Jake's lack of language development had become painfully obvious when I compared his talking (one to two words at a time) with another 3-year-old at HMH. An assessment by child health services revealed that although he was a bright, intelligent child, his language and behavioural development was quite limited — in some instances he rated as a 1- to 2-year-old.

We commenced visits to Child and Adolescent Mental Health Services (CAMHS) for speech therapy and behavioural therapy. Jake had been going to childcare 3 days per week since he had come to live with me. His social skills had improved immensely but he still occasionally showed aggressive signs. We have never been able to leave him in the same room with Susanna without one of us present, for fear he may act aggressively toward her.

However, with time and the stability and routine that are established, Jake has developed his lovely sunny nature (albeit very mischievous) and appears to love Susanna, and not consider her the rival he at first thought. As this sibling behaviour is to be expected in general, the occasional posturing to take attention away from the baby is seen as quite normal. He is popular at childcare, and his language skills are coming along very well. He now completes sentences, and although he has not 'caught up', I have no doubt that he will.

Life for me has changed, it would seem, forever. I had come to Adelaide to 'escape' my children, and now three of them live here and I have two small children to raise. I am 63 years old; when Jake is 10, I will be seventy. Margaret's illness had put some strain on my available free time, especially once she became pregnant with Susanna. But that was as nothing compared to the way things are at present.

When the question of care of the children was first mooted, my (and my son's) only reaction was that there was, indeed, no question. Foster care was and is not an option. The children's welfare is currently officially in the hands of the State Minister for Families and Communities, and I am primary carer. There is very little free time. Jake is currently going through the 'terrible twos' syndrome. He pushes most of my buttons, most of the time. (Told you he was smart!)

I no longer have a place to go to in my home which is mine. Susanna shares my bedroom, Jake shares my office. When it becomes possible, they will share the ex-office and I will move my desk and computer into my bedroom. At the moment, that won't work because Jake would climb into Susanna's cot and wake her up at any time. My ex-lounge room is the playroom, with toys scattered all over.

I am coping. It does seem some days that we are slowly getting used to the huge changes. I am so lucky that my son is here to relieve the pressure, and afford me windows of time-out, but these are fraught with worry until I get home and see that all is well. My child protection services contact person is organising respite care for me, and I have agreed at last, because I cannot afford to go under. I resisted at first because I did not want Jake's routine to be changed yet again. (Apart from two or three short terms with her mother, Susanna has been with me for most of her 6 months of life.)

Getting along with Margaret (who is now home at her house) is another problem. We have to work with access visits, which at the moment are mostly at my house. When she doesn't do the right thing in this respect, I feel very resentful and I know that I should not, because it is the illness and not the person.

Helen Mayo House, child protection, child health, CAMHS, various care organisations, my own GP, my son and friends all support me. I feel really lucky that there are so many people who care, including staff of much maligned government agencies. Helen Mayo House has been truly wonderful, keeping contact with me and providing assessment of Susanna long after she left there. They are always ready to help if I ring for advice.

Life has changed, indeed, but after an easier day with Jake, including more cuddles than he used to give, and feeding Susanna (world's most perfect baby), I know that we are doing what we have to, and want to, which begs the question: how do mentally ill mothers and their children cope if they do not have the same support?

Thru Innocent Eyes

Nichole Whiting

———

M y name is Nichole Whiting and I am 39 years old. I had my first drug-induced psychosis in the mid-1980s and this started a further decline of my mental health, which led to several more admissions before I was finally diagnosed with bipolar disorder at the age of 31.

At the age of 33 I began to volunteer at the James Fletcher Hospital in Newcastle, hoping to become an advocate. In 2005, this dream became a reality and I now also work at Maitland Hospital and at Morisset Hospital. However it has been a long road.

I first became a single parent at the age of 23 and, due to my own childhood experiences, emotional state and an underlying illness, I was not the same parent that I have been able to be to my second son who was born in 1996, after I had been diagnosed and had begun counselling and rehabilitation for my drug and alcohol abuse.

The cold reality of the different ways in which I was able to raise my two sons has still left a significant impact today on the way they relate to one another and to me. My eldest son is envious and shows signs of jealousy toward his younger brother, and has also taken on the opinion that it was he who made my life so difficult. He learnt to blame himself for my tears, my outbursts of anger and unpredictable behaviour. How can our infant children begin to understand what is happening inside to the parent to whom they are instinctively connected, the sole reason for their existence, their first impression of life and love?

The truth is, I was a woman who tried to do the best she could, living one day at a time, trying to survive the rollercoaster of the madness and sorrow that was my life. I realise now I did not walk this journey alone; my children accompanied my every step. They became my little soldiers, and together we fought through the demons and the unpredictable highs and lows of my mental health.

From the time my eldest son was born, I slowly replaced his unconditional love with fear, sadness, anger and confusion. You may ask how I know I did this, when we are talking about babies, children who can barely speak or crawl. Inside the infant lies the brain, working perfectly doing its job, its sole purpose to absorb information and process data.. The reality of my life soon became his life, complete with all of the obvious damage that I alone would cause in times of madness and confusion, which led to the emotional abuse and neglect of my children.

Today, I am still a witness to the devastating effects that my life and my illness has had on my children, and for all they have had to endure. In times of crisis, when I was upset, I would hold them as I cried, especially my eldest son — and it was not a silent cry. Sometimes it would be a loud cry begging for comfort and acknowledgment of my pain, pouring my fear and my sadness into their souls, so I was not alone and, as they cried, I would rock them thinking to myself, 'I will protect you, I will keep you safe'. I swore that they would never have to go through such pain and sorrow in their lives.

I often made very poor decisions due to my mental health issues and emotional state. If I became angry or was having an argument at a friend's or family member's house the first thing I would do was to go and pick up my son. This would be done in such a quick and abrupt fashion that it must have been so frightening for him. I thought someone would try to take him from me — he certainly became a possession at times and a weapon I could use against all who loved him. I would continue to yell and threaten whomever I was in conflict with while still holding my son in my arms.

A mother learns to distinguish between the different cries their children make and this allows the parent to attend to the needs of the child; unfortunately, in times that my sons were afraid I realise I found it very difficult to comfort them because my own rage and circumstances came first. When my eldest son was afraid, he would kick his legs and throw his arms around and bounce up and down, and at times become as stiff as a board with spasm-like screaming in my arms. It was as though his natural instincts were telling him to throw himself out of my arms so he would be safe and yet I never thought that it was me he was afraid of — me he so desperately wanted to get away from — I naturally assumed he was just upset and feeling the same emotions that I was for exactly the same reasons.

By the time I was diagnosed my eldest son was 8 years old, and while I was in hospital he went to live with his father. We both agreed it was best for him to continue living there until I had recovered; my son never returned and this was his choice. Today my son has many emotional and social problems and I know this has been caused by me — anger, low self-esteem, and he has no sense of fear or discipline.

Thankfully though, after much dedication and therapy, I now have the skills to not only cope when I am under stress but to thrive. My mental health is very stable and I maintain a healthy therapeutic lifestyle and can now be a good mother and enjoy all of the normality and happiness that is associated with life. Every day, because of my lifestyle changes, I am able to make a difference in the lives of parents and people living with a mental illness in times of crisis.

I believe that it is essential to provide adequate support to both the parent and the children after discharge from hospital, to ensure that the child's needs are adequately catered for. A follow-up phone call or a brief intervention is not sufficient time spent to assess either the parent or the child's state of mind and welfare, especially after a psychotic episode. Having experienced psychosis many times myself, I can assure you we are more than capable when we are unwell to be quite cunning, and can give quite the performance, leaving mental health workers in the community to believe we are doing fine and all is going well, when in fact this is not so. What would you do to protect your freedom, to keep your children with you?

I am proud of the person that I am now. The wisdom and the insight that I have gained and experienced through my journey has given me the confidence to be able to help, sympathise and assist other people living with a mental illness. However, let us never underestimate mental illness and the devastating effects that it can cause to our children when we are unwell.

10

A Sibling's Story From 3 to 7 Years of Age

Paola Mason

~~~

My mother's mental illness had huge effects on my whole life. My earliest *recollection really is at the age of 2. I remember being in my cot with my teddy bear and potty under the bed. I have one vivid recollection of needing to go to the toilet and not finding the pot but my father's shoe (which sufficed at the time, even though I did find out that he wasn't very happy about it the next day).*

At this early age I do not recall my mum being unwell. That began after my little sister was born (I was 3½ years old). I remember mum coming home from hospital with a baby and that the baby cried a lot — actually, she seemed to cry all the time. I remember trying to help comfort her by rocking the cradle/pram and that she wouldn't stop. I also remember rocking it so much that she fell out and that I got into a lot of trouble (I wasn't smacked or anything like that though).

As I have explained my baby sister was an unsettled baby. I didn't know why, but I do remember Mum getting upset and being tired. I remember that my sister used to have a rash that required cream that Mum had permanently at the ready, placed in her bra, to apply. I also remember my aunt coming over sometimes, but again I didn't understand why. My little sister had a rash on her head that never seemed to go away. (I now know that it was severe cradle cap.) I remember mum forgot to feed me and that I would put one chair upon another to get to the biscuit tin when I got hungry. I remember being frightened of climbing and falling (I am still afraid of heights).I can now see lots of things happened because Mum wasn't well enough to look after all our needs, even though I know she wanted the best for us.

When my sister was 2½ years old (I was 6) she got to the stove and managed to spill boiling water all over herself and had to go to hospital. I remember having nightmares about her dying and being put into a big basket and taken away. I also recall going to visit her, but not being allowed to go into the room, and then watching Mum put on a gown to go in and watching them through little glass windows. Mum was always upset and angry after that. When my little sister came home from hospital she had hardly any hair and they said it may never grow back (I heard adults talking about this) but gratefully she grew the most wonderful head of hair.

Not long after all of this happened mum began to get sadder and sadder until one day these people came to take Mum (we lived on a main road, and she was in the front yard yelling). I was really scared because all of these adults were yelling so I hid under my parents' bed. I stayed there until my uncle managed to get me out and explained that Mum went to hospital. I have discussed this with my little sister who said to me 'I was at the front door watching Mum'; remember, she was just over 2½ years of age. I recall that when we were young and there seemed to be more adults coming to visit, I also remember that there seemed to be a lot of arguments (adults raising their voices) even though I wasn't always present.

I recall at one stage that Mum became involved with a religious group and that a number of books with pictures of hell seemed to be around the house — and also that hell was where I was going if I wasn't good! I remember Mum started to talk to people that weren't really there. What I recall from this time in particular was that I wasn't sure what was real and what wasn't. I was afraid of the dark and slept with the blind open because 'if they were going to get me, I wanted to see them first'.

My little sister slept in the cot until she was 3 and then we were in the same room together. I remember that she didn't always sleep very well and that sometimes she would talk in her sleep, so I would put a pillow over my head to not hear noises or things. There were times when Mum seemed okay (she was happy, she would sing and she could be very funny) and then she could be very, very sad, cry, wail at times and then she would start to talk to herself. I remember feeling really sad myself when she was sad, and I would cry. I remember also being scared when she would talk to herself because some of the things she would say didn't make sense. It was worse when she would say things like 'leave me alone', 'I am dying', 'I want to kill myself'. I remember these things upsetting me a lot. At these times my little sister and I would go and play outside, go to the playground, go down the lane behind our house or into the shed. We had guinea pigs and we could play with them and make wonderful bran pies with grapes for them to eat. Many things occurred in my childhood, but one in particular that really upset me was the time my mother threatened my father with a knife. I recall shaking, screaming and running outside and then down the road. I don't know what happened but it was my father that came and got me. I remember how relieved I was and how sad Mum was when we got home.

As I got older I left my little sister behind in many ways — I made my own friends and would visit them (this doesn't at all mean that I wasn't worried about her or Mum) and she would be home with Mum. I would ride my bike for hours and hours, often alone. Again, my sister was at home. I suppose her view on things may be different to mine. We are quite different in personalities and yet we are both in the 'people professions'. She is now a nurse, I am in sales and consultancy. I live with and care for Mum, and even though my little sister lives independently, she shares in the care for Mum. We have been through a great deal individually and as a family, but ultimately we are all we have, and that is what matters. We all do the best we can.

I look back on my childhood and think about the effects of those events I can remember. It has been very helpful for me to understand more about mental illness. My concern for children growing up as I did and not understanding what was going on is so strong that it has led me to give my time to help these children (I also like to believe that I am helping parents too) — and perhaps others like me who are now adults and didn't have that help back then. Perhaps I learned a lot about staying strong and helping others from the things that happened — I know that working for Children of Mentally Ill Consumers (COMIC) has led me to see how challenging the effects of mental illness can be on children and makes me feel good at times that I can help some people. My experiences may have hurt me in some ways but they have also strengthened me.

Raising Sam*

The Experience of a Grandmother Raising Her Grandson From Infancy

Harriet

*Sam and Harriet are pseudonym

---

*I*f there is one day in my life that I will remember above all others, it is *November 3, 1993. I was preparing a lunch party for family and close friends to celebrate my mother's 80th birthday. My 16-year-old son and his girlfriend arrived before the guests, and announced that they were to be parents. I kept this news to myself and managed to host a lovely day.*

My son had had a difficult few years and was living with other young people in a house close to home. I suspected they were using drugs but I had no idea to what extent. My son's girlfriend had run away from home when she was 12 and had little contact with her mother. Both had been raised in homes without a father and I was well aware of the disadvantages this can have, particularly in regard to respect for authority and discipline.

My son's girlfriend often behaved erratically and I was informed shortly before my grandson's birth that she had been previously diagnosed with schizophrenia, and had a history of hospitalisation and treatment.

They were just 17 when Sam* was born prematurely and his mother had already moved back to where she grew up and was being helped by her mother and family. Most weekends I travelled some distance so that I could see Sam, and help out where possible. My son commuted at weekends as he was still studying in Sydney.

Sam's mother was given a Department of Housing flat that was very comfortable, and gave the family stability. Within a year all had turned to grief. She had met someone else and my son, who adored his little boy, was told to go. I bought a house in Newcastle as a place for my son to live, and to have his visits with Sam. My son was very capable with Sam and was spending more and more time with him. Within a year Sam's mother had abandoned him and gone to Queensland where she was arrested and admitted to a psychiatric hospital.

Sam was 2 years old when I took him to Queensland for her birthday and a pre-Christmas visit. We stayed for a week in a motel and visited twice each day. Sam loved seeing his mother and one of our saddest days was the final goodbye, watching him waving to her as we left. Sam remembers this visit, and I suspect that it is one of his earliest memories. My son obtained full custody of Sam and I moved to Newcastle to live with them.

At about this time I realised that my son was using heroin. The home situation became very volatile and he moved into his own place nearby. In spite of this my son was very capable and a good parent and I supported him having Sam to stay often. I decided to stop working and found the transition easy as I threw myself into renovating the house and doing the garden. I had just turned 50 and I missed my friends and workmates, but kept in touch by phone.

Sam spent a few days each week at Family Day Care, commencing when he was about 2½, and he thrived on the contact with other children. He then attended preschool, prior to starting school. He was a very happy little boy and rarely threw a tantrum or cried. I always encouraged his friends to visit and stay over and I made good friends with the young parents of these children. We also had lots of children living in our street and his early years were full of games and good company. Because I did not work I was able to attend most school functions and be more involved with sporting activities. I was not able to do this when my son was at school and I realised what we had both missed out on. Sam and I have had lots of adventures and holidays away together.

Sam's mother has spent long periods of time in institutions and it is unlikely that she will recover. When Sam sees her she is never able to fully engage or focus on him; she rarely hugs him or kisses him goodbye. He worries about her safety when she is not in a hospital being cared for, and I am concerned about his emotional wellbeing as I have rarely seen him cry. Sometimes I just wish he would break down and let it all out, but he silently keeps his feelings to himself. I have consulted a number of child social workers who tell me that he does open up more with them, so I am grateful for their help and we will continue to consult them. I know he would dearly have loved to have his mother look after him — I could never replace her and I haven't tried to. I have a close relationship with her and do all I can to make her life easier and help Sam stay in contact. My family and close friends have criticised me for allowing this contact for the negative effects it has on him, but my argument is that, for better or worse, she is his mother and we have to deal with that reality and I know that when he is older he will want to be her protector and help her all he can. This is beginning to be evident now.

Being 'mother' to my grandchild is quite a different experience to that of raising my son. I have more patience, wisdom, tolerance and time. I enjoy the routine and I love having the time to cook more interesting meals, look after clothing more carefully and do mundane tasks at my leisure. Raising my son was very much done in the fast lane and I missed so much of the little pleasures.

The years are racing by and now that Sam is a teenager I am experiencing different emotions. I sometimes feel resentful when he displays teenage selfishness and is rude to me. He wants more independence and freedom to hang out with his friends and I am enjoying having more time to myself to enjoy with my friends, and to care for my elderly mother and aunt.

Over the years I have had moments when I've resented my loss of freedom and felt that I did not choose the path I am on, but the things I have missed out on are superficial and I've had great pleasure and satisfaction from caring for my only grandchild. Naturally, I have fears for Sam's future and worry about peer pressure, drugs and alcohol and the effect his parents' drug problems have had on him. He is very close to his father who is finally doing well and studying. I hope that by directing Sam into healthy teenage pursuits he will continue to develop into a happy young man with good values and a positive self-identity. That would be all the reward I need for any sacrifices I have made.

Life rarely goes to plan and I feel very pleased with myself that I have met the challenge with love, acceptance, optimism and energy. I look forward to the coming years and know that there will be ups and downs, but I know that with good health I will continue to enjoy the ride.

Political and Cultural Influences

Children Are Our Future

Understanding the Needs of Aboriginal Children and Their Families

Helen Milroy

—◦—

'Mothers and Fathers'

We may not always choose to become parents, but once we behold that precious little bundle, our lives are changed forever. Becoming a parent is an amazing experience that includes some of the most intense emotions that one can ever undergo in life. Babies don't come with instructions, and yet so much of what happens is innate. One can never be completely prepared for what will happen and yet life goes on. Parenting is generational, and how we are as parents occurs in the broader context of our own experiences of our parents, communities and society. The best we can hope for is that we will recognise our mistakes, accept support from others and be prepared to let the world see just how remarkable our children really are.

Children are our future, our hopes and aspirations, as peoples of this world rests on their shoulders and they will carry us with them as they grow and develop, as they walk the path we have created for them and, in turn, they will prepare a place for us on which to rest in our later years. The importance of children, however, is far beyond them taking up their place in society. Children keep us grounded. They help us to enjoy the simple things in life and give to us the greatest gift of all, the chance to love and nurture a new little spirit, a little person who will be totally dependent on our care. In turn they will look at us and smile, bring light into our lives and give us the opportunity to experience unfettered joy as they reach out and touch our hearts.

We must give our children the best start, the right start in life and development. We all have many stories to tell, many more to share and some yet to be created as we begin our journey as parents, gazing upon the wonder that is creation.

Introduction

Very little formal research has been carried out on distinct groups of Aboriginal infants in compromised families. In this chapter, an empirical approach based on clinical experience will be shared, to improve the understanding of the needs of Aboriginal children and their families for clinicians working in a crosscultural context. Working with Aboriginal families can be both challenging and rewarding and, particularly when working with Aboriginal mothers and infants, understanding cultural frameworks will greatly assist better outcomes — in many cases making working relationships possible.

In addition to good practice guidelines, clinicians need awareness of some specific issues influencing and impacting on Aboriginal families. These include understanding the history and ongoing impact of colonisation; the current levels of disadvantage, morbidity and mortality; and the cultural influences on family, health and recovery. Following a general overview, three case examples will be used to illustrate the various issues and ways of working with Aboriginal families. Ideally, when working with specific communities, clinicians will undertake crosscultural training and seek out local orientation and protocols.

Overview

Indigenous Australians

The Indigenous peoples of Australia comprise two groups, namely Aboriginal peoples from mainland Australia and surrounding small islands, and Torres Strait Islanders originating from the islands in the Torres Strait and the northern coast of Queensland. Although Aboriginal peoples and Torres Strait Islanders share many of the same experiences of colonisation, they are quite distinct cultural groups with very different origins, customs and family structures. This chapter will focus on the experiences of Aboriginal peoples and, although some of the information will be relevant, additional specific information and guidance will be required in understanding Torres Strait Islander families. Although use of the term 'Aboriginal' is generally accepted, it is a collective term that was imposed with colonisation.

Aboriginal peoples comprise many distinct groups with separate languages, customs and beliefs. However, groups also share common experiences of history as well as connections through ancestry, spirituality, song and story lines, and ceremony. In general, Aboriginal people prefer to use their clan group's names such as Koori, or Murri, as part of their identity as Aboriginal peoples. The currently accepted Australian government definition of who is Aboriginal — as used for example for ABSTUDY (Australian Government Department of Education, Science and Training, 2007) — has three major components. An Australian Aboriginal or Torres Strait Islander person:

- is one who is of Aboriginal or Torres Strait Islander descent
- identifies as an Australian Aboriginal or Torres Strait Islander person
- is accepted as such by the community in which they live or have lived.

Because of the diversity of culture as well as experience, the needs of individuals, families and communities vary enormously and a range of approaches and services are required. Although some generic principles may apply, understanding and working with the local community is of the utmost importance when developing best practice approaches to improve outcomes for Aboriginal families.

History

Aboriginal peoples are acknowledged as the oldest continuous living culture in the world, with histories dating back many thousands of years; Aboriginal peoples remain the cultural and spiritual custodians of the world's oldest sacred sites as well as their homelands. At the time of colonisation, Aboriginal peoples were viewed as healthier than most Europeans, with little evidence of the chronic disease or distress states found today. With colonisation came a number of significant events and changes imposed on Aboriginal peoples including the:

- imposition of a foreign culture, law, language and society
- decimation of the Aboriginal population through massacres, deliberate poisoning, introduction of disease and starvation
- dispossession of Aboriginal peoples from their homelands into missions and reserves
- denigration and denial of Aboriginal culture, spirituality, identity and traditional law

- fragmentation and destruction of families and communities through high rates of death, incarceration and removal of children
- racially-based legislative control over all aspects of Aboriginal people's lives including work, marriage and guardianship of children.

This traumatic history was widespread and sustained over many decades. As a result, there is significant trauma and loss that has accumulated over generations. The sense of extreme powerlessness that many families feel in the face of great adversity, racism and discrimination must be acknowledged. With the release of the Bringing Them Home Report (Human Rights and Equal Opportunity Commission, 1997), the impact of the 'Stolen Generations' is only now being fully realised. The historical legacy is still apparent today with many unresolved issues such as sovereignty and native title, reconciliation, equity and compensation. However, history also reveals the strengths of Aboriginal people to survive such adversity. Resiliency and endurance, connection to land, culture and spirituality, and kinship and knowledge systems are predominant strengths.

Demographics

From the Australian Bureau of Statistics Census data (2002, 2007), Indigenous people make up about 2.3% of the total population of Australia. Of this, 90% were of Aboriginal origin only, 6% Torres Strait Islander origin only and 4% were of both Aboriginal and Torres Strait Islander origin. The largest proportion of Indigenous people live in New South Wales, followed by Queensland and Western Australia. However, in the Northern Territory, Indigenous people make up 32% of the population whereas in most states, it is less than 4% and in Victoria Indigenous people account for only 0.6% of the state population.

The population is quite dispersed with 53% of Indigenous people living in major cities or inner regional areas and 24% living in remote or very remote regions. The relative visibility of population groups is important to understand as it influences attitudes and beliefs and can impact on service delivery. Although a large proportion of the Indigenous population live in the larger urban centres, families can be easily overlooked and, despite proximity to services, health and wellbeing outcomes are much the same for all levels of geographical isolation (Australian Institute of Health and Welfare, 2005).

The Indigenous population has a significantly different age distribution, with a median age of 21 years compared with 36 years for the non-Indigenous population. There are significantly higher numbers of young people, with 39% aged less than 15 years compared with 20% for the non-Indigenous population and relatively fewer elders with only 3% aged over 65 years compared with 13% in the non-Indigenous population (Australian Bureau of Statistics, 2002). This means there are relatively more children than adults in the population and the usual buffering for families through availability of extended family members to assist parents and children does not exist to the same extent. Hence, even taking into consideration cultural and kinship obligations, the important role in childcare played by the small number of elders available is far greater than would be expected because of the loss of human capital.

Understanding Aboriginal Health, Wellbeing and Healing: From Definition to Cultural Understanding

The Aboriginal view of health is holistic and interconnected with mind, body, spirit and nature in balance. The most commonly cited definition of health from an Aboriginal perspective comes from the first National Aboriginal Health Strategy (1989a) and states:

> [Health is] ... not just the physical wellbeing of the individual but the social, emotional, and cultural wellbeing of the whole community. This is a whole-of-life view and it also includes the cyclical concept of life-death-life. (National Aboriginal Health Strategy Working Party, 1989a, p. x)

What is interesting about this definition is the earlier discussion from the working party, established to develop the National Aboriginal Health Strategy, on trying to define health as follows:

> In Aboriginal society there was no word, term or expression for 'health' as it is understood in Western society. It would be difficult from the Aboriginal perception to conceptualise 'health' as one aspect of life. The word as it is used in Western society almost defies translation but the nearest translation in an Aboriginal context would probably be a term such as 'life is health is life'. (National Health Strategy Working Party, 1989b, p. 1)

In the *Ways Forward* report, Swan and Raphael (1995) expanded on the notion of health under Guiding Principles:

> The Aboriginal concept of health is holistic, encompassing mental health and physical, cultural and spiritual health. Land is central to wellbeing. This holistic concept does not merely refer to the 'whole body' but in fact is steeped in the harmonised interrelations which constitute cultural wellbeing. These interrelating factors can be categorised largely as spiritual, environmental, ideological, political, social, economic, mental and physical. Crucially, it must be understood that when the harmony of these interrelations is disrupted, Aboriginal ill-health will persist. (Swan & Raphael, 1995, Part 1, p. 13)

Although these definitions are helpful, understanding the cultural context of health is more difficult. Cultural beliefs and experiences can impact on the way a person:

- understands illness and causal pathways
- attributes meaning
- develops symptoms and experiences phenomena
- develops coping mechanisms and behaviour
- accepts treatment and views recovery from illness.

As Aboriginal people, including children from very early in life, can experience an array of auditory and visual phenomena as part of normal cultural life, these could be easily misconstrued in a psychiatric setting (Parker & Milroy, 2003). Sheldon (2001) noted the importance of understanding cultural norms when assessing symptoms and behaviour and the value of involving Aboriginal mental health workers throughout the process. The person's or community's previous experiences with services and authority figures can also influence how a person responds in the clinical setting, particularly given the historical levels of discrimination. Problems in cross-cultural communication can result in an inappropriate interview process, invalid assessment and create further barriers for the family to access health care and may lead to families avoiding contact with services altogether.

To understand Aboriginal mental health it is also important to have some understanding of Aboriginal knowledge systems and worldview, custom and beliefs, cultural experiences and behaviour, and methods of healing. For example, from an Aboriginal perspective, wellbeing is about balance and harmony rather than symptom reduction or restoring function. The concept is community-centred rather than individually focused, with the use of strengths to promote recovery as opposed to risk reduction. Priority setting may also be different and attending appointments may be of less importance than fulfilling cultural, ceremonial or family obligations. The use of traditional healers is still widespread, and working in conjunction with cultural knowledge systems is essential for good outcomes. In central Australia, Ngangkaris are employed to provide traditional healing practices in mental health for their communities, and often work in consultation with the local health and mental health service (Ngaanyatjarra Pitjantjatjara Yankunytjatjara Women's Council Aboriginal Corporation, 2003).

Understanding Aboriginal Family Systems

Historically, Aboriginal families were connected through extensive systems of kinship and skin groupings. These systems locate individuals in the community and neighbouring clans within relationships of caring, sharing, obligation and reciprocity. Essentially, the kinship system provided a very secure attachment system that established caring relationships so that everyone grew up with multiple carers and attachment figures and, in turn, provided care for others. The system was also circular in that it provided obligation for younger adults to care for elders and hence the system was both comprehensive and generational. With these kinship social rules, children could never be considered as orphans as someone within the system would be obliged to fulfil a mother relationship with the child. For example, a mother's sister was considered as a mother rather than an aunt and was expected to take on the same responsibility as the biological mother, with no distinction between biological children and nieces and nephews. This was the same for fathers and grandparents. Aunts and uncles were also part of the system but sometimes played different roles from parents, such as providing discipline under certain circumstances. Likewise, children generally considered their cousins as siblings and acted accordingly, often with the older children providing a protective and caring role for younger children. The socialisation of Aboriginal children is quite different, as pointed out by Enembaru (Dudgeon, Garvey, & Pickett, 2000, p. 178), Aboriginal infants are seen as 'autonomous individuals capable of indicating their needs'; they are 'indulged in many aspects' of care and 'early self-reliance' is encouraged.

The following genogram provides an example of how a kinship system may be organised, although clinicians need to work within the framework of the particular cultural group as there are many different systems still operating.

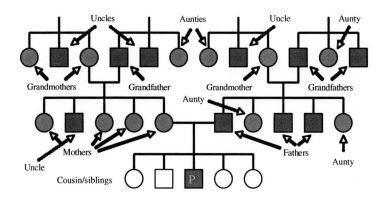

Figure 1
Kinship systems (Milroy, 2002).

The terms 'aunty' or 'uncle' can also be used today to denote a mark of respect for senior people within the community, regardless of family ties, and hence will be respected by all adults and children. From a traditional perspective, kinship obligations were taken very seriously, with great concern arising if obligations were not carried out appropriately. Kinship systems still operate in most communities today but perhaps with less strict adherence. In contemporary society, kinship obligations can create a significant burden for some families, especially grandmothers trying to fulfil their cultural obligations to a large number of children with grossly inadequate supports and resources. Hammil (2001) argues that the health and welfare of the grandmothers is crucial for the survival of communities, and support is needed to prevent 'burnout' among the older women. However, kinship systems do offer a broad base of support for children and mothers.

Social rules regarding family relationships also determined social behaviour, to some degree. Depending on the relationship, some family members would be in avoidance relationships; that is, they were not meant to speak to each other directly or be in close proximity. Other social behaviours may include who could speak for the family or give an opinion. From a clinical perspective, it is important to map the family's kinship system as this will establish the broader nature of attachment relationships and what roles others play in the family system. It will also be easier to locate the client as they may move between support systems. It may be difficult to establish who the biological parents are, as opposed to the 'bringing them up' parents, and rules of kinship add complexity to understanding issues of confidentiality, consent, custody and guardianship.

The skin groupings are a related but different system that were allocated everyone within the community, and neighbouring clans, into different groups for purposes such as ensuring everyone is part of a community of belonging, and also for systems of marriage. Parents and children belong to different groups, but children could belong to the same group as their grandparents. Skin groupings vary around Australia; for instance, the number of skin groups could vary from a four- to an eight-group system. The social rules governing skin groups were similar in providing a family system of relationships for each member in the skin group (not necessarily biologically related) and hence guidance and assistance, even for newcomers, after skin allocation.

It is most likely that due to the allocation of its members, skin groupings would have contributed to maintaining a healthy genetic pool. Traditionally, there were significant cultural rules associated with marriage, and couples who chose to enter into a 'wrong' marriage could be punished by the community. Although skin systems still operate today, there is enormous variation between communities and families regarding the nature of social rules, adherence to and structure of the kinship and skin group systems.

Working collaboratively with local community and cultural consultants enables clinicians to understand these complex family and kinship relationships that continue to influence Aboriginal families.

Social, Emotional and Physical Wellbeing

Currently, on all socioeconomic, health and welfare indicators, Aboriginal people are the most disadvantaged population group in Australia. The Australian Institute of Health and Welfare report (2005) on the health and welfare of Australia's Aboriginal and Torres Strait Islander peoples suggest that, overall, Aboriginal people are more likely to be unemployed; have lower household incomes; experience poorer housing with significant problems with overcrowding, poor sanitation and water supply; have lower levels of school attendance and completion to high school, with lower numeracy and literacy levels; are more likely to be incarcerated or have children removed under care and protection orders; and will experience more major life stress events than the non-Indigenous population.

The report also found significant health issues in comparison with the non-Indigenous population. For Indigenous peoples in Australia:

- Most major illnesses and chronic diseases are overrepresented, with age-specific death rates being higher, especially in the young and middle adult groups with 75% of male and 65% of female deaths before the age of 65 years.

- Infants continue to have lower birth weights and higher mortality rates and maternal mortality rates are also higher.

- Life expectancy continues to be reported as 17–20 years less.

- When compared to other Indigenous groups in New Zealand and Canada, Australian Aboriginal peoples are by far the most disadvantaged with the highest levels of morbidity and mortality and the greatest level of health inequities.

There are also a number of increased health risk factors present in the Aboriginal community, including smoking, hazardous drinking, drug use, obesity, poor nutrition and multiple life events. Although Indigenous people are less likely to consume alcohol compared to the non-Indigenous population, those who do are more likely to drink hazardously. The high rates of smoking among pregnant Indigenous women contribute to the low birthweights in infants (Australian Institute of Health and Welfare, 2005). Hence the risk for early onset of chronic disease and mental health problems starts early in life and is compounded throughout development.

Mental Health

The available mental health morbidity data on Indigenous peoples suggests increased rates of depression and trauma-related problems as well as higher rates of suicide, especially in young men. Although hospital admission data suggest increased rates of hospitalisation for psychosis, this may represent the impact of substance use (Thomson, Burns, Burrow, & Kirov, 2004). There is frequent comorbidity, with physical health problems such as diabetes and other risk factors occurring more frequently, including grief and loss, domestic violence, incarceration and poverty. There are a number of confounding issues to consider when viewing mental illness in Indigenous populations, including cultural and historical factors, and high levels of socioeconomic disadvantage.

Hunter (1993) argues while it is important not to 'pathologise' culture within the transcultural context, it is equally important not to miss significant illness and the important gains to be made in treating severe illness appropriately. Clinicians need to be careful not to overdiagnose illness in the face of significant disadvantage and discrimination, but also be cognisant of the very real impact of colonisation and racism on mental health and wellbeing for Indigenous peoples. The *Ways Forward* report (Swan & Raphael, 1995) highlighted the general lack of knowledge and understanding of Indigenous mental health and raised many important issues in regard to the mislabelling and further traumatisation of Indigenous peoples within inadequate and culturally inappropriate mental health systems, during periods of incarceration or out-of- home care. It can be very difficult for clinicians to tease out what constitutes illness as opposed to the general levels of discrimination and social disadvantage affecting people's lives.

Aboriginal Children and Their Social and Emotional Wellbeing

The Western Australian Aboriginal Child Health Survey (Zubrick et al., 2005) showed the number of life stress events was the factor most strongly associated with high risk of clinically significant behavioural and emotional difficulties for Aboriginal children. The survey found 22% of Aboriginal children were living in families where seven or more major life stress events had occurred over the preceding 12 months, placing them at 5.5 times the risk of developing emotional and behavioural difficulties. Up to 70% of families had experienced three or more major life stress events, suggesting the majority of the population is at considerable risk. This places considerable strain on child development and could impact adversely on health, wellbeing and educational outcomes. The survey also found that children cared for by a primary carer with a long-term and limiting medical condition were 3.5 times as likely to be at high risk and there is mounting evidence showing the transgenerational impact on children cared for by carers who had been forcibly removed as children under past government policies (Atkinson, 2002; De Maio et al., 2005; Haebich, 2000).

Three case examples illustrate the need for understanding the cultural context that influences the health and wellbeing of Indigenous infants and their families.

Case 1: Marcus, Troy and Brenda: Understanding the Historical Legacy

Marcus, aged 6, and his brother Troy, aged 3, were cared for by their grandmother, Brenda, following the death of their mother, Susan, in a motor vehicle accident 6 months after Troy's birth. Brenda was a 48-year-old Aboriginal woman with recurrent depression and unstable diabetes. Marcus had become increasingly difficult to manage, with oppositional behaviour, refusing to attend school and showing aggression in the playground. Troy was more introverted and mostly stayed close to Brenda, sleeping in her bed at night. Brenda had been struggling to cope and was hospitalised for 2 weeks recently for her diabetes, with the children placed in temporary foster care. Problems at home with both the children had escalated since her admission. Brenda was referred back to the mental health service for review of her antidepressant medication, where further discussion ensued over Brenda's concerns for Marcus and Troy.

Brenda grew up in a mission as part of the 'Stolen Generations' and had little contact with her own parents after leaving the mission at age 16 years. Brenda's mother died from renal failure just after Susan's birth and her father died from a heart attack the following year. She worked as a domestic on pastoral properties until marrying Ralph at age 21 years when pregnant with their first child. Brenda had several miscarriages before having a second child, Colin, born prematurely at 30 weeks' gestation. Colin had many developmental difficulties from birth and was diagnosed with cerebral palsy. Colin lived in a residential facility since late adolescence when Brenda was no longer able to manage his care at home. Brenda's marriage broke up shortly after Colin's birth and she remained single.

Brenda had several siblings who remained in the community with their family. As Brenda had 'lighter' skin, she was removed to the mission, and attended the mission school until Year 7. Although she had tried to connect back to the community, she always felt she didn't really fit in and was not confident in her own identity as an

Aboriginal woman. She still had contact with some of the 'mission kids' but otherwise had spent most of her life caring for her own children and grandchildren. She suffered severe depression following the death of her daughter and believed life would not be the same any more. She was however, committed to ensuring her grandsons grew up well and had been thinking recently about taking them back to her community to find out about their Aboriginal heritage.

Marcus and Troy had already suffered the loss of their mother, and were now at high risk of losing their primary carer. Marcus's development of externalising behaviours was not surprising: Marcus had significant separation anxiety and unresolved grief over the loss of his mother and believed he had to protect the family. Brenda's significant ill-health, with the attendant threat of either her death or perhaps an inability to continue caring for the children, was highly anxiety-provoking. It was appropriate to understand why Marcus refused to go to school and acted out in the playground, rather than mislabelling his aggressive behaviours as conduct or attentional disorders. We needed to ensure that Marcus did not become his grandmother's carer, a not infrequent outcome for Aboriginal children.

Troy appeared more apathetic and withdrawn, and concern for his wellbeing was expressed by Brenda and his foster mother. Although Troy's behaviour was less disruptive, his infancy was traumatic with the loss of his mother when he was 6 months old, and the subsequent depression and chronic illness of his grandmother. These impacted significantly on his attachment relationships and development of self-regulation. He was difficult to engage, and appeared aimless yet 'busy' in his play, moving from object to object, always keeping an eye on his grandmother.

Brenda had suffered multiple losses, including her family of origin and, in effect, both of her children. The prospect of losing her grandchildren was a very real threat. This intensified her anxiety and some noncompliance as she avoided further scrutiny as a parent. Identifying these issues and assisting Brenda to resolve her own identity issues and strengthening her community connections was important to assist the children's developing cultural identity, broaden their attachment to family and provide a greater sense of security for the future.

Supporting the children through school was also significant given Brenda's poor education and the children's reluctance to leave the home. The school system has the potential to offer important social supports to both children.

Brenda was comforted in her own grief by holding Troy as an infant, setting up a role-reversal situation for Troy to contain his carer's (Brenda) emotions at the expense of his own healthy development. Troy's emotional and psychological needs were potentially easy to overlook as Brenda, like many parents, assumed he was too young to understand and would 'cope'.

It was important to assist Brenda in her understanding of child development and the importance of stable, consistent long-term relationships for the children to avoid further loss or abandonment. We also arranged some home support and helped create opportunities for the children to play and participate in the wider community. Ensuring ongoing health, educational and welfare support with this family was challenging, but possible and necessary to ensure the optimal development of Marcus and Troy.

Acknowledging the continuing impact of Brenda's history of removal from her family led to contact with services to assist in family reunification and counselling. There are a variety of such services including Link-up, Bringing Them Home Counsellors and Social and Emotional Wellbeing workers. The mental health workers acknowledged they were not fully equipped to deal adequately with the complexities that Brenda faced, especially around the issue of removal, and they worked collaboratively with Aboriginal Community Controlled Organisations to provide the range of services needed. Understanding the historical frame of reference helped the workers to understand some of the levels of difficulty for this family, and potentially lead the children towards a positive sense of identity as Aboriginal Australians.

Case 2: Sarah, Amy and Jonah: Understanding Kinship and Communication

Sarah, a 17-year-old Aboriginal woman, was first seen 5 days post delivery of her second child, Jonah. Her first child, Amy, aged 2 years, lived with an aunty in a remote community and Sarah had occasional contact. The delivery was unremarkable; however, Sarah had received minimal antenatal care and had significant anaemia during the pregnancy. She had been living with her mother in a community on the outskirts of town with no heating, poor cooking facilities and overcrowding, as several extended family members also stayed in the house. She was not keen to return home as many family members drank alcohol and smoked and she was concerned for her infant's welfare. Despite this, she wished to leave hospital as soon as possible and planned to stay with friends locally. She did not have a partner and would not disclose the baby's father.

Sarah's background was traumatic with significant domestic violence and sexual abuse during her early life. She had lived with many different family members and only moved back to live with her mother a year previously. She attended multiple schools and failed to make the transition to high school, preferring to hang out with friends instead. She had never been employed but often looked after younger children in her kinship network. During her early teens, she had minor offences for drug use and stealing and was well known to Family and Children's Services. There was no previous contact with mental health services.

On the ward, staff noted Sarah was not very communicative, had difficulty breastfeeding and left Jonah for long periods in the nursery. In interview, Sarah insisted she would manage once she was out of hospital and would comply with any recommendations. She avoided eye contact, looking down at the ground and appeared restricted in her affect. She held Jonah away from her face but was confident with general routines of changing nappies and bathing. Jonah himself was physically healthy and alert, and quite responsive to his mother's nurturing. She reported that Amy was developing well, although could not provide details of this.

Sarah had many risk factors for postnatal depression, which also needed a cross-cultural perspective. It is common for Aboriginal girls to have children from a young age, yet this can be easily used in making judgments about behaviour and personality.

Children can be reared by other family members and this does not necessarily denote abandonment or poor attachment. Currently, attachment classifications have not been validated for Aboriginal families, as parenting beliefs and practices clearly differ from 'Western' norms. Young women from remote communities can also be very shy and not show communication styles expected, and affective responses and personal hygiene standards can vary. If there is any doubt, someone from the person's home community or an Aboriginal mental health worker may be able to assist in identifying whether the behaviour is abnormal or not. Lack of eye contact could be part of cultural behaviour and may be a sign of respect. Long silences or pauses after questions can also be culturally appropriate, but could easily be misconstrued in a mental status examination. Miscommunication and poor understanding of language can also complicate the picture. In a study by Watson, Hodson, Johnson and Kemp (2002) on the maternity experiences of Indigenous women in the Northern Territory, miscommunication, lack of empathy and cultural and spiritual misunderstandings were noted as major concerns. In some cases, Aboriginal people will answer 'yes' to everything to be polite, but this does not mean there is agreement; and 'no' to questions can be used in the same way. English was not Sarah's first language; Aboriginal English can have different meanings and Sarah's educational level was low. It was important therefore to use simple language, without jargon but without talking 'down' to her.

As Aboriginal children often grow up with a great deal of early autonomy and self-reliance, Sarah was resilient in looking after herself and providing for the baby even without stable accommodation. Nevertheless, with her limited resources, it was important to consider ways of enriching the early experience of this adolescent mother and her infant. Sarah's preexisting anaemia and other medical concerns also required treatment.

We needed to ensure that follow-up plans were realistic and achievable, and acceptable to Sarah. Expecting a young woman with a newborn to catch buses and trains across town to attend a short appointment was unreasonable and could lead to inappropriate labels as unreliable or noncompliant. Sarah was referred to the female Aboriginal liaison worker for support. Sarah's behaviour was quite different with the Aboriginal staff member. She appeared more relaxed, conversed easily, making jokes, talking and playing with the baby. She was also more receptive to discussing her plans and welcomed help with finding suitable accommodation. Sarah considered staying with her aunty for contact with her first child but could not afford to travel to the community.

Case 3: John, Cassie and Their Infants:
Understanding Contemporary Aboriginal Realities and Cultural Influences

John was a 23-year-old Aboriginal male recently admitted for a possible drug-induced psychosis following increasing marijuana use. This was his fourth admission in the last 3 years and there was concern he may have an underlying psychotic illness, as the intervals between admissions had shortened and recovery was less than optimal. John lived with his partner of 5 years, Cassie aged 21 years, and they had three children, girls aged 4 and 3 years and a boy aged 9 months. John had become increasingly violent and possessive over the past 2 years, mostly related to bouts of alcohol use, and John and Cassie had been arguing constantly. John had also been seeing 'spirit' figures and talking to ancestors about the special gifts he was receiving and his beliefs of his growing importance in the community. John was from the local area, but Cassie wanted to take the kids back to her homelands in a remote town so she could be closer to her mother. However, she feared that if she left something 'bad' like 'payback' may happen to her and the children or to her extended family. John had also threatened to kill himself if she left with the children. Both the girls were very shy and reserved and the infant was described as irritable and difficult to settle. Cassie had few supports, mostly staying at home caring for her children.

John's early life was unremarkable and he was considered a bright student at school. John's mother always worked to support the family, hence John was mostly brought up by his older sisters. His drug use began in his early teens with the twin influences of peer pressure and his father's cardiovascular death, and escalated after witnessing the suicide of a close friend at age 16 years. John had tried an apprenticeship but was too distracted and unreliable at work and, after attempting labouring jobs, gave up altogether, with inevitable financial strains. John's family tried to help but his four sisters all had children of their own to manage under difficult circumstances.

The challenge in managing this young family with multiple issues was balancing the individual needs with those of the children and family unit, while incorporating a cultural perspective. It was easy to see this young man as the 'problem' and for Cassie and the children to return to her extended family for support. Of course this would exacerbate John's sense of loss and abandonment, already a recurring theme in his life. John's threat of suicide needed focused risk assessment, viewed in the broader context of loss and grief, trauma and illness. John had also struggled with his role as a father, exacerbated by the unresolved grief from his father's death and his multiple separations for psychiatric treatment. The cultural issues present in his symptoms required careful assessment, assisting John's emerging identity as a young man, husband and father in his community.

His partner, Cassie, was a young, relatively unsupported mother of three, away from close family, with significant current stressors and many risk factors for postnatal depression requiring assessment in her own right. She was concerned about her own and the children's safety and fearful that if she was assessed, clinicians would see her as an unfit mother. It was important to provide nonintrusive support for Cassie. She needed tangible support with transport, day care, and paying bills before any therapeutic engagement. The treating team, with the help of cultural consultants, began to consider how the kinship network of both these parents from different places could be used to assist the family, what roles other family members could play and how elders or males in the community could strengthen the development of John's male cultural identity and assist him in changing his maladaptive behaviour.

The children were assessed physically and their developmental milestones mapped using a Denver developmental screen, but the main work for this family revolved around stabilising 'big picture' issues in Cassie and John's lives, taking into account the needs of these three high-risk infants.

All three children had been exposed to violence, drug use and psychotic behaviour within the family context. Although the children had been protected by their mother, their experience of their father was frightening. The infant was considered at particular risk, with the escalation of stressors and an uncertainty about Cassie's perceptions of having a son, who was already described as irritable. Cassie received support with her attachment relationship with him, and encouragement to allow him to develop his own unique identity.

Aboriginal children may experience cultural phenomena from birth — including the ability to see and hear ancestors. Given the nature of John's illness, having a clear understanding of the differences between cultural phenomena and illness, as well as treatment options, was important for the family and clinician to improve the therapeutic alliance and reduce fears about the future.

For John, Cassie and the children, comprehensive health screening was essential. Although John appeared physically healthy, the risks for chronic disease outlined earlier in this chapter were high, and would potentially compound his mental health problems. Cassie and the children were also at risk and finding safe places to play and develop was important in their care.

Concluding Remarks

From the available data, it is clear that the majority of the Aboriginal population sits at the moderate-to-severe end for risk of poor outcomes and consequently services set up for a normally distributed population with human capital and buffering are grossly inadequate for most Aboriginal families. Given the level of burden and risk in families and communities is extremely high and virtually universal, (Commonwealth Department of Health and Aged Care, 2000) the resources required to overcome the backlog of disadvantage and inequity is enormous, hence providing adequate support for the healthy development of children is essential. Working with families with high levels of burden and trauma can be challenging and clinicians need to maintain good self-care and a sense of hope to avoid feeling overwhelmed. Aboriginal children can be remarkably resilient and often form strong attachments in therapy allowing them to bounce back quite quickly, given the right circumstances. It is important to recognise the endurance, tolerance and strengths within families and communities. Given the level of risk, many families are doing remarkably well and understanding success stories may assist in helping others.

When reflecting on working with Aboriginal families, a number of questions should be considered including:

- Has the family been understood in the context of Australian history, contemporary disadvantage, and within their own cultural knowledge and belief system?

- Have the family's strengths been identified and utilised?

- Has the treating team sufficient training and expertise for working with Aboriginal families in a crosscultural setting?

- Are the models of assessment and treatment comprehensive, holistic and culturally appropriate?

- Has an Aboriginal mental health worker or cultural consultant been engaged to assist with assessment or treatment?

- And finally, are there personal, systemic or other barriers preventing access, engagement or equitable outcomes and if so what accountability mechanisms are in place to effect change?

When working in the crosscultural context with Aboriginal families it is important to understand and maintain cultural protocols for engagement, value and share knowledge, be prepared to work in partnership and in collaboration with Aboriginal community workers and organisations. It is equally important to understand the relative power imbalances, representational issues, equity, access and resource implications within services and communities. There are many barriers that still exist for Aboriginal families in accessing and benefitting from services. Emphasis needs to be given to workforce training and capacity building, development of culturally appropriate models of care, and accountability for outcomes. Supporting Aboriginal families in a safe and appropriate way to cope with the many issues they face is important for the healthy development of children and for the sustainability of future generations. In February 2008 at the opening of Parliament, the 'Apology' delivered by the Prime Minister of Australia for the immense harm caused to Aboriginal societies paved the way for a new relationship based on respect and a genuine commitment to improve the health and wellbeing of Aboriginal communities. For this to really take effect, however, it must be matched by an ongoing commitment at all levels to work to better the lives and opportunities for Aboriginal children and their families.

Author Note

The case studies are based on a composite of common clinical presentations and any identifying information has been removed.

References

National Health Strategy Working Party. (1989a). *A National Aboriginal Health Strategy. Report of The National Health Strategy Working Party.* Retrieved October 30, 2007, from http://www.health.gov.au/internet/wcms/publishing.nsf/Content/health-oatsih-pubs-healthstrategy.htm

National Health Strategy Working Party. (1989b). *A National Aboriginal Health Strategy. Report of The National Health Strategy Working Party.* Retrieved October 30, 2007, from http://www.health.gov.au/internet/wcms/publishing.nsf/Content/health-oatsih-pubs-healthstrategy.htm

Atkinson, J. (2002). *Trauma trails, recreating song lines: The transgenerational effects of trauma in Indigenous Australia.* Melbourne, Australia: Spinifex.

Australian Bureau of Statistics. (2002). *Population distribution, Aboriginal and Torres Strait Islander Australians, 2001.* (Cat No. 4705.0). Canberra, Australia: Australian Bureau of Statistics.

Australian Bureau of Statistics. (2007). *2006 Census Quickstats Australia.* Retrieved October 30, 2007, from http://www.censusdata.abs.gov.au/ABSNavigation/prenav/ViewData

Australian Government Department of Education, Science and Training. (2007). *Primary eligibility criteria for ABSTUDY chapter 10: Aboriginality or Torres Strait Islander status.* Retrieved January 11, 2008, from http://www.dest.gov.au/sectors/indigenous_education/publications_resources/abstudy/primary_eligibility_criteria_for_abstudy/aboriginality_or_torres_strait_islander_status.htm

Australian Institute of Health and Welfare. (2005). *The health and welfare of Australia's Aboriginal and Torres Strait Islander peoples* (Cat No 4704.0). Canberra, Australia: Australian Bureau of Statistics.

Commonwealth Department of Health and Aged Care. (2000). *Promotion, prevention and early intervention for mental health—A monograph.* Canberra, Australia: Mental Health and Special Programs Branch, Commonwealth Department of Health and Aged Care.

De Maio, J.A., Zubrick, S.R., Silburn, S.R., Lawrence, D.M., Mitrou, F.G., Dalby, R.B. et al. (2005). *The Western Australian Aboriginal child health survey: Measuring the social and emotional wellbeing of Aboriginal children and the intergenerational effects of forced separation.* Perth, Australia: Curtin University of Technology and Telethon Institute for Child Health Research.

Dudgeon, P., Garvey, D., & Pickett, H. (Eds.). (2000). *Working with Indigenous Australians: A handbook for psychologists.* Perth, Australia: Gunada Press.

Haebich, A. (2000). *Broken circles: Fragmenting Indigenous families 1800–2000.* Fremantle, Australia: Fremantle Arts Centre Press.

Hammil, J. (2001). Granny rights: Combating the granny burnout syndrome among Australian Indigenous communities. *Development, 44*(2), 69–74

Human Rights and Equal Opportunity Commission. (1997). *Bringing them home: Report of the National Inquiry into the Separation of Aboriginal and Torres Strait Islander Children from Their Families.* Canberra, Australia: Australian Government Publishing Service.

Hunter, E. (1993). *Aboriginal health and history: Power and prejudice in remote Australia.* Cambridge: Cambridge University Press.

Milroy, H. (2002, May). *The dance of life: The bio–psycho–social–cultural–spiritual model from an Indigenous perspective.* Paper presented at the meeting of the Inaugural Pacific Rim Indigenous Doctors Conference, Hawaii.

Ngaanyatjarra Pitjantjatjara Yankunytjatjara Women's Council Aboriginal Corporation. (2003). *Ngangkari Work-Anangu Way: Traditional Healers of Central Australia,* Retrieved January 20, 2008, from http://www.tjanpiaboriginalbaskets.com/NPY%20Council/npycouncil.htm

Parker, R., & Milroy, H. (2003). Schizophrenia and related psychosis in Aboriginal and Torres Strait Islander People. *Aboriginal and Islander Health Worker Journal, 27,* 17–19.

Sheldon, M. (2001). Psychiatric assessment in remote Aboriginal communities. *Australian and New Zealand Journal of Psychiatry, 35,* 435–442.

Swan, P., & Raphael, B. (1995). *Ways Forward, National Consultancy Report on Aboriginal and Torres Strait Islander Mental Health 1995: Part 1.* Retrieved October 30, 2007, from http://www.health.gov.au/internet/wcms/publishing.nsf/Content/mental-pubs-w-wayforw

Thomson N., Burns J., Burrow, S., & Kirov E. (2004). *Overview of Australian Indigenous health.* Retrieved October 30, 2007, from http://www.healthinfonet.ecu.edu.au/html/html_overviews/overview.pdf

Watson, J., Hodson, K., Johnson, R., & Kemp, K. (2002). The maternity experiences of Indigenous women admitted to an acute care setting. *Australian Journal of Rural Health, 10*(3), 154–160.

Zubrick, S.R., Silburn, S.R., Lawrence, D. M., Mitrou, F.G., Dalby. R.B., Blair, E.M. et al. (2005). *The Western Australian Aboriginal child health survey: The social and emotional wellbeing of Aboriginal children and young people.* Perth, Australia: Curtin University of Technology and Telethon Institute for Child Health Research.

Infants in Refugee and Asylum-Seeker Families

Sarah Mares and Rosalind Powrie

⸻

Forced migration has become a major world problem, with increasing armed conflict between and within nations leading to vast numbers of refugees, asylum seekers and displaced persons. The United Nations High Commissioner for Refugees (UNHCR, 2007) identified 32.9 million people as 'of concern' at the end of 2006. Roughly half of the refugee population is female, although the proportions vary greatly depending on the refugee situation, region of asylum and age distribution. Information on the age breakdown is incomplete but suggests that 45% of refugees are children under the age of 18; 11% of them being under the age of five (UNHCR, 2007).

This chapter will explore the particular developmental risk and protective factors impacting on infants and young children in families who, as a result of forced migration, seek refuge or asylum in countries other than their own. We will summarise the sparse empirical data and use case examples to consider the implications for clinicians working with refugee infants and families in health and early childhood services. The particular impact of Australia's policies on asylum seekers, including children and families, will also be discussed.

Under the Geneva Convention (UNHCR, 1951) a refugee is defined as a person who

> owing to a well-founded fear of being persecuted for reasons of
> race, religion, nationality, membership of a particular social group,

> or political opinion, is outside the country of his nationality, and is
> unable to or, owing to such fear, is unwilling to avail himself of the
> protection of that country … (UNHCR, 1951, p. 16)

Asylum seekers are persons who have applied for asylum or refugee status, but who have not yet received a final decision on their application. In Australia, the term is used to identify those who arrive on shore without an existing refugee determination or valid visa.

Early childhood development occurs within the context of care-giving relationships, usually the family, and families exist and are influenced by the wider social and cultural context (Bronfenbrenner, 1979). Circumstances of war, political upheaval and forced migration impose considerable stress on individuals and on family systems. The capacity of the caregiver(s) to respond to and meet the infant's changing needs is influenced by aspects of the parent's own functioning, which can be compromised as a result of trauma, cultural dislocation and loss of support and social networks. War and forced migration frequently result in women parenting alone.

> Migration can change the role of women as mothers. If previously
> mothers were the main caregiver for their children within a circle of
> others, in exile they become the sole caregiver … This creates great
> pressure for these women. (Hardi, 2005, p. 154)

Infants bring their own innate capacities to cope with change and stress and are most sensitive to environmental experiences closest to them, but can also be indirectly affected by more distant events and disruptions filtered through the care-giving environment.

Models and Theories of Trauma in Refugee Populations

There has been considerable recent discussion about the conceptual models that inform the literature on the mental health impacts of trauma in refugee populations. These models have an inevitable effect on interventions and service provision to exposed populations. Ingelby (2005) outlines in detail and summarises these frameworks. The Trauma Model has tended to dominate in the last decade, with a focus on individual psychopathology. Critiques of this model include inappropriate diagnoses of trauma in whole populations on the basis of exposure, the medicalising of normal suffering by use of DSM (*Diagnostic and Statistical Manual for Mental Disorders*) type diagnostic categories, the risks of importing Western-style individual models of intervention and counselling and potentially undermining communal and culturally relevant strategies for social recovery (Silove, 2005). We would add an inadequate focus and understanding of the developmental aspects and family impacts of trauma exposure, and the implications of this for timely intervention, particularly in very young children (Weine et al., 2004).

Another area of debate is the focus on pathology, rather than the resilience and adaptation shown by many families and individuals (Barwick et al., 2002). Lustig et al. (2004) in their review of the literature found that the reactions of children and adolescents to conflict-related trauma are mediated by exposure, coping strategies, belief systems and social relations. For infants and young children the coping capacity of relatives, family and the care-giving system is of primary importance in mediating the effects, meaning and consequences of trauma. The psychological literature on refugees rarely describes the family, and it is argued that there is excessive focus on suffering and deficits, with little research on nonclinical populations (Weine et al., 2004).

Culture, Parenting and Mental Illness

Birth and Parenting in the Early Years

Infants learn about their culture from birth through the daily caretaking rituals and behaviours of and interactions with their caregivers. This includes how they are held, touched, talked to and looked at; and feeding, weaning and sleeping rituals and arrangements. In turn, caregivers bring to the infant all the learned conscious and unintentional ways of being with and rearing their infant that are culturally determined and transmitted across generations. Pregnancy and childbirth are rites of passage in every culture and are accompanied by certain rituals undertaken by the family, health system and society ('lying in' periods for mothers in many cultures, christening or baptism, burying of the placenta in 'Country' by traditional Australian Aboriginal families). These are designed to not only ensure the health and survival of mother and infant but also to initiate, connect and welcome the child into their society and parents into their new roles.

While attachment behaviours are universal phenomena, the meaning of certain behaviours is culturally constructed according to the desirable end point of child rearing and socioemotional development (Harwood, Miller, & Irizarry, 1995; Small, 1999). For instance, in some cultures interdependence of infants and children with the caregiver (as in Japan with the concept of 'amae') is privileged over developing independence of the infant/child (as is the focus in mainstream Australian families). Assessment of the attachment relationship and behaviours observed, as well as the meaning of this to the parents, need to be understood within the cultural context.

Culture is thus the overarching 'holding environment' for infants and their families and gives meaning to the experiences of this developmental stage of life. With the enormous dislocation from their normal life and culture of origin that refugee families suffer, the holding environment can become fragile and tenuous or distorted, depending on what is happening for the family and the timing of a child's birth.

Mental Illness

Another level of complexity in relation to refugees and their mental health is the impact of culture on the development, presentation and diagnosis of mental illness (Silove, 2005). The field of transcultural psychiatry and cross-cultural research has identified how culture influences the expression of distress and illness and the way it is explained, 'labelled' and treated, and the acceptability and efficacy of treatment. Ethnicity also plays a part in differential responses to psychotropic medications as reflected in the growing research on ethno-psychopharmacology (Alarcon, Westermeyer, Foulkes, & Ruiz, 1999). These issues need consideration in order to accurately diagnose and treat mental health disorders in a given cross-cultural situation, but importantly, to also understand the meaning of symptoms or concerns to an individual or family. Questions that elicit an explanation of the symptoms will help to understand problems from within a cultural perspective (Kleinman, 1980), rather than attempt to apply a 'universalist' view, which in our society will show an inherent 'western' bias — that is, the biomedical model with explanations based around individual psychopathology. An example may be, 'What do you call the problem, why is it happening now and what do you think caused it?'

Parental Mental Health and Children's Functioning

There is a substantial association between parental and, in particular, maternal mental health and children's adjustment. Perinatal mental illness has been shown to have potential long-term negative developmental consequences for infants and children, especially in combination with other risk factors (Goodman & Gotlib, 2002; Murray, Cooper, Wilson, & Romaniuk, 2003; Radke-Yarrow & Klimes-Dougan, 2002). Refugee populations have a high prevalence of posttraumatic stress disorder (PTSD) compared with non-refugee populations, and exposure to trauma and mass violence increase risk for depressive and anxiety disorders (Bruce, 2003). There is also evidence of the adverse impact of maternal mental health on children's functioning, both in situations of war trauma (Qouta, Runamäki, & Eyad, 2005; Smith, Perrin, Yule, & Rabe-Hesketh, 2001), while seeking asylum (Mares & Jureidini, 2004; Mares, Newman, Dudley, & Gale, 2002; Steel et al., 2004), and following resettlement (Almquist & Broberg, 1999).

The following vignette demonstrates the interactions between symptoms of psychosis and PTSD, cultural difference and upheaval in a family and the difficulties in formulating an appropriate clinical understanding of these factors.

> Ms M and her four children from Somalia were referred for psychiatric assessment after the children were removed from her care under child protection legislation 18 months after the family were resettled in rural Australia under the UNHCR humanitarian program. They had endured 2 years in the Kakuma refugee camp in Kenya, where they had experienced significant trauma, including sexual violence. The family had moved seven times since arriving in Australia, resulting in school disruption for the older children and loss of any developing social networks. Each move was preceded by Ms M's belief that people were either not giving her what she was entitled to, or were in fact stealing her money and possessions. When child protection services became involved, the family was barricaded in a hotel room, because Ms M believed she and her children were being poisoned. The youngest child, aged 2 years, was breastfeeding. Her removal particularly distressed Ms M, adding to her sense of persecution and risk. Her husband had been killed 3½ years earlier. Despite this she related that all the children, including the youngest, were her husband's, and that the baby had 'stayed in my womb until it was safe to be born'. This could be considered a delusional belief, but it seemed more appropriately understood as protective for mother and child in current circumstances. Trusting no-one and remaining hypervigilant had been necessary and had served her and her children well prior to arriving in Australia. Her experience of ongoing persecution and insecurity, and her inability to accept available services and help needed a contextual understanding. A psychiatric diagnosis was appropriate but insufficient.

Phases of the Refugee Experience

Phases of the refugee experience can be summarised as preflight, flight and resettlement (Fazel & Stein, 2002; Lustig et al., 2004). It is important to consider the impact of events, stressors and experience on families at each phase to help understand the significance for infants and young children, including the circumstances of a child's conception, time and place, as in the vignette above. The history of these events and experiences must be obtained sensitively, taking care not to appear to interrogate or retraumatise vulnerable family members.

Preflight

Asylum seekers and refugees are very diverse, coming from many different cultural, ethnic, religious backgrounds and regions of the world. There is often great diversity within the same cultural or country of origin group, influenced by levels of education, family structure and support; language group; ethnic, tribal or religious affiliations; and the inherent differences in levels of resilience between individuals and families.

Premigration experiences also vary widely, but with inevitable degrees of exposure to violence (direct and witnessed), trauma, civil strife, family dislocation and loss and often, for many families, years spent in substandard living conditions in refugee camps (Berman, 2001). Physical deprivations including hunger and malnutrition and general poverty may impact on pregnant and lactating women and young children, leading to poor obstetric and health outcomes and developmental disorders with preschoolers most at risk (Dybdahl, 2001). Exposure to multiple adverse social risk factors known to affect infant mental health is common (Sameroff & Fiese, 2000).

This period is characterised for adults and older children by social and political upheaval, fear and, depending on circumstances, exposure to war and violence and injury and death to loved ones. Younger children experience a disruption to usual routines, and the anxiety or absence of the adults who care for them, as well as possible direct exposure to violence. Toddlers may also witness anger, violence and fear but have little way of making sense of it cognitively, and adults who could help them with this may be preoccupied and vulnerable themselves.

Flight

Flight experiences for asylum seekers can be extremely traumatic, unpredictable, dangerous and financially costly, as seen in the wave of smuggling by boat of asylum-seekers from Afghanistan, Iraq and Iran through Indonesia to the northern offshore waters of Australia between 1999 and 2003. The well-publicised events at this time, of overcrowded or sinking boats, many with young children on board, can only give a small snapshot of the life and death struggles many of these families have experienced (Kevin, 2004). For refugees settled under the UNHCR schemes the flight experiences are equally traumatic.

> A young mother aged 14 whose parents had been murdered by rebel soldiers had to walk 120 kilometres alone while heavily pregnant to reach a UNHCR camp in a neighbouring African country. It then took 2 years before she was able to be resettled in Australia with her young child.

Families with infants born during the flight phases of the refugee experience may have experienced considerable physical hardship and insecurity with a lack of health services, particularly during labour and delivery and a lack or absence of usual family and social supports.

Resettlement

The resettlement phase varies considerably depending on the welcome extended to arriving refugee families, the attitudes of the community and host culture and the way refugees are represented in the media and political debates. Marginalisation and racism, or the further traumatisation and uncertainty during detention and the visa determination process, impact adversely on the health and psychological wellbeing of families and their young children.

As well as the difficult process of negotiating cultural and language differences there may be a sense of hope and safety, providing adequate resources and support are provided. There is evidence that postsettlement experiences have a major impact on long-term psychosocial adjustment of refugees and asylum seekers, (Silove & Ekblad, 2002; Silove, Sinnerbrink, Field, Manicavasagar, & Steel, 1997).

Along with hope, resettlement brings stress — termed acculturative stress by Berry, Kim, Minde and Mok (1987). The crisis of adjustment entails challenges such as learning and understanding a new social, health and welfare system; understanding and learning different customs and language; mastering transport systems; adjusting to differing expectations regarding gender roles and child-rearing values; parenting behaviours and norms; finding accommodation and employment; and stress due to social isolation.

> Mr and Mrs S are refugees and were referred by child protection services for psychiatric assessment after their 3-week-old baby was admitted for sleep apnoea. After returning home they were reported by a family support worker for noncompliance with the use of a monitor, the father instead choosing to stay up all night to watch his baby. Intervention by child protection workers escalated into a state of threatening conflict with the father in which police intervened and their child was temporarily removed. Mr S had been a victim of torture and imprisonment, and although not a recent arrival had remained relatively isolated. His wife had arrived more recently, neither had any family support in Australia, and they were struggling financially. A psychiatric assessment showed that Mr S had significant trauma symptoms and was deeply suspicious of authority figures. His interaction with health and child protection services triggered his symptoms and led to the escalation of conflict and initial noncompliance with treatment. He had no sense of connection with a wider

'holding environment' of family or culture to offset and moderate his mistrust and hypervigilance. The response of professionals, rather than acting to contain and reassure this traumatised family, added to their distress and escalated the problem.

Moro (2003), in her work with infants in the migratory context, asks us first to think about what it means to be an infant, mother or father in any particular cultural context and how this is changed in the context of migration. She uses the term 'transcultural risk' as a specific factor for infants who bear the traumatic family experience of migration. The initial motivation for fleeing their home country might have been primarily for their children's welfare.

A Hazara family, a persecuted minority in Iran, fled to save the father from imprisonment, protect their sons from army service and to seek access to education for their daughters. The father's depression and anxiety compounded during the family's several year detention in Woomera Detention Centre, during which time no education was provided, the children were exposed to violence, and the language development of the 3-year-old was delayed.

Clearly, refugee families vary in their ability to cope with loss, trauma and dislocation — some being remarkably resilient and adaptive, others more vulnerable. There is also evidence that families who have opportunities to reconnect with their culture, to honour important celebrations, and participate in significant religious and community events and rituals are able to recover better from trauma and adapt more easily to their new environment. Their children too, acquire a better capacity to develop a healthy bicultural identity (Eisenbruch, 1992).

Infants and young children are at risk because of their vulnerability to parental stress, which may last for months if not years. Refugee families have not migrated voluntarily. Many live unwillingly in exile with attendant ambivalent feelings about resettlement and the permanency of their new home. This is exacerbated in circumstances where uncertainty continues about permanent protection, where asylum claims are protracted or refused or, as in Australia since 1999, temporary protection visas (TPV) are offered. Continuing uncertainty compounds lack of support and resources. The feelings of displacement and prolonged and unresolved loss may interfere with many of the functions of parenting. For new mothers the loss of natural support systems, particularly in extended family cultures, can be devastating. This creates a higher risk for development of perinatal depression.

A Sudanese mother of three young children was admitted to an antenatal ward at 28 weeks for premature labour. She was referred for assessment of depression and revealed that she has been experiencing prolonged grief for her mother — she hadn't seen her for 3 years and hadn't yet been able to obtain a visa for her to visit. Her husband, due to his traditional gender role, did not help her with domestic and child-rearing tasks and she felt increasingly unable to cope.

Research on children of holocaust survivors, shows that infants born during resettlement and even many years afterwards, may be influenced by experiences related to displacement, survival and forced migration, and the transgenerational transmission of trauma (Fonagy, 2002).

The Importance of Government Policies and Practice

Government policies can support or hinder the resettlement process and Australian policies over time provide examples of both. After the Vietnam war, for example, a welcome was extended to 'boat people', who were offered considerable government support to resettle in Australia. This included English classes, financial and housing assistance. Two generations later, the Vietnamese in Australia have relatively low rates of mental health problems (Steel, 2002).

In the last decade, the welcome and support offered to boat people, this time predominantly arriving from the Middle East, has been very different, with a progressive toughening of Department of Immigration policy and practice and the express intention of policies that deliberately deter or discourage others attempting to seek asylum in Australia. This has included policies of indefinite mandatory detention, often for many years, despite this breaching Australia's human rights obligations. Some families have been detained in remote detention centres and on offshore islands, like Nauru, with limited access to health, legal and other services and often complete social isolation. Temporary protection, as the name implies, provides a few years of refuge but with limited rights and supports and no ongoing security.

These policies have demonstrably had considerable negative mental health and developmental consequences for individual adults and children and families detained (Mares & Jureidini, 2004; Momartin et al., 2006; Steel et al., 2004, 2006). Australia has received much criticism from international bodies, including the Human Rights and Equal Opportunity Commission (HREOC, 2004), and these policies have resulted in sustained legal challenge and community protest (Gosden, 2006; Mares & Newman, 2007). There have been some changes. For example, since July 2006, indefinite detention of children is no longer policy, but overall immigration policy and law remain essentially unaltered and the policy of deterrence, with the consequent human rights and mental health implications, remains in place.

In the 4 years from January 1999 to December 2003, 71 infants were born in immigration detention in Australia and in June 2000 there were 164 infants in immigration detention. The total number of infants (aged 0–4) detained in Australia over the last decade is unknown. Some have spent more than half their lives in detention, mainly in remote centres with little access to adequate services, and exposed to depressed, self-harming adults and sometimes violent protest (HREOC, 2004).

> Ms A arrived by boat in northern Australia with her husband and two young children, having fled war and persecution. They were detained for over 3½ years before being granted protection visas. During this time two children were born, the first while the family were in a remote centre, 7 months after arrival in Australia. Ms A was emotionally traumatised by the birth of her third child, as policy dictated her transfer to the nearest maternity hospital for delivery 1 month (under continuous guarding) before her due date. She had little understanding of the process, with inadequate interpreter services, and her husband was absent for the birth. She became mute and depressed, her older children developed behaviour problems and her husband became depressed and angry. When first assessed by a psychiatrist, the baby, now 6 months old was left in a stroller facing the wall, appearing neglected and withdrawn.
>
> No action was taken on recommendations to release the family because of the severity of their symptoms, ongoing environmental risk to the children by exposure to violence and self-harm by other detainees, and lack of play and exploration opportunities. Eighteen months later, another child was born and better managed in a city-based maternity hospital, although still under guard, with an Arabic-speaking doctor and husband present. However, by then the parents were significantly compromised by their own mental health problems and their children demonstrated substantial emotional and developmental difficulties. The family were returned to the detention facility after an initial improvement in the mother's functioning while in a family admission unit. Advocating for the developmental needs of their young children became a primary focus of intervention but was often frustrated by the complex system. Their experiences in immigration detention added considerably to their difficulties.

General Approaches to Assessment of Refugee Families

For parents who have suffered significant trauma and political persecution, in particular, lack of trust, mostly in others who hold positions of authority or power, can be an impediment to direct and open communication. For women, talking to males may be culturally inappropriate, intimidating and traumatising, particularly if they have experienced sexual assault. Assessment of parental distress and functioning therefore needs to occur sensitively, with ample time available and in a setting that affords greatest security, safety and confidentiality and takes into account gender issues. A clear explanation of the interviewer's position, role, and professional code of confidentiality and goals of the assessment is important from the outset.

The use of a support worker and/or cultural consultant may also be very helpful for the family and may provide important information for the interviewer about normative aspects of parenting, beliefs, family functioning and gender roles in the particular cultural group, as well as the social and historical influences on the family from their country of origin. Interpreters should be used when necessary (as is mostly the case) and it is desirable for them to be trained in interpreting in mental health settings.

A skilful balance is needed to allow parents to tell their story, without retraumatising them, while focusing on issues relevant to parenting and their children. This will include timing and pace of questions; avoiding an interrogative style; and paying close attention to anxiety levels, lapses in memory, coherence of conversation and other mental state cues which might signal reemergence of traumatic memories. Parents need to be given permission to stop the interview, take a break or do what is necessary to contain strong feelings. When interviewing parents with their children, ample permission should be given to attending to their children's needs and to appropriate provision of facilities, and toys. The more naturalistic the setting, the more relevant observations and information can be obtained about the important day-to-day care young children receive from their parents.

Assessment of Infants and Young Children

While it is essential to consider the family and social impacts of displacement, trauma exposure and migration, this contextual focus should not be at the expense of considering the baby or young child. It is essential in any assessment and intervention to hold the infant and her experience in mind, often in the face of overwhelming parental needs and feelings. Doing this supports the parent in beginning, where necessary, to refocus herself on her infant, something that may have been lost in response to parental depression and a struggle for survival.

Infants and young children can and do suffer the effects of direct and indirect exposure to trauma, and forced migration may mean that children have been neglected or maltreated both physically and emotionally. A comprehensive physical and developmental assessment and appropriate interventions are also required so that the physical and nutritional effects of war and dislocation are not overlooked. While most trauma for infants and toddlers occurs within the interpersonal context, this is not always so for refugee children who may have been exposed directly to violence between unrelated adults.

Symptoms of trauma in infants and toddlers are outlined in the axial classificatory System for Disorders in Infancy and Early Childhood, DC 0–3 R (Zero to 3, 2005). Traumatised infants can exhibit behaviours, including developmental delays, that are hard to diagnose and for parents to understand and that may perpetuate difficult parent–child interactions and further impair social and emotional development and relationships. A diagnosis, or at least an understanding, of a child's symptoms in light of their exposure to trauma can be helpful for parents and child carers faced with difficult or contradictory behaviours.

Interventions

Once assessment has concluded, appropriate mental health interventions will be undertaken with the infant and family, depending on diagnosis and culturally informed formulation. The location of the family and availability of professional resources will also influence what is able to be offered to the family. Those families who are detained or separated as a consequence of detention, or granted temporary protection, have particularly limited access to services and intervention. At times, advocacy for a family's rights, safety and wellbeing may be the priority before mental health interventions can be undertaken.

Implications for Advocacy

Advocacy is speaking, acting and writing with minimal conflict of interest on behalf of the sincerely perceived interests of a disadvantaged person or group to promote, protect and defend their welfare and justice (QPPD, 2007).

Refugee families require advocacy on a number of different levels according to their needs and circumstances, and there are a number of specialist organisations, funded and voluntary, who fulfil this role in Australia. Infants 'cannot wait' for long periods until parents or the wider systems impacting on parental care-giving are able to provide good enough care or support the young child's recovery from neglect or abuse. Thus tensions will inevitably arise for professionals in health, welfare and education when working with refugee families, when individual advocacy for these most vulnerable infants seems the best pathway.

> The complex situation and clinical presentation of Ms A and her family (whose story was described earlier) resulted in escalating tensions in and between the many treatment, advocacy and other professionals and services involved in their care, despite attempts at systemic and collaborative approaches to the family's needs. These continued long after the family were eventually granted protection visas and living in the community and illustrate the inherent complexity and difficulty of some of this work.

At times, professionals will see a clear role for advocacy with fruitful results:

> Mr and Mrs J, both young professionals, fled to Australia from their home country in the Middle East fearing persecution because of their religious beliefs. During the 3½ years they spent in immigration detention, Mrs J gave birth to their first child after suffering constant nausea during the pregnancy. She became frustrated by the slow response of authorities to infant feeding problems and the lack of autonomy they had as parents in this environment, and soon developed postnatal depression. Mr J became severely depressed and despairing as numerous attempts to obtain a protection visa failed. The family were first assessed psychiatrically while in detention and a limited clinical intervention plus advocacy for their release followed. They were finally granted a bridging visa when their son was 20 months old and could now live together in the community. A second baby was born, but they were prohibited from working and their entire support came from nongovernment services and advocates. Their ongoing lobbying finally saw the granting of a permanent visa 9 months later. Mrs J recovered and Mr J's depression gradually lifted with the support of a men's refugee group. Both parents showed remarkable resilience in the face of this adversity and uncertainty. They were able to put their children's needs first, as evidenced by their sensitive and responsive parenting, despite their own feelings of frustration and helplessness. The children now attend local childcare and are doing well.
>
> This family had many strengths but were also exposed to considerable adversity in their home country and then while seeking asylum in Australia. The children were born into a high-risk environment with parental depression and many uncertainties. Active support and advocacy enabled them to move from this to an increasingly settled and productive family life in Australia. It appears that they and their children are doing well.

Many professionals undertake political advocacy because of their concerns about the clear negative effects on the mental health and development of infants and their families. The important role of professional and personal advocacy against such policies, but also the high personal cost, is outlined in Mares and Newman (2007). Issues of professional boundaries, vicarious traumatisation, supervision and networking for support are inherent in the nature of advocacy for the social and emotional needs of young children in refugee families. This requires ongoing attention and acknowledgment of the capacity of workers to make time to reflect on, process and learn from their experiences.

Conclusions

Refugees and asylum seekers are an extremely diverse population with a wide range of vulnerabilities and resources. In common, these families and their infants have the experience of displacement, or forced migration, in response to war or persecution in their homeland. Infants and young children are dependent on their caregivers for basic care and protection and for help in making sense of the world. Assessment and interventions with these communities and families need to be culturally informed, comprehensive and sensitively delivered, with a broad contextual focus as well as a capacity to hold the infant or young child and their needs and experiences in mind.

Resilient and supported families show excellent abilities to overcome the stresses of their refugee status and adapt to Australian life.

References

Alarcon, R.D., Westermeyer J., Foulkes, E.F., & Ruiz P. (1999). Clinical relevance of contemporary cultural psychiatry. *Journal of Nervous and Mental Disease, 187,* 465–471.

Almquist, K., & Broberg, A.G. (1999). Mental health and social adjustment in young refugee children 3½ years after their arrival in Sweden. *Journal of the American Academy of Child and Adolescent Psychiatry, 38,* 723–30.

Barwick, C.L., Beiser, M., & Edwards, G. (2002). Refugee children and their families: Exploring mental health risks and protective factors. In F.J.C. Azima & N. Grizenko (Eds.), *Immigrant and refugee children and their families: Clinical, research and training issues* (pp. 37–66). Madison, CT: International Universities Press.

Berman, H. (2001). Children and war: Current understandings and future directions. *Public Health Nursing, 18,* 243–252.

Berry, J.W., Kim, U., Minde, T., & Mok, D. (1987). Comparative studies of acculturative stress. *International Migration Review, 21,* 491–511.

Bronfenbrenner, U. (1979). *The ecology of human development: Experiments by nature and design.* Cambridge, MA: Harvard University Press.

Bruce, A. (2003). The unmaking of the world: Mental health and resettled refugees from the Horn of Africa. In D. Barnes (Ed.), *Asylum seekers and refugees in Australia: Issues of mental health and wellbeing* (pp. 102–134). Sydney, Australia: Transcultural Mental Health Centre.

Dybdahl, R. (2001). Children and mothers in war: An outcome study of a psychosocial intervention program. *Child Development, 72,* 1214–1230.

Eisenbruch, M. (1992). Toward a culturally sensitive DSM: Cultural bereavement in Cambodian refugees and the traditional healer as taxonomist. *Journal of Nervous and Mental Diseases, 180,* 8–10.

Fazel. M., & Stein, A. (2002). The mental health of refugee children. *Archives of Disease in Childhood, 87,* 366–370.

Fonagy, P. (2002). The transgenerational transmission of holocaust trauma: Lessons learned from the analysis of an adolescent with obsessive compulsive disorder. In C. Covington, P. Williams, J. Arundale & J. Knox (Eds.), *Terrorism and war: unconscious dynamics of political violence* (pp. 329–352). London: Karnac.

Goodman, S.H., & Gotlib, I.H. (2002). *Children of depressed parents: Mechanisms of risk and implications for treatment* Washington, DC: American Psychological Association.

Gosden, D. (2006). What if no one had spoken out against this policy? The rise of asylum seeker and refugee advocacy in Australia. *Portal, 3,* 1.

Hardi, C. (2005). Kurdish women refugees: Obstacles and opportunities. In D. Ingelby (Ed.), *Forced migration and mental health: Rethinking the care of refugees and displaced persons* (pp. 149–168). New York: Springer.

Harwood, R.L., Miller, J.G., & Irizarry, L. (1995). *Culture and attachment: Perceptions of the child in context.* New York: Guilford Press.

Human Rights and Equal Opportunity Commission (HREOC). (2004). *A last resort? National inquiry into children in immigration detention.* Sydney, Australia: HREOC.

Ingelby, D. (Ed.). (2005). *Forced migration and mental health: Rethinking the care of refugees and displaced persons.* New York: Springer.

Kevin, T. (2004). *A certain maritime incident: The sinking of SEIV X.* Melbourne, Australia: Scribe Publications.

Kleinman, A. (1980). *Patients and healers in the context of culture.* Berkeley: University of California.

Lustig, S., Keating, M., Grant, K.W., Geltman, P., Ellis, H., Kinzie, D., Keane, T., & Saxe, G. (2004). Review of child and adolescent refugee mental health. *Journal of the American Academy of Child & Adolescent Psychiatry, 43,* 24–36.

Mares, S., & Jureidini, J. (2004). Psychiatric assessment of children and families in immigration detention: Clinical, administrative and ethical issues. *Australian and New Zealand Journal of Public Health, 28*(6), 16–22.

Mares, S., & Newman, L. (2007). *Acting from the heart: Australian advocates for asylum seekers tell their stories.* Sydney, Australia: Finch Publishing.

Mares, S., Newman, L., Dudley, M., & Gale, F. (2002). Seeking refuge, losing hope: Parents and children in immigration detention. *Australasian Psychiatry, 10,* 91–96.

Momartin, S., Steel, Z., Coello, M., Aroche, J., Silove, D.M., & Brooks, R. (2006). A comparison of the mental health of refugees with temporary versus permanent protection visas. *Medical Journal of Australia, 185,* 357–361.

Moro, M. R. (2003). Parents and infants in changing cultural context: Immigration, trauma, and risk. *Infant Mental Health Journal, 24,* 240–264.

Murray, L., Cooper, P.J. Wilson, A., & Romaniuk, H. (2003). Controlled trial of the short and long term effect of psychological treatment of post partum depression II: Impact on the mother–child relationship and child outcome. *British Journal of Psychiatry, 182,* 420–427.

Qouta, S., Runamäki, R-L., & Eyad, E.S. (2005). Mother-child expression of psychological distress in war trauma. *Clinical Child Psychology and Psychiatry, 10,* 135–156.

QPPD (Queensland Parents for People with a Disability Inc.). (2008). Available at http://www.qppd.org/About/advocacy.htm

Radke-Yarrow, M., & Klimes-Dougan, M. (2002). Parental depression and offspring disorders: A developmental perspective. In S.H. Goodman & I.H. Gotlib (Eds.), *Children of depressed parents: Mechanisms of risk and implications for treatment* (pp. 155–174). Washington DC: American Psychological Association.

Sameroff, A.J., & Fiese, B. (2000). Models of development and developmental risk. In C.H. Zeanah (Ed.), *Handbook of infant mental health* (2nd ed.). New York: Guilford Press.

Silove, D., Sinnerbrink, I., Field, A., Manicavasagar, V., & Steel, Z. (1997). Anxiety, depression and PTSD in asylum seekers: Associations with premigration trauma and post migration stressors. *British Journal of Psychiatry, 170,* 351–357.

Silove, D., & Ekblad, S. (2002). How well do refugees adapt after resettlement in Western countries? *Acta Psychiatrica Scandinavica, 106,* 401–402.

Silove, D. (2005). From trauma to survival and adaptation: Towards a framework for guiding mental health initiatives in post conflict societies. In D. Ingelby (Ed.), *Forced migration and mental health: Rethinking the care of refugees and displaced persons* (pp. 29–52). New York: Springer.

Small, M. (1999). *Our babies, ourselves: How biology and culture shape the way we parent.* New York: Anchor.

Smith, P., Perrin, S., Yule, W., & Rabe-Hesketh, S. (2001). War exposure and maternal reactions in the psychological adjustment of children from Bosnia-Hercegovina. *Journal of Child Psychology and Psychiatry, 4,* 395–404.

Steel, Z. (2002). Long-term effect of psychological trauma on the mental health of Vietnamese refugees resettled in Australia: A population-based study. *The Lancet, 360*(9339), 1056–1062.

Steel, Z., Momartin, S., Bateman, C., Hafshejani, A., Silove, D., Everson, N. et al. (2004). Psychiatric status of asylum seeker families held for a protracted period in a remote detention centre in Australia. *Australian and New Zealand Journal of Public Health, 28*, 520–526.

Steel, Z., Silove, D., Brooks, R., Momartin, S., Alzuhairi, B., & Susljik, I. (2006). Impact of immigration detention and temporary protection on the mental health of refugees. *British Journal of Psychiatry, 188*, 58–64.

United Nations High Commissioner for Refugees (UNHCR). (1951). *The 1951 Convention Relating to the Status of Refugees*. Geneva: United Nations.

United Nations High Commissioner for Refugees (UNHCR). (2007). *Statistical yearbook 2006. Trends in displacement, protection and solutions*. Retrieved August 10, 2007, from http://www.unhcr.org/statistics.html

Weine, S., Muzurovic, N., Kulauzovic, Y., Besic, S., Lezic A., Mujagic, A., et al. (2004). Family consequences of refugee trauma. *Family Process, 43*, 147–160.

Zero to Three. (2005). *Diagnostic classification of mental health and developmental disorders of infancy and early childhood: revised edition* (DC: 0–3R). Washington, DC: Zero to Three Press.

Working With Infants and Their Parents With Specific Disorders

Mummy Has an Illness Called Schizophrenia

Thinking With Infants and Their Parents With Mental Illness

Julie Stone

T he baby has a mind. This is perhaps the single most important contribution the field of infant mental health has made to our understanding of the baby and her experience (Thomson Salo, 2005). The baby has a mind and arrives in the world receptive and ready to engage with her human partners. It is in and through her relationships with her caregivers that a child develops her sense of self and begins to make sense of the world. These vital early relationships shape and mould the child's ability to be and behave in relationship with others. The caregiver's role is central in facilitating the child's healthy development in all spheres: physical, intellectual, emotional, social and spiritual.

The relationship between parent and child is always complex. These complexities are invariably intensified when the parent has a mental illness. So too the complexities and challenges in the relationships between patient, or client, and mental health professionals are intensified when the patient is a parent and when their infant's emotional wellbeing is embraced as an aspect of responsible care.

The nature of mental illness is that it perturbs the mind's functioning — cognition and affect are disturbed. Ways of perceiving self and others and the world become distorted. These disturbances have far-reaching implications for a parent with mental illness in the role of caring for an infant or a very young child. In their profound and compassionate treatise, *Madness and the Loss of Motherhood*, Apfel and Handel (1993) remind us:

> Mothers who have major mental illness are a heterogeneous group and treatment planning must reflect each individual situation. Despite the many emotional and social handicaps that these women endure, they usually respond best to an approach that appreciates the unique psychology of the person being treated.
>
> The problems facing the mother with long-term mental illness are multifactorial and need thorough assessment. The psychological, fiscal, social, cultural, psychiatric, medical and domestic situation must be included in any assessment.
>
> … Ethical, moral, and emotional issues inevitably confront the staff caring for these patients. Openly addressing these issues is vital to patient care. (pp. 148–149)

Confronting the ethical, moral, and emotional issues that we inevitably meet in our work with families where a parent has a mental illness is often painful, for the parent and for the mental health workers. In this chapter, I will explore some of the complexities and challenges I have struggled with in my experience as an infant, child and family psychiatrist in the role of leader of a multi-disciplinary team, providing a mental health service for families with children under 5 years of age.

Apfel and Handel (1993) make clear that the focus of their writing is from the perspective of the parent with mental illness. While highlighting that the children 'need attention and work' these concerns are outside, though not ignored, in the scope of their book (p. xxvii). The focus of this book is infants and their parents with mental illness, and this chapter will focus particularly on the perspective and needs of infants of parents with severe mental illnesses.

Winnicott famously reminds us, 'there is no such thing as a baby' (Winnicott, 1964, p. 88); to survive, a baby must have a caregiver. In infant–parent work we must find a place for the baby and those who care for her.

So, as well as embracing the 'unique psychology' of the parents, it is important to remember that the infant with her experience is also unique. Thomson Salo and Paul (2007) enhance our thinking about the subjective experience of babies. Someone must hold the infant, her particular experiences and her needs in the centre of their mind. The clinical challenge is to simultaneously hold the infant, her mother, her father and their needs, individually and as a couple, in mind, without pitting the needs of parent(s) against those of the child.

Infants and Their Parents: Three Case Studies[1]

Sue and her Daughter Rosie

When we first met Rosie and her mother, Sue, Rosie had just celebrated her second birthday. Sue was in her late 30s and had been diagnosed with schizophrenia in her twenties. Rosie was her third child; her other two children, a daughter 10 and a son 7, lived in foster care. Sue and Rosie rarely saw them.

Sue's illness was well managed. She no longer experienced any 'positive' (i.e., overt) psychotic symptoms such as delusions and hallucinations, but the negative symptoms of withdrawal and lack of energy were significant and marked. Her mood was stable yet chronically dysthymic. Sue's face was expressionless and gave the impression that she was absent and disinterested in life around her. This was not the truth. Sue was a thoughtful woman, and her daughter brought some joy to her otherwise quiet and limited life.

Throughout her pregnancy with Rosie, Sue had been well supported by her local community-based adult mental health service. Sue liked and trusted the team so when, after consultation with us, the team's childcare worker Patricia suggested it might be important for Rosie's development for Sue to accept a referral to the infant mental health service, she agreed to come and meet us.

Ostensibly Sue and Rosie were doing well. The Adult Team was very pleased that they had managed Sue's illness without any relapse, or need for hospitalisation throughout the pregnancy or in the 2 years following Rosie's birth. They understood the central importance of parenting in the lives of their patients and had worked collaboratively with the child protection service and allayed immediate concerns about Rosie's wellbeing in the care of her mother.

Rosie was a very serious little girl. Although slightly built, Rosie was growing and meeting her physical milestones well enough. She watched closely, seemed to listen carefully, but said nothing. It was her silence that had begun to concern Patricia. It had been hard for Patricia to talk with Sue about her concerns. She had worked closely and well with Sue since Rosie was a baby, supporting and encouraging Sue in her role as Rosie's mother. When concern and doubt about Rosie's development crept into Patricia's thinking, she was fearful that Sue would feel criticised and undermined. She knew that Sue was frightened that she would 'lose Rosie' as she had lost her elder children, despite Patricia's view that she was a 'good enough mother'. She and the team also believed that Sue's positive connection with her daughter was a strong and important motivating force in helping Sue remain well and engaged with life. It got her out of bed in the morning, albeit sometimes with a struggle.

Catherine, Errol and Their Son Gareth

Gareth was 3 when he, his mother, Catherine and his father, Errol, came to meet us for the first time, referred by Catherine's treating psychiatrist. Catherine was in her early 30s and had been married to Errol for nearly 10 years before this long-awaited first baby arrived. Their relationship was tense and strained. Since Gareth's birth, at times it was stretched to near breaking point. There was frequent heated and hostile debate between the parental couple about the raising of their son.

Catherine had been referred to an adult mental health service following concerns raised by the maternal and child health nurse who visited Catherine and Gareth during his first year. The treating psychiatrist had found Catherine something of a diagnostic puzzle and, despite his thoughtful treatment plans and exploration of various medications, which he suspected she did not take, her symptoms persisted. He believed Gareth seemed to be developing well, but he knew that Catherine's preoccupation with him eating enough and the mounting tension between his parents, must be taking their toll on Gareth.

Catherine had become unwell in the final months of her pregnancy and she had not regained her health. She was so focused on getting Gareth to eat, that her interaction with him was intrusive and often bizarre. Initially, Catherine was thought to have a depressive illness with marked anxiety. As her belief about Gareth's health became more entrenched, it became clear that she had a psychotic illness. The medical history suggested it was some years since she had been functioning well.

Catherine had taken Gareth to several different paediatricians and other allied health professionals in a search for confirmation of her fears about her son's imperilled nutritional status. Their kindly reassurances did nothing to settle her worry. Errol's own mother had had a history of mental illness, the details of which remained vague. Errol was very wary about psychiatric services becoming involved with his family, and especially fearful of what this might mean for Gareth. He was adamant that despite Catherine's fears, Gareth was doing fine.

Errol's understandable attempts to support Catherine and to limit her intrusiveness with their son led him to become increasingly controlling of their interactions. He left detailed instructions of how and what Catherine should do during the day and became frustrated and angry when she did not comply with his plans. His anger was further fuelled when Catherine began drinking, no doubt as a way to help her survive her tense and difficult days.

Gareth was a healthy looking little boy, clearly well nourished. He was a serious child, watching carefully, and interacting in a rather formal and stiff way. His language was well developed and he communicated clearly, though often with a stutter. He seemed to manage his mother's intrusiveness by blocking her out, denying her eye contact and only rarely approaching her or responding to her frequent overtures to him. With his father he was compliant and seemed biddable to his father's frequent requests for him to perform for us. We believed Errol's anxiety to prove to us that Gareth was developing well led to these requests.

Valerie, Alan and Their Son Jack

Valerie was diagnosed as suffering from bipolar affective disorder in her late teens. Her frequent bouts of severe depression and occasional manic episodes had derailed her plans to qualify as a nurse. She met Alan when she was 25. They began a relationship and Alan took on the role of caring for Valerie, who quietly accepted her role as invalid.

As she neared her 30th birthday, Valerie's longing for a baby intensified. Alan was worried about how she would cope with motherhood, but finally agreed to support her wish. They worked closely with the mental health team to manage Valerie's medication. Quite soon Valerie was pregnant with twins.

Valerie was severely depressed throughout the pregnancy. The twins were born precipitously at 32 weeks. The firstborn, a little girl named Gemma, died after 36 hours. Jack had a very difficult neonatal course, but was eventually discharged home after 7 weeks in hospital. Alan was delighted with his son, and took on the role of caring for Jack with gusto.

Valerie was heartbroken by Gemma's death. Alan did not understand her mourning and became impatient with her. He wanted her to join him in celebrating the live baby they had. Valerie said she struggled to find her place in caring for Jack, and her mourning moved into a further severe depression. After three unhappy months, she left the family.

Valerie's departure prompted Alan to move interstate, close to his parents. He soon found work and Jack spent 3 days each week with his grandmother. The other days he was cared for in a small home-based childcare centre. Jack grew into a robust little boy whose early, difficult beginning seemed to leave few scars. His physical and social developmental milestones were age-appropriate and his father proudly described him as 'fearless'.

Soon after leaving Jack and Alan, Valerie was admitted to a psychiatric hospital and spent many months there. She said it was a life-saving admission. As well as preventing her suicide, the care she received helped her come to a new understanding of many things about her self and her life. With the encouragement of her primary therapist, Valerie tentatively made contact with Alan and Jack. Initially, Alan refused to speak with her, telling her that as far as he and Jack were concerned, she was dead. Valerie persisted and slowly over the months the communication between them increased. As Jack's first birthday approached, Alan accepted her request to visit and then invited her to stay.

The couple had a great deal to negotiate. Valerie had changed. Alan was not at all sure he liked the changes and he was wary of allowing her to make a place for herself in their son's life. He was also unsure of how to relate to her, as Valerie was no longer willing to simply do as she was told. Alan's fears about Valerie's vulnerability and fragility seemed to be confirmed when she was again hospitalised 6 months after returning to live with them. It was during this brief hospitalisation that Valerie, Alan and Jack were referred to the infant mental health service.

On meeting the family for the first time we were struck by our observation of how well Jack seemed to relate to both his parents, and how well they communicated with this stocky, busy 18-month-old boy.

Beyond the Mother–Infant Dyad

Sue, Catherine and Valerie were very different women. The similarity in their lives and experience was simply that they were all mothers of young children and they all suffered from a severe mental illness; their psychology, however, was unique and, of course, each father was different. Sue was very guarded about Rosie's father. She said he had nothing to do with them and was unwilling to share any information about him; for instance, whether Rosie shared the same father as her older children. There seemed to be no creative way of further exploring this important person in Rosie's life.

Errol and Alan played a central and important place in their sons' lives. Although each of them exhibited frustration, ambivalence and, at times, open hostility toward their partners, there was no doubting that they were deeply committed to their children.

The teams caring for Sue and Catherine, and to a lesser extent Valerie, were open to thinking about the infants and their needs. They were curious and interested in what an infant mental health service might have to offer the families of the patients in their care. Other colleagues seemed to feel persecuted by our suggestion that they consider the emotional wellbeing of the young children of their patients. They were often hostile to the suggestion that it was an important issue in its own right, or that the child's development may impact upon the health and wellbeing of their parents.

The struggles of Emanuel (2002) to share her understanding of children's emotional experiences with colleagues in a social services agency provide an excellent perspective of the tensions between different service agendas. I experienced similar struggles to Emanuel and found it a taxing part of my role. Emanuel encountered staff who were overworked and underresourced, and who seemed to feel misunderstood and unappreciated by the organisation they worked for. They seemed defensive and suspicious that in offering a different way of thinking she was somehow critical of their work; some became enraged that she should ask them to think about the children's emotional experience. Similarly, with some adult teams I failed to find a way to engage with them so that we could think together about the infant and her experience in her family.

Psychodynamic theories provide the theoretical frame in which I hold my clinical thinking. These theories invite us to create a therapeutic space in which all things can be thought about and talked about. They offer us a way to contain and think about the experience of the families we work with and the stresses and strains of the systems we work within.

Perhaps because we have all been infants and, in some part, identify with the infant's vulnerability, strong feelings are often evoked when we broach the subject of lost dreams and the, sometimes vast, distance between the longed for and the experienced, in caring for young infants. Rightly, there is a good deal of concern about 'mother blaming'. However, the pursuit of not blaming may blind us to the reality of the ways in which the day-to-day experience of living with a major mental illness may impinge upon a parent's capacity to be a 'good enough' parent at particular ages and stages or phases in their children's development.

Infant observation has provided me with useful perspectives for this work, and the powerful emotions aroused in working with infants of mentally ill mothers often mirror the observer's place in infant observation.

> The observer [therapist] needs to be able to think about what she is witnessing. But the freedom to think is inhibited when emotions run strong. The observer [therapist] may take refuge in judgment and blame. Blame is not creative, and when we know we shouldn't be blaming we can get caught in the pursuit of not blaming. The observer [therapist] needs to be free to think about what might appear to be blameful. Seminar discussion [supervision] can often assist the observer [therapist] in coming to understand her response, in reaching a place of compassion to embrace insufficiency. Compassion comes from thought. (Bolton, Griffiths, Stone, & Thomson Salo, 2007, p. 139)

While it is imperative that as mental health clinicians we are thoughtful, compassionate and respectful in our relationships with the patients or clients we work with, it is also essential that we share our knowledge, understanding and concerns openly with them. Building on the strengths of parents, supporting them and helping them to establish a more robust and mutually enjoyable relationship with their children is the focus and intent of infant–parent work. However, building on strengths must not be at the expense of creating a space in which the limitations, difficulties and deficits that may be caused by, or compounded by, the parent's illness, can be thought about and talked about, openly and honestly. Creating the space for this dialogue is perhaps the major challenge in working with parents with a mental illness and their infant children.

> Motherhood wishes and fantasies are universal and central to female identity. The possibilities and actualities of motherhood for women with mental illness may not be the same as for women who are not so disabled. The discrepancy that exists between the desires for this normal experience and the realities of their ability to carry out the role of motherhood creates additional emotional pain for the patients ...
>
> The psychotic inability to distinguish fantasy from reality may be reflected in the patient's fantasy of being normal while, in fact, he or she is very far from acting or appearing normal. The continual therapeutic challenge is how to acknowledge both fantasies and realities and to help the patient to realise whatever dreams of normalcy can be implemented and to mourn those that cannot be. (Apfel & Handel, 1993, p. xxvi, p. 8)

Some clinicians who work with infants and their families seem reticent to develop a direct relationship with the baby. They fear that the parent may become anxious that their insufficiency is being highlighted or that they are being displaced or criticised. However, this is not my experience. Most frequently, a mother whose capacity to engage joyfully with her infant is impaired, for whatever reason, is pleased when another takes an active and lively interest in her child, and is often delighted, and sometimes relieved, when she sees her infant enter energetically into the invitation that is offered to her.

When the mother has a major mental illness, direct work with the infant is an important part of the assessment or the ongoing infant–parent work. Sue, Catherine and Valerie all expressed their pleasure in seeing their children enjoy the relationships they developed with members of the infant mental health team — from the warm greeting from the receptionist, to the therapists who worked more directly with them.

Working With the Families

Rosie and Her Mummy

Part of our work with Sue, Rosie and Patricia was to explore Sue's fear that Rosie would be taken from her, and also to listen to the depth of her heartbreak at her estrangement from her older two children. In the past, when Sue was floridly psychotic and frequently unable to care for her children, she felt she had been brutally and inhumanely dismissed by the child protection service. She said they never talked with her, seemed to assume that she was totally incompetent, and that because she was unable to care for her children that she did not love them. Bereft of children, and worn down by failed attempts to see them, she was left feeling vilified and deeply ashamed of her failure as a mother. This past seemed to blind Sue, and Patricia, to the potential for the creative contribution that the child protection service might now make in supporting Sue in her role as Rosie's mother and in providing services that would contribute to Rosie's healthy development.

Rosie was initially solemn, silent and watchful and slept through much of the first meeting. Her mother said she slept long hours in the morning and afternoon, and also slept well at night. I was concerned and wondered if Rosie was depressed. However, slowly over the following weeks of meeting with Rosie, her affect brightened and she proved to be a lively and enthusiastic play partner. Initially, she kept close to her mother then gradually explored more of the play room and became enlivened by the language-rich and imaginative play that was shared with Rosie and her mother. As Rosie became more energetic, her language and her play became more expressive.

Two co-therapists worked side-by-side, with one focused on Sue, the other focused on Rosie. The infant mental health clinicians kept track of both conversations, and shared aspects of the conversations between mother and daughter. For example, 'Mummy is feeling very sad. She is telling me that she misses your big brother and sister very much. She wishes she could see them more often'. In later meetings there was a chance to build on this narrative with Rosie and Sue, for instance, describing in age-appropriate language why her siblings lived elsewhere, and the meaning for Sue and Rosie of Sue's mental illness

Rosie was told mummy had an illness, called schizophrenia, and that having schizophrenia meant that mummy's face could not always show Rosie how she was feeling and that sometimes mummy got very tired. Sue was encouraged to talk with Rosie about how she was feeling. The speech pathology trained/family therapy trained infant mental health clinician developed some games with Rosie and Sue that helped them play together and build upon their conversation and sharing with one another.

Initially reluctant to have anyone else, other than the mental health team, visit her home, Sue finally agreed to two play-based early development services visiting her and Rosie at home. She also agreed to our recommendation that Rosie spend several afternoons a week at a childcare centre, where she could have some interaction with other children and adults.

After 4 months of working together, Sue was pleased to stop working with the infant mental health team. She was appreciative of what had been achieved, but relieved that Rosie was not being 'labelled'. Understandably, many parents with a mental illness are fearful of what their illness means for their children, and they are often wary of their children becoming involved with mental health services. It is a fear that needs to be revisited frequently throughout their children's development.

Gareth and His Parents

With little insight into her illness, Catherine also just wanted to be left alone to care for Gareth. Unhappy in her marriage, she toyed with leaving Errol, but was frightened that he would enact his threat that if she did leave them, she would never again see her son. Exploring the painful obstetric history shared by this couple, talking with Catherine about her, at times, almost paralysing fear that Gareth would die, and listening to Errol's disappointment and frustration with his wife, was important in our work with this family. Coming to a place of trust in our relationship with them, where the domestic violence in their relationship could be talked about and thought about was crucial, particularly as the impact of the violence on Gareth could be openly discussed. Catherine came to understand that her refuge in alcohol really did make things worse for her and for Gareth, and for Errol, and she stopped her drinking. After many conversations, and with the encouragement and support of our team together with her treating team, Catherine finally agreed to accept a trial of depot antipsychotic medication. Over the ensuing months her mental state slowly improved. Her anxiety lessened, and she became less intensely preoccupied with her son's health. She became much less intrusive and intense in her communication with Gareth, and he responded by inviting his mother more enthusiastically into his play.

Gareth's family life was complex. One of the early tasks was to help his parents think about what was grown-ups' business and what was appropriate for their 3-year-old son to hear and to see. The problems in the marital relationship were clearly grown-ups' business. Gareth appeared relieved when he was told that one of the team was going to meet with mummy and daddy to talk with them about their fighting and other grown-up business. He quickly developed a strong positive alliance with Rachel, the clinician who played with him during this time. Both of Gareth's parents were concerned by his aggression and during these play sessions the toy animals fought some ferocious battles, and the mummy and baby animals were often in conflict over food.

Gareth and Catherine were also seen together for infant–parent therapy with Rachel and another therapist. Rachel took the opportunity of the joint sessions to tell Catherine about some of the themes of the play. The story of the mother–son muddle about food formed a central theme. Despite having limited insight into her illness, Catherine accepted the team's explanation to herself and Gareth that her thinking got mixed up, and that she worried that he was hungry and tried to feed him even when his tummy was already full. They explained to Gareth that they were seeing mummy to try and help mummy's worries get smaller and smaller as they were too big for her to handle alone.

Rachel was warm and gentle with Catherine. She respectfully negotiated with Gareth about inviting Mummy into some of their games; different ones to the ones they played together. Many of the shared games involved food, and sometimes Gareth tried to feed his mummy too much food. Rachel used humour to help heal some of the anxiety and anger that was associated with the history of Catherine's intrusive feeding. She also helped their communication by giving words to Gareth's behaviour that told his mum to 'back off' and encouraging him to use his words to tell his mummy when he had had enough. She helped Catherine become more attuned to Gareth by reading the signs that he gave to her and thinking with them together about what his behaviour might be trying to communicate.

Catherine was heartbroken when we recommended that Gareth spend some time at day care. Errol was also reluctant for this to happen, disparaging of day care and forcefully stating his belief that Catherine should be able to look after Gareth. We persisted, because Gareth had no opportunity to play with other children and also because we felt that he needed some respite from his parents' intense focus upon him. The director of the centre we suggested to Catherine became an integral member to the care team, and contributed richly to some family meetings and case conferences. She engaged Catherine well, fielded her frequent telephone calls and she was respectful and clear when she suspected Catherine had been drinking heavily and was not safe to drive and collect Gareth.

Gareth and his mum loved coming to the infant mental health service. They attended regularly for more than a year and clearly began to enjoy their relationship with each other more. It was delightful to see this little boy shrug off some of his hypervigilance and grow more confident in his engagement with the world. Catherine's symptoms lessened once she accepted the depot antipsychotic medication and, with encouragement, she took some tentative steps toward joining a craft group and building some friendships within this group of women

Errol did not often visit after the initial months. However, he usually came to case review meetings and expressed his appreciation of what the service had given him and his family as Catherine stopped her drinking and her psychotic preoccupation and intrusiveness with Gareth lessened. Despite this, marital tensions persisted. Errol was very proud of his son's achievement and was looking forward to 'encouraging Gareth's academic success'.

Jack's Family

Alan had been deeply wounded when Valerie left; his anger and resentment about how hard it had been for him continued to seethe close to the surface. In listening intently to his experience, it became clear that returning to live near to his parents had been very difficult for Alan. His feelings about his mother, Betty, were complex and painful. She had never liked Valerie and she now seemed to have a vested interest in keeping her son's anger with Valerie alive. Alan joked that it probably kept the heat off him. Both Alan and Valerie were grateful for the contribution Betty made to caring for Jack. Jack was said to adore his grandmother, and he still spent regular time with her.

Valerie was much more able to see the world from Jack's point of view than Alan. She could appreciate the emotionally torrid journey her son had travelled in his short life. She was also able to hear our concern that Jack's 'fearlessness' may be a mask for his fears and welcomed the opportunity to think about ways she could talk with Jack to help him heal his hurts and build an authentic and honest relationship with him.

Together as a couple, with Valerie taking the lead and encouraging Alan to join her, they courageously accepted the opportunity to talk about their relationship and its future. Intermittent alcohol abuse and violence were also part of Alan and Valerie's history, so too were longstanding sexual difficulties compounded by Valerie's previously unspoken experience of having been sexually abused by her stepfather. After several meetings with a family therapist in the infant mental health team, Alan and Valerie accepted a referral to a relationship counsellor elsewhere.

Jack was a busy 18-month-old when we first met him. He seemed fiercely independent and some of his motor development was well ahead of his age — a remarkable achievement given his shaky neonatal course. His bright affect was engaging, but had a brittle feel to it. I was concerned that Jack had no way of expressing his fear or vulnerability and suspected his rush at the world covered over a good deal of anxiety.

Alan often called his son 'buddy' and frequently told him he was a 'big boy'. The work with Jack was to allow him a space in which he could be a little boy, who had lived through lots of scary, sad and potentially very confusing times.

It was painful for Alan to think about what it might mean for Jack to have been a twin. He wanted to dismiss the possibility that this experience had any impact upon Jack, or upon him. Piontelli (2002) offers us a wonderful window into intrauterine life, and her descriptions of the twin pregnancies she studied leave no doubt that Gemma's presence will have impacted upon Jack. Alan wept silently as we spoke to his son about his mummy's sadness when he was a little baby, because his sister, who shared his mummy's tummy where they grew together, had died when they were born. The therapist also told Jack that remembering made his father sad.

Helping Jack's parents' think about his particular vulnerability in the context of the challenges that all children face was very important for them all, particularly for Jack. Alan defended against his own hurt, and so found it difficult to embrace the reality that Valerie's illness, their marital separation, the interstate move, and his own escape into working hard, were all part of Jack's experience. We challenged him and said that blaming Valerie was unlikely to be helpful for any of them.

Part of the story shared with Jack was that his daddy wanted him to be well and happy, and sometimes when he was worried, daddy forgot that Jack was only a little boy, not yet 2. Jack was told that he would stay with grandma while mummy and daddy came to think about some grown-up business with infant mental health team members. Valerie's illness was talked about and named, and Jack was told that the doctors and nurses would help Mummy to get better when she was sick.

With the help of the infant mental health clinicians, Valerie and Jack developed some creative games they enjoyed together. Valerie became a competent storyteller for Jack, helping to create an honest and coherent life narrative of his experience with him and for him. She had wondered how to talk with Jack about Gemma, and about leaving him when he was 3 months old. She was pleased to have found a way of talking with him about their journey together. She was surprised to discover that his story became Jack's favourite story.

Conclusion

Finding the courage and the space to think about the needs of parent and child and the ways in which these needs may at times diverge or seem to compete, is the challenge of our work with infants and their parents with mental illness. It is a complex therapeutic task, and there are parallels in the diverging and competing needs in the organisation of the systems in which we work.

Historically, there has been a strict demarcation between mental health services that attend to the mental health needs of adults and those that care for children. Budgets are usually separate and compete for limited funding. Mother–baby units, where they exist, are frequently administered as part of an adult service. Priorities and agendas can, and do, differ in services addressing the needs of adults and those servicing the needs of children. One of the most pressing challenges for me in my role in leading the development of an infant mental health service as part of a statewide mental health service was to find a respectful way to negotiate these differing priorities.

It is the privilege of our work that people share with us their deepest longings and some of the most intimate details of their experience. I am indebted to the families I have met over the years, and to all they have taught me. Our patients are our best teachers. My hope is that the stories of Sue and her daughter Rose, Gareth and his parents Catherine and Errol, and Valerie, Alan and their son Jack, will help bring further understanding, particularly of the infant's experience, to others who struggle in their work with families where one or both parents suffer from a major mental illness. In the complexity of caring for people with mental illness, the child can easily be lost or overlooked amidst the concern about the parents. These parents love their children and they need and want the support of those caring for them to ensure that their children not only survive, but that they are given the chance to flourish. We must do what we can to best help this.

Endnote

1   The case studies are based on actual events, with names changed and identifying information removed.

References

Apfel, R.J., & Handel, M.H. (1993). *Madness and loss of motherhood: Sexuality, reproduction, and long-term mental illness.* Washington, DC: American Psychiatric Press.

Bolton, C., Griffiths, J., Stone, J., & Thomson Salo, F. (2007). The experience of infant observation: A theme and variations for four voices. *Infant Observation, 10,* 129–141.

Emanuel, L. (2002). Deprivation x 3: The contribution of organizational dynamics to the triple deprivation of looked-after children. *Journal of Child Psychotherapy, 28,* 163–179.

Piontelli A. (2002). *Twins: From fetus to childhood.* London: Routledge.

Thomson Salo, F. (2005). *You and your baby: A baby's emotional life.* London: Karnac Books.

Thomson Salo, F., & Paul, C. (Eds.). (2007). *The baby as subject: New directions in infant–parent therapy from the Royal Children's Hospital, Melbourne* (2nd ed.). Melbourne, Australia: Stonnington Press.

Winnicott, D.W. (1964). *The child, the family, and the outside world.* Harmondsworth, England: Penguin.

15

Working With Severely Mentally Ill Mothers and Their Infants in a Mother–Baby Inpatient Unit

Anne Sved Williams, Sue Ellershaw, Lynly Mader and Mandy Seyfang

— ᘉ —

When parents of infants become severely unwell with a mental illness, admission to a mental health facility may be required. In Australia, as well as many other western countries, it is considered highly desirable to admit the parent(s) with their infant to such a facility, to continue and sometimes enhance ongoing attachment between mother and infant. There are also other considerations — particularly ensuring that the parent is able to care adequately for the infant by the time of discharge, and that the infant is developing appropriately.

In an earlier review (Sved Williams, 2004), the possible risks for infants of mentally ill parents were described. To reduce or prevent physical and emotional risk or to introduce early intervention strategies for those infants where risks are evident, a comprehensive care plan is essential for both mother and child.

This chapter will describe the work of a parent–baby unit, Helen Mayo House. The unit is an inpatient facility for parents with mental illness (mostly mothers) and their infant/s up to the age of 3 years. We will describe the rationale for admissions to the unit, the evaluations used, the techniques of treatment and outcomes. Case descriptions are used to illustrate the work of the unit. We will also describe some of the challenges and struggles involved in working with this population.

The South Australian Perinatal and Infant Mental Health Service (PIMHS)

The state of South Australia has a population of approximately 1,600,000 people, and with recent reorganisations the Children, Youth and Women's Health Service (CYWHS) takes responsibility for the health of infants, women and children. Helen Mayo House (HMH), the acute admission unit, has existed in its current form for approximately 20 years and has always been a statewide service, providing treatment for parents throughout South Australia. The service has the following components:

1. Inpatient unit which provides:
   * inpatient treatment for six adults and six or more infants under the age of 3 years
   * telephone counselling around the clock provided by nursing staff to consumers
   * support to community professionals, including advice on relevant resources, medication use, and so on
   * teaching to trainees and students in psychiatry, medicine, psychology, occupational therapy, social work, nursing and midwifery
   * development of staff expertise and research opportunities.
2. Consultation-liaison service to the obstetric and neonatal intensive care units of CYWHS.
3. Community services which include:
   * teaching services to community staff at many primary and secondary care sites via annual conference, seminars and teaching packages
   * community group programs developed to complement or replace inpatient care and include groups for postnatal depression and mother–infant play
   * family home visiting program of substantial length and intensity, developed in conjunction with a church-based welfare program and funded by the state government. Workers employed in this service attend weekly team meetings at Helen Mayo House, meet clients prior to discharge and can receive ongoing supervision from HMH staff

- outpatient work including assessments on referral from GPs and mother–infant and family therapy clinics
- joint mother–infant admissions.

Rationale

Barnett and Morgan (1996) explored the comparative advantages and disadvantages of joint admission, and while noting the cost of such treatment, posed the question 'Can we afford not to provide it?' They suggest that further research must provide the answer about whether joint admission makes a statistically significant, positive influence on longer term outcomes for both mother and infant. Thus far little evidence exists to prove the case either way. Attempts to look at child outcomes by Wai Wan, Warburton, Appleby and Abel (2007) and Leung (1999) each principally proved that following up these groups is extraordinarily difficult for many reasons: mobility, current mental illness, children living elsewhere, and the fear of revealing problems that may lead to child removal. Wai Wan and colleagues also found, in their limited sample, that positive outcomes are more likely for girls than boys, especially if the mother is currently well. Leung similarly noted more current behaviour difficulties 3 to 5 years after discharge if the mother was currently depressed, particularly if there was perceived lack of support. Clearly, hospitalisation is a short time period in the lives of both parent and infant but is also a great crisis; the opportunity must be taken to minimise harm for family members and maximise outcomes as they leave on their journey after discharge.

What Does Joint Admission Provide?

Specialised care in a mother-baby unit provides:
- expert treatment by specialist staff with an understanding of all the complexities of physical, psychological and emotional support for both mother and infant
- safe treatment of mother and baby together at a time that attachment is growing between them. Staff support in the unit facilitates the mother's increasing confidence in her care for her baby.
- biopsychosocial elements of the mental illness can be addressed in one setting regardless of whether the mother is detained under the mental health act or admitted voluntarily.

Clearly, expertise can be provided on a day patient basis or with community care, particularly when there is good family support and the maternal illness is less severe. When there are sleep and/or emotional regulation difficulties for mother and/or infant and ambivalence in the maternal–infant relationship, the benefits of hospitalisation with staff availability around the clock become very apparent.

On occasions an inpatient stay will be requested by the state welfare/ child protection authority, to assess the parenting capacity of a woman with a significant mental illness. The assessments are carried out only when the mental state of the mother is viewed by staff as being sufficiently stable in order for the assessment to be conducted. Strict guidelines are followed to ensure the role of the unit staff and the role of child protection staff are clearly defined, for example decisions concerning removal of a child into care are made by child protection staff.

Models of Care

While a biopsychosocial framework is used to understand a woman's illness, staff must work with formal diagnostic frameworks. To fully understand the woman, her partner and infant, attachment theory and systems theory form the basic model. Staff bring with them training and orientations from many other fields, as well as backgrounds based in all the mental health disciplines, which provides a rich web of understandings for our patients. Mental health consumer and carer networks are often consulted for their opinions to ensure the unit is appropriately responsive of their viewpoints. Inpatient, outpatient, community and group care are all available as modes of treatment, whichever seems most necessary and appropriate. Inpatient care may be the only option for those living in rural districts where relatively little appropriate community care is available.

Staffing

The service is staffed by a multidisciplinary team consisting of consultant psychiatrists, psychiatric trainee, nursing staff, psychologist, social worker and occupational therapist (at least one of whom has specialist infant mental health expertise) as well as ancillary staff.

The Work of the Helen Mayo House Mother–Baby Unit[1]

Case 1: Maternal Depression — Tiffany and Briony

> Tiffany was a first time mother aged 36, and had been with Joe for 8 years. Tiffany was on maternity leave from her senior nurse position. Her pregnancy was long-planned and assisted by a fertility clinic, but was marred by an abnormal blood level suggestive of

a foetal abnormality, although in fact Briony had no noticeable physical problems at the age of 3 months. Tiffany had been referred by her general practitioner, as she was depressed to the point of contemplating suicide. While clear that she would never harm Briony, she nevertheless questioned whether her feelings for Briony were appropriate. Briony appeared well cared for on all physical parameters, and was developmentally advanced on screening with the Denver Developmental Screen (Frankenburg & Bresnick, 1998). However, she was often irritable and it was observed that Tiffany was often irritable when with her. Briony responded to her mother with marked gaze avoidance, and a general restlessness when held by Tiffany. Tiffany voiced her disappointment with motherhood, acknowledging how every step of the way from conception, through the pregnancy, to failed breastfeeding had convinced her that she should never have been a mother.

Tiffany's family history was also relevant. Her maternal grandmother had committed suicide in the postnatal period, and her mother had told Tiffany that she herself had been uncertain about how to parent her children. Tiffany had vowed 'to do better' than her mother, who she felt had pushed her away, but she felt dejected at her own failures, and rejected by Briony. She was tempted to 'put her in full-time childcare and go back to full-time work where I feel wanted and competent'. Her depression interfered with her concentration, her sleep and energy were much diminished, and she could not see how she could manage her old job as she used to.

A diagnosis of major depression was made and the compromised mother–infant relationship explored. The nursing staff also found that it was difficult to settle Briony. The following management plan was prepared.

- Tiffany's antidepressant medication was changed from the selective serotonin reuptake inhibitor prescribed for the last 2 months to a combined serotonin and noradrenaline medication regime.
- Briony initially slept in the nursery despite Tiffany's concerns that she 'ought' to be having direct care of Briony. At first Briony woke several times during the night but quickly settled into a routine of 12 hours sleep.
- Tiffany and Briony commenced mother–infant therapy with the staff infant mental health specialist using the Circle of Security model (Marvin, Cooper, Hoffman, & Powell, 2002) as an underpinning with frequent video feedback. Tiffany could clearly see her own avoidance of contact with Briony and lack of interest in playing with her. She discussed this openly with

staff and asked for guidance regarding play. Nursing staff initially were close at hand to guide Tiffany in Briony's care and take over when Briony's irritability was persistent, a not infrequent situation early in the admission.

- Tiffany and Joe spoke to the social worker who had interviewed Joe alone and found that he too was struggling with this unexpected outcome of their planned parenting. While Joe and Tiffany previously had an excellent relationship, the stressors of the last 2 years had 'driven wedges' between them and there was a lot of unexpressed anger. They welcomed the opportunity to discuss their problems, and began to express their needs more freely to each other.

After 2 weeks, Tiffany understood that 'good-enough' mothering (Winnicott, 1951) was good enough, and was better at resisting her failed attempts to be 'perfect'. Briony's eyes sought out her mother's, and play together was hesitant but more interactive. Briony cried much less during the day, and both Tiffany and Briony were sleeping through the night. Joe and Tiffany had been out on a 'date' together and expressed hope for the future as Tiffany's mood had significantly lifted.

They were discharged from inpatient care and agreed to a follow-up plan which included:

- ongoing outpatient mother–infant therapy
- attendance at a group run by other members of the team (a 9-week structured group for women with postnatal depression that encourages women to understand their needs, look after themselves, assert their views and find support from others in a similar situation to themselves—an 'instant village')
- private psychiatric referral
- attendance at her GP who had attended the ward round on invitation to ensure that she knew details of Tiffany's hospitalisation and ongoing plans.

Tiffany left the unit after weekend leave had convinced her that she could manage at home nearly as well as she has managed in hospital. Her appreciation of care received was rewarding for staff.

Dual Diagnosis: Mental Illness and Substance Abuse

The statistics from Helen Mayo House show approximately 120 admissions every year, with an average length of stay of 3 weeks. An in-depth study of 33 consecutive admissions to Helen Mayo House (diBella, 2003) showed that 34%

Table 1

Psychiatric Diagnoses of 38 Clients of Helen Mayo House (di Bella, 2003)

Number of Clients	Diagnosis
Axis 1	
15	Major depression (1 with psychotic features)
4	Dysthymia
7	Adjustment disorder with depressed mood
4	Anxiety disorder
4	BPAD (3 manic phase, 1 depressive) (bipolar affective disorder)
3	Psychotic disorders (1 schizophrenia, 1 schizoaffective, 1 not otherwise specified [NOS])
1	Alcohol dependence
Dual Diagnosis	
	Comorbid substance use disorders ($n = 13$)
1	Benzodiazepine misuse
2	THC use (cannabis)
3	THC dependence (cannabis)
3	ETOH abuse (alcohol)
3	Amphetamine abuse
1	Opiate abuse
Axis II	
13	Borderline personality disorder
3	Borderline traits
2	Dependent personality disorder

of this group had a dual diagnosis — both a mental illness and a substance abuse diagnosis (Table 1). This combination of problems has been noted throughout mental health services in Australia in the last 2 decades as substance abuse has become more prevalent.

Other features of note were:

· the high number of older children in this sample who did not live with their mother; of these 38 women 12 mothers had in total 22 older children permanently cared for by others

· the large percentage of infants for whom there are multiple environmental risk factors. The Rochester Longitudinal Study examined outcomes at age 18 years for children from a variety of backgrounds and confirmed that as the number of environmental risk factors increased (Table 2), the negative consequences increased substantially (Sameroff, 1998). Many of the infants who leave Helen Mayo House return to an environment characterised by many of these risks (Table 3).

Table 2

Multiple Risk Factors Followed in Rochester Longitudinal Study
(Sameroff, 1998)

- History of maternal mental illness
- High maternal anxiety
- Parental perspectives reflecting rigidity in attitudes and beliefs about child's development
- Few observed positive parent–child interactions
- Head of household unskilled occupation
- Minimal maternal education
- Disadvantaged minority group
- Single parenthood
- Stressful life events
- Large family size

Table 3

Environmental Risk Factors for Helen Mayo House Population (di Bella, 2003)

- Anxiety (Beck Anxiety Scale): 16 severe, 12 moderate (74%)
- Compromised interaction with child: severe compromise on self-assessment 8/38 (21%)
- Single parents: 15 (39%)
- Income: 17/24 live-in partners in unskilled occupation or on social security (71%)
- Maternal education: 19 (50%) had less than high school qualifications
- Other current stressors: 5 current Family Court dispute, 8 current domestic violence relationship, 6 infants with failure to thrive or developmental delay

Case 2: Dual Diagnosis — Margaret and Rosie

Margaret, 24, was admitted to the unit with Rosie, 4 weeks old. Margaret's parents separated when she was 2 years old, and she was sexually abused by several of her mother's subsequent partners. Margaret ran away from home in her early teens, and lived as a 'street kid'. Her first child, a boy, aged 5, lived with his father, and Margaret had occasional contact with him. Margaret had not worked for several years, and had continued to misuse alcohol and illicit substances, which led to the development of a psychotic illness.

In the early stages of her pregnancy with Rosie, Margaret's partner abandoned her. She decided that she would strive to keep her child, and she reduced her substance abuse but could not give it up altogether. The symptoms of Margaret's psychotic illness recurred in late pregnancy, and she spent 3 weeks in a psychiatric inpatient unit. When Rosie was born, the staff at the obstetric hospital expressed concern about her ability to care for Rosie, as she would often leave Rosie alone while she went outside to smoke. Margaret's moods alternated from very distressed to calm and happy, causing staff to suspect she was using marijuana. Her mental state deteriorated significantly, and admission of Margaret and Rosie to the unit was requested both by the consultation–liaison team of PIMHS who work at the hospital's obstetric service and the state child protection agency.

On arrival at Helen Mayo House, staff found that Margaret was suffering delusions, with beliefs that she had special powers to keep herself and her infant safe, even if neither of them ate any food. Her affect was very variable throughout the initial interview, with elation and tears that were not always consistent with the content of her conversation. She attempted to care for her infant, but clearly could not do so consistently, and reluctantly accepted help from staff. The diagnosis was not completely clear at admission as it was possible that she had either a substance-induced psychosis or a bipolar mood disorder, a diagnosis consistent with the time course of the occurrence of her 'puerperal psychosis'. Margaret's detention order (under the state *Mental Health Act*) was confirmed as she would not remain voluntarily.

Over the first few days, Margaret provided little of Rosie's care as she could not concentrate, and found it difficult to take care of herself. She did not like taking medication and the nursing staff had to stand with her to ensure that she swallowed her tablets. Margaret gradually began to understand that she needed to keep her infant in mind when thinking about her illness and refusing her medication. She consistently stated that she wanted to care for Rosie and believed she was parenting her adequately, but staff observed that she became restless within minutes of offering Rosie a bottle, preferring still to move outside to smoke. While she clearly loved her daughter and handled her gently most of the time, she was also heard to say that Rosie was deliberately trying to 'get her upset'. Rosie was surprisingly settled, feeding well with either Margaret or the nursing staff who undertook most of her care.

With antipsychotic medication beginning to take effect, Margaret became calmer and more able to complete Rosie's feeds. On occasions Margaret seemed to be distrustful of staff but was grateful for their help. She especially relied on them to help with Rosie at night as she needed to sleep.

Margaret's mother Maureen visited the unit and indicated her willingness to help Margaret. Maureen was in a stable relationship with Des, and they invited Margaret and Rosie to stay with them. Margaret refused this offer, and expressed rage at what she perceived was her mother's failure to help her when she was a child. She said she could manage by herself. Staff gently but firmly challenged this, pointing out the demands of single parenthood, and the effects of substance abuse on a parent's capability to care for their infant child. As the medication continued to minimise Margaret's symptoms, her trust with staff increased, and her attachment with Rosie became stronger. Margaret agreed to joint problem-solving sessions with Maureen and Des. The psychiatrist and social worker used a strengths-based family therapy approach (Erickson & Kurz-Reimer, 1999) that facilitated the airing of tensions, and rebuilding of their relationships.

After 33 days in the unit, Margaret and Rosie went for overnight leave with Maureen and Des. It did not work out well, and Margaret was angry and despairing, and regressed in her mood and behaviour. By the following weekend she was optimistic and calmer and asked for overnight leave again. This time it worked out well, and Margaret and Rosie were discharged to live with Maureen and Des. Rosie continued to progress appropriately, and behaved comfortably with her mother, looking and smiling at her and snuggling.

Follow-up plans for Margaret were comprehensive. A case worker from the local area mental health service was assigned to work with Margaret, and she also agreed to meet with a worker from the drug and alcohol service. Margaret had moved into the contemplation phase of quitting her substance abuse (Miller & Rollnick, 2002), and alternated between denial regarding her drug abuse and its effects to clear statements about what she would do for the sake of Rosie. Child protection workers arranged to see her at home soon after discharge to clarify with Margaret that they would continue to work with her intensively until they were satisfied with the adequacy of safety and care issues for Rosie.

Margaret also accepted referral to a program based at a childcare centre that provided group counselling for parents (see Chapter 19). Margaret had begun to reflect on her own experience as a child and showed interest in learning how to parent differently. Margaret initially rejected childcare, stating that she would never 'abandon' her child as she herself felt abandoned. During her lengthy hospitalisation, however, she had realised that a day each week in childcare may be beneficial for both mother and infant.

Maureen and Des showed a keen interest in the program, with Maureen expressing guilt about how little she had known when, as a teenager with multiple difficulties, she herself gave birth to Margaret. With maturity, and support from Des, Maureen saw that helping Margaret and Rosie was a chance for some reparation.

Working in a Mother–Baby Unit With Mentally Ill Women and Their Partners Where There is Risk of Violence

Fathers are clearly important in the lives of their partners and infants, and have widely varying attitudes, skills and needs as described by Peter Ballard (Chapter 7). The experience at Helen Mayo House is that, not infrequently, the behaviour of a woman's partner causes great concern as it poses risks to all in the unit. The relationship between mother and partner is often unstable, with the men reluctant for contact with the staff. Sometimes the staff are also reluctant for contact because of the substantial possibility of violence. Safety care plans must be negotiated prior to the partner spending periods of time in the unit, because of safety concerns for the woman and her child, and sometimes the other patients and their infants, and staff.

Case 3: Pamela, Haydon and Laura

Pamela had a long history of a schizoaffective illness, and had been in a relationship with Haydon for 7 years. There were incidents of domestic violence, with presentations to emergency departments after 'falls' for treatment of bruising, and a fractured finger. Haydon had a job, had provided a home for Pamela over an extended period of time, and expressed love for his daughter Laura who was 14 months old at the time of admission. Alcohol had a major role in their lives, with most episodes of domestic violence occurring on Saturdays following Haydon's return home from watching sport at the pub. It was unclear why Pamela had become psychotic just prior to admission. Possible causes were Pamela's noncompliance with medication, an angry outburst by Haydon, and Laura's increasing independence.

On admission, Laura was slightly underweight, progressing well with development of gross motor skills, but not speaking/babbling in accordance with her age range. She clung to her mother, became quite distressed when separated from her, and yet interacted relatively little with her verbally.

Interventions during Pamela's twenty day admission to HMH included:

- changing her medication to a depot medication to ensure compliance
- successful representation to the Guardianship Board for an ongoing Community Treatment Order under the state *Mental Health Act*, which ensured follow up by a community mental health worker after discharge
- discussion of the domestic violence with Pamela who gradually accepted the impacts on Laura. Later, domestic violence was also discussed jointly at a session with Haydon. Staff alerted security guards of the possibility that Haydon may be violent, as Pamela predicted he would respond this way. Careful planning and the number of staff in the room limited the initial shouting and denial. Haydon began to cry and expressed concern at his behaviour. He agreed that Pamela could contact domestic violence services, and said that he would 'look into' anger management programs if provided with a list of contacts. He was not prepared to make any further commitments at that time.
- mother–infant therapy, using the Circle of Security model which addressed 'top half' difficulties of letting go of Laura and 'bottom half' problems in providing a safe haven. Staff also undertook a triadic play assessment (Fivaz-Depeursinge, Corboz-Warnery, & Keren, 2004) later in the admission when Haydon had begun to take responsibility for his violent behaviour. It was clear that Haydon could play well with Laura although needing to exclude Pamela from this play. Pamela and Haydon agreed to return to HMH parent–infant therapy service as outpatients after discharge, but rejected the suggestion they attend a group operating in a community setting.
- involvement of the state child protection service, who suggested limited monitoring following discharge.

Intake, Assessment and Treatment

Intake Criteria for Helen Mayo House

Ideally, specialised care should be available to all mothers with mental health difficulties whose problems warrant hospitalisation but, as there is limited capacity to meet the demand, an admission priority system has been created:

- High priority: currently psychotic; chronic mental illness exacerbated by recent delivery; thoughts of suicide and/or infanticide; acute postnatal depression; younger baby who is breastfed.
- Moderate priority: depression of lesser severity and multiple psychosocial problems
- Lower priority: requested parenting assessment, untreated abuse in parent's history that is impacting her parenting capacity, parent facing multiple psychosocial stressors that are compromising her capacity to parent and have created significant mental health symptomatology.

Assessment

1. Psychiatric assessment of the parent.

The trainee psychiatrist, in conjunction with nursing staff, undertakes a comprehensive history and mental state examination of the admitted parent. This is complemented by the findings of all clinical staff over the first few days of admission. Emphasis is given to the experience around parenting, the history of the parent's attachment relationships, perceived struggles and losses, and the parent's own priorities for treatment. The stressors and supports in the community are examined, for example housing, financial concerns, domestic violence, and substance use.

2. A client care management plan is formulated.

The plan is formulated with input from the whole team that addresses inpatient goals, longer term goals and means of connecting the client into appropriate community services. Key organisations already involved with the family are invited to contribute and may attend weekly reviews. The client care management plan addresses the needs of the parent in her own right as an adult, as a parent and, where relevant, as an individual in a relationship with a partner. The plan must also include the identified needs of the infant or children cared for by the client.

3. The infant's needs are identified through a physical examination and a range of structured assessments including:

- the Denver Developmental Screen II (Frankenburg & Bresnick, 1998) is a brief checklist that aims to identify areas of concern or delay with the child's development that might prompt further assessment or intervention. It covers the age range from 0 to 6 years and looks at gross motor skills, fine motor adaptive skills, personal and social functioning and language.

- the Modified Alarm Distress Baby scale (Matthey, Črnčec, & Guedeney, 2006) assesses the social behaviour of infants and may indicate infant social withdrawal in reference to the assessor. It has been adapted from the original longer scale of Guedeney and Fermanian (2001) and rates the extent and nature of facial expressiveness, eye contact, vocalisation, and physical activity towards an observer including the observer's perception of the infant's ability to engage in a relationship with him/her.

- further observations of the infant's ability to self regulate around emotions, sleep, feeding and general settling are also considered as part of the infant assessment.

4. The relationship between parent and child is of great significance and is assessed by a combination of:

- a developmental history from conception to present day with identification of any disruption and loss between parent and child through ill health during pregnancy or trauma before, during and after birth

- observation of the interaction between parent and child relating to the parent's ability to support the child's exploration and the infant's sense of security in the relationship, along with the ability of the parent to take charge when necessary

- at times a modified format of the Strange Situation Procedure (Ainsworth, Blehar, Waters, & Wall, 1978) is used to give greater clarity around the attachment issues of the infant

- staff also use the Louis Macro Scale (Louis, Condon, Shute, & Elzinga, 1997), which measures safety, physical and emotional care while considering infant characteristics and mother's mental state

- video taping of parent–infant interactions that may illustrate the level of parental reflective functioning, emotional availability and attunement with the infant. As well as forming a component of assessment the video recordings may be used as an intervention with the mother by watching and discussing with her the interactions between herself and her baby.

Techniques for Treatment

Treatment is multifaceted and frequently includes pharmacology and a range of interpersonal counselling approaches. A number of factors influence the extent to which goals can be achieved during an inpatient stay, such as the symptomatology of the parent, issues relating to partner and family members, and the extent to which a parent is able to think about the needs of her infant at this time. Some work can only be carried out after discharge as many parents are too unwell during admission for in-depth therapy.

The team works to provide an environment that gives safety and space for women to reflect upon their experience of mothering, and the needs of them-selves and their families. To establish and maintain such a ward milieu requires a high degree of professional reflection and skill. The team provides positive parenting role modelling and assists the mother to:

- read the cues from her infant
- develop positive developmentally appropriate responses and interactions.

Staff aim to provide a secure base and, frequently, an alternative attachment experience for the adult around containment of arousal and anxiety states (Adshead, 1998). Parents are encouraged to engage in the form of counselling that is most appropriate. Approaches may include cognitive–behavioural approaches (Greenberger & Padesky, 1995), psychoeducation (Lukens & McFarlane, 2004), narrative influenced individual and family therapy (White & Epston, 1990), and motivational interviewing (Miller & Rollnick, 2002).

In the case presentations we have described joint work with mother and baby. Parent–infant therapy has been highly influenced by interactional guidance (McDonough, 2004), Wait, Watch and Wonder (Muir, Lojkasek, & Cohen, 1999), Circle of Security (Marvin et al., 2002) and Parallel Parent Child Narratives (Chambers, Amos, Allison, & Roeger, 2006). Video recording and playback of dyadic and triadic (Fivaz-Depeursinge et al., 2004) interactions are often used as a means to promote self-reflection within, and between, the participants.

The degree to which these techniques are applied is influenced not only by length of stay but the often fluctuating nature of the mother's mental state. Careful attention must be given to the impact of medication, the degree and intrusiveness of external stressors and the ability of the woman and the team to manage the inevitable emotional flux that mother–infant therapy creates. The structure of the unit must allow for individual and team supervision so that the inherent tensions of this work may be addressed. Staff know that their own attachment templates are reactivated as soon as they begin work with a client's internal representations. The brevity of patient stay and vicarious traumatisa-tion arising from the women's stories combine with these frequent reactivations to make this work emotionally intense. However, the work is also highly reward-ing when change occurs in an environment that is safe for families and staff.

Staff Matters: Working With Mentally Ill Women, Their Partners and Their Infants

As already noted, challenges abound for staff working with this client group. Issues faced include:

- general issues of working with people with severe mental illness, including burnout, and dealing with stigma and marginalisation for the client group
- violence and personal safety issues with regard to partners, particularly where substance abuse and drug 'dealing' are evident
- the possibility of professional objectivity giving way to the distress of the mother, leading to conflicting decisions about aspects of treatment. This can be minimised by the team working together to implement the treatment plan.
- vicarious traumatisation with the continuing flow of histories from multiply traumatised patients
- more demands for service than personnel can manage
- interagency difficulties, particularly with child protection services, which are not only extremely underresourced but (appropriately) infant-focused, sometimes without an understanding of the effects and prognosis of the mental illness. HMH staff must advocate for the woman *and* her infant. This can particularly be an issue with illnesses such as bipolar mood disorder, which may be alarming in the early stages when a mother can be acutely psychotic and may pose a risk to her infant in the short term. With treatment the symptoms can settle, leading to reasonable long-term outcomes for both mother and infant (Radke-Yarrow, Nottelmann, Martinez, Fox, & Belmont, 1992).
- related to this are the general ethical issues for both mother and infant, well discussed by Seeman (2004).

Staff work well when they are reflective, supported, and well trained, particularly in understanding not only psychiatric illness, but also systems and attachment theories, and how to sustain a consistent team approach in following through with a care plan for mother and baby. Ward rounds in Helen Mayo House are sometimes scenes of hilarity, as a sense of humour can provide a new perspective on major challenges and struggles staff experience in their work. Holidays, staff training, group and individual supervision and support are all essential to maintain the balance between the clinical needs of mothers and babies and the needs of staff as professionals working in an emotionally demanding environment.

Conclusion

Women with significant mental illness often find parenting difficult, although this is not universally the situation. Case discussions have been chosen to highlight both the severity and complexity of the mental illnesses, and also the potential difficulties that mother–infant pairs may have. Techniques have been described for taking the relationship in more positive directions and therefore diminishing risks to the infant as they grow.

The possibility exists to identify potential problems early in some cases, and to intervene quickly in most cases. Thus an ideal comprehensive service for mentally ill women and their babies would include:

- illness identification in pregnancy or the early postnatal period with appropriate management plans made and enacted
- extended family home visiting services postnatally by nurses or family home visitors in conjunction with mental health staff, GPs, child protection workers and other primary care-givers
- specialised mother–baby unit for acute inpatient care when needed
- supported accommodation for those women with severe mental illness and small children who are well enough to parent, but who need substantial care in the long term for best outcomes for themselves and their children.

Working in this area is demanding but rewarding, and a team of committed people can develop relevant expertise for this vulnerable population.

There is a significant body of knowledge regarding the risks to infants, and greater awareness of interventions that can achieve positive outcomes. The capacity to implement a full range of services depends on committed workers with relevant knowledge and experience, but also on a government that supports such services with relevant funding, as costs are often substantial. When viewed through the lens of cost, however, it is clear that for each dollar spent now, less will need to be spent in the future. This is always difficult for governments to hear, as the results of interventions may be one or more generations on and, of course, no government lasts this distance. It is, however, well known that neither the mentally ill nor infants have a significant voice in government. Those of us who work in this area must therefore not only speak with and learn from our clients about how services can be developed and improved but, where possible, collaborate with them to make representations to those with political power so that long-term outcomes for the infants, children and their families ensure their healthy development and wellbeing.

Endnote

1   The case studies are based on actual events, with names changed and identifying information changed or removed.

References

Ainsworth, M.D.S., Blehar, M.C., Waters, E., & Wall, S. (1978). *Patterns of attachment: A psychological study of the strange situation.* Hillsdale, NJ: Erlbaum.

Adshead, G. (1998). Psychiatric staff as attachment figures. *British Journal of Psychiatry, 172,* 64–69.

Barnett B., & Morgan, M. (1996). Postpartum psychiatric disorder: Who should be admitted and to which hospital. *Australian and New Zealand Journal of Psychiatry 30,* 709–714

Chambers, H., Amos, J., Allison, S., & Roeger, L. (2006). Parent and child therapy: An attachment-based intervention of children with challenging problems. *Australian and New Zealand Journal of Family Therapy, 27,* 68–74.

diBella, I. (2003, August). *Mothers and infants … and fathers.* Paper presented at the Australian Association of Infant Mental Health Annual Conference, Adelaide, South Australia.

Erickson, M.F., & Kurz-Reimer, K. (1999). *Infants, toddlers and families: A framework for support and intervention.* New York: Guilford Publications.

Fivaz-Depeursinge, E., Corboz-Warnery, A, & Keren, M., (2004). The primary triangle: Treating infants in their families. In A.J. Sameroff, S.C. McDonough & K.L. Rosenblum (Eds.), *Treating parent–infant relationship problems.* New York: Guilford.

Frankenburg W.K., & Bresnick,¡B. (1998). *Denver II Prescreening Questionnaire (PDQII).* Denver CO: Denver Developmental Materials Inc.

Greenberger, D., & Padesky, C. (1995). *Mind over mood: Change how you feel by changing the way you think.* New York: Guilford Press.

Guedeney A., & Fermanian J. (2001). A validity and reliability study of assessment and screening for sustained withdrawal reaction in infancy: The alarm distress baby scale. *Infant Mental Health Journal, 5,* 559–575.

Leung N. (1999). *The relationship between social support, child behaviour and maternal depression.* Unpublished honours thesis, the University of Adelaide, South Australia.

Louis, A., Condon, J., Shute, R., & Elzinga, R. (1997). The development of Louis MACRO (Mother And Child Risk Observation) forms: Assessing parent–infant–child risk in the presence of maternal mental illness. *Child Abuse & Neglect: The International Journal, 21,* 589–606.

Lukens, E.P., & McFarlane, W.R. (2004). Psychoeducation as evidence-based practice: Considerations for practice, research, and policy. *Brief Treatment of Crisis Intervention, 4*, 202–25.

McDonough, S.C. (2004). Interaction guidance: Promoting and nurturing the caregiving relationship. In A.J. Sameroff, S.C. McDonough, & K.L. Rosenblum (Eds.), *Treating parent–infant relationship problems.* New York: Guilford.

Marvin R., Cooper G., Hoffman K., & Powell B. (2002). The Circle of Security Project: Attachment-based interventions with caregiver–preschool child dyads. *Attachment and Human Development, 4*, 107–124.

Matthey, S., Črnčec, R., & Guedeney, A. (2006, July). *The modified ADBB (m-ADBB): Assessing for infant withdrawal during routine examinations.* Poster session presented at the World Association for Infant Mental Health Congress, Paris.

Miller R.M., & Rollnick S. (2002). *Motivational interviewing: Preparing people for change.* New York: Guilford Press.

Muir E., Lojkasek M., & Cohen N. (1999). Watch, Wait and Wonder. *A manual describing a dyadic infant led approach to problems in infancy and early childhood.* Toronto, Canada: The Hincks-Dellcrest Centre and the Hincks-Dellcrest Institute.

Radke-Yarrow M., Nottelmann E., Martinez P., Fox M.B., & Belmont B. (1992). Young children of affectively ill parents: A longitudinal study of psychosocial development. *Journal of the American Academy of Child & Adolescent Psychiatry, 31*, 68–77.

Sameroff, A.J. (1998). Environmental risk factors in infancy. *Pediatrics, 102*(5, Suppl.), 1287–1292.

Seeman M. (2004). Relational ethics: When mothers suffer from psychosis. *Archives of Women's Mental Health, 7*, 201–210.

Sved Williams A. (2004). Infants of mothers with mental illness. In V. Cowling (Ed.), *Children of parents with mental illness: Personal and clinical perspectives* (pp. 17–40). Melbourne: ACER Press.

Wai Wan M., Warburton A., Appleby L., & Abel K. (2007). Mother and baby unit admissions: Feasibility study examining child outcomes 4–6 years on. *Australian and New Zealand Journal of Psychiatry, 41*, 150–156.

White, M., & Epston, D. (1990). *Narrative means to therapeutic ends.* New York: Norton.

Winnicott, D. (1951). Transitional objects and transitional phenomena. *International Journal of Psychoanalysis, 34*, 89–97.

Infants of Parents
Who Misuse Drugs

Nichola Coombs

～～

The following is an extract from an article by Julie-Anne Davies, published in *The Age* (Melbourne) in March 1999. The article explores the life of a methadone[1]-maintained mother of three and her new baby, Taylor, born opiate-addicted and suffering neonatal abstinence syndrome (withdrawal).

> Taylor rarely opens his eyes and, more worrying for a full-term infant, shows no inclination to suckle, neither a teat nor his mother's breast. So he is being tube-fed every 3 hours. This is called gavaging and is painful to watch. A clear plastic length of tubing about as wide as a straw is passed down his throat into his stomach and formula or breast milk is slowly syringed in. The most extraordinary part of what is essentially force feeding is how little Taylor reacts to having a tube poked down his throat. He doesn't even gag. He's too out of it to notice … when you hold him you feel the involuntary jerking; you feel his 2-inch-long heart thundering away rapidly inside his chest and know it is beating unusually fast (a side-effect of morphine); you grab the starfish-shaped hands as they strain against nothing. And still he won't look at anyone; he keeps his eyes closed against the world.
>
> … Just after midnight Taylor's scores climb back up to 16,[2] he's not even a week old and he's hanging out for another hit of

methadone. He is jerky, tense, trembling in his sleep and sneezing — another sign of withdrawal. The nurses are tube-feeding him every three hours because he won't suckle. The decision is made to raise his morphine dose again ... The morphine is not holding the withdrawal symptoms in check; he shakes and jerks in his sleep. He trembles and sneezes while waking ... The screaming has now started, Taylor is letting the world know that he's here and he's doing it hard.

(Reprinted with permission from Julie-Anne Davies and *The Age*)

Taylor is one of a substantial population of babies exposed to illicit substances in utero and consequently their first weeks or months of life are spent painfully withdrawing from the drug in a special care nursery; subjected to traumatic, intrusive bodily experiences and medical interventions. The symptoms of neonatal abstinence syndrome (NAS) or withdrawal include irritability and poor feeding, experienced up to 6 months after birth. Opiate-exposed infants are difficult to engage and console and exhibit unpredictable behavioural responses, all of which can compromise the development of the maternal–infant relationship. For drug-exposed infants, difficulties may continue beyond the neonatal period in the form of inattentive, ill-attuned parenting and exposure to high-risk drug-using environments. These babies are therefore faced with a double jeopardy: being born physically compromised, irritable and possibly more demanding than other babies; in addition, their primary carer may be limited in her capacity to respond sensitively to their cues and communications, because of the pharmacological effect of the drug and underlying psychopathology.

For the purpose of this chapter the author has focused on the infants of opiate-addicted mothers, encompassing those who are using heroin and those who are methadone-maintained. This chapter begins with a review of the researched outcomes for children born opiate-addicted and raised by substance-affected parents. Psychoanalytic and developmental theory will be used to explore the infant's experience of opiate withdrawal as well as the potential for ongoing trauma within a relationship with a substance-affected parent and the ramifications for child development. Clinical case material will be used to illustrate an infant's experience, and possible interventions explored.

Prenatal Drug Exposure and Development

Recognition that the use of opiates during pregnancy has potentially harmful effects to the foetus extends back to antiquity; Hippocrates noted that 'uterine suffocation' occurred in conjunction with maternal opium use (Zagon & McLaughlin, 1984). More recently, arising from public concern about foetal alcohol syndrome in the 1970s and the 'crack baby epidemic' of the 1980s, a considerable body of research has been devoted to understanding the impact of prenatal drug exposure on the cognitive, social and emotional development of children (de Cubas & Field, 1993; Householder, Hatcher, Burns, & Chasnoff, 1982; Griffith, Azuma, & Chasnoff, 1994). For the most part, this research has explored the possible teratogenic (birth-defect forming) effects of prenatal exposure to drugs or alcohol with maternal and environmental variables being treated as confounding factors, rather than as a primary focus for investigation and understanding. Understanding the findings in research on infants/children exposed to drugs is complicated because of the need to disentangle the prenatal, perinatal, and environmental factors contributing to developmental outcomes.

Neonatal Withdrawal

It is known that opiates (heroin and methadone) in a pregnant woman's bloodstream pass through the placental barrier (Khoo, 2000). Evidence of intrauterine stress on the developing foetus is shown in reports of violent kicking of the foetus when the mother is denied narcotics (Householder et al., 1982). This kicking subsides when the mother is administered a dose of the narcotic, indicating the foetus may undergo periodic withdrawal in utero. Consequently, infants of women using opiates during pregnancy are born physiologically addicted to the drug, and after their supply is cut off at birth they are at high risk for NAS. Neonatal abstinence syndrome symptoms can include: restlessness, incessant shrill crying, inability to sleep, poor feeding, hyperactive reflexes, tremors and, in severe cases, generalised convulsions. Other symptoms include yawning, sneezing, fever, rapid respiration, stretching, sweating, nasal stuffiness and skin pallor. In some infants, constant squirming causes excoriation of the skin (Hans & Jeremy 2001; Pruitt, Jacobs, & Schydlower, 1990).

One wonders about the newborn's subjective experience of the seemingly painful withdrawal just described. The newborn's task in the first 3 months of life is achievement of psychophysiological homeostasis (Greenspan, 1990) — state control, habituation and establishment of sleep–wake cycles. The withdrawing infant is postulated to have difficulty with this task, being compromised in his ability to modulate his arousal in response to stimuli and transit smoothly between different states. It is hypothesised that even 'normal' experiences of bodily function and sensation can be experienced as startling, overwhelming or frightening to the newborn (Jordan, 2000). It is therefore assumed that the infant withdrawing from narcotics suffers more, and feels more impinged upon, and presumably more 'misunderstood'.

As well as the withdrawal symptoms being distressing for the infant, they complicate the task of the new mother in learning to recognise and interpret her infant's needs. In addition, the guilt, shame and blame a mother may feel at this time can be devastating for the beginning of this relationship, with mothers frequently feeling too distressed even to spend time with their withdrawing infants.

Play

Substance-exposed toddlers have been found to be more disturbed, disorganised and deficient in their play with toys. Research shows these toddlers demonstrating less representational play and that their play behaviours reveal disorganisation characterised by scattering, batting, picking up, and putting down toys — rather than sustained combining of toys, fantasy play, or curious exploration (Beckwith et al., 1994; Metosky & Vondra, 1995; Rodning, Beckwith, & Howards, 1989).

In addition to the possible teratological effects of substance exposure, the maternal environment, explored later in this chapter, may hold the key to some explanation of why substance-exposed toddlers might demonstrate problems in playing. Bowlby (1973) suggests that a lack of maternal 'emotional availability' and responsiveness can deny the child a sense of security, which can lead to inhibiting their exploration. Thus, healthy emotional development during which the infant uses the mother as a 'secure base' (Ainsworth, Blehar, Waters, & Wall, 1978; Marvin, Cooper, Hoffman, & Powell, 2002) or for 'checking back' (Mahler, Pine, & Bergman, 1975) may not occur. The degree of exploration of the infant of a drug-using mother and the engagement with the environment in play and with others may consequently be interfered with or interrupted.

Cognition and Motor Development

Bion (1962) posited a process by which mothers help their babies learn to think. He suggested that a mother, through her attention and support, is able to get in contact with her baby's state of mind, and enable the baby to 'think' and grow psychologically. He called this relationship *container–contained* whereby the mother's mind acts as a container for the baby. A mother's free-floating, calm and receptive state of mind is seen as a prerequisite for the mother to function as a good container that could take on the baby's feelings and give them meaning through her understanding. Through repeated experiences of having someone tuning into his experience, reflecting upon it and then responding, the baby gradually begins to identify with this function of his caregiver and begins to develop his own capacity to think and be able to reflect upon his own emotional experience.

In a review, de Cubas and Field (1993) summarise that children of methadone-dependent women 'frequently show a constellation of "soft" neurological signs typically associated with mild cerebral dysfunction and may be reflected in later attention deficit disorders or learning difficulties' (p. 266). Hans (1989) reported that methadone-exposed infants, who had shown delayed motor development at 4 months, continued to show motor deficits in subsequent years only if they were from families of high socioenvironmental risk, living in extremely impoverished circumstances. The author proposes that in utero methadone exposure may not cause a cognitive deficit, but may create a vulnerability in the children that then makes them more susceptible to impoverished environments.

Furthermore, Hans and Jeremy (2001) found that drug-exposed children showed significantly poorer cognitive and motor development during the first two years of life than a group of unexposed, high-risk socioenvironmentally comparable nondrug-exposed children. More significant was the steady drop in mental performance during the second year of life, providing further evidence of the importance of the environment on child development. The researchers hypothesise that much of the effect of maternal opiate use on mental development of their offspring is exacerbated with exposure to impoverished living conditions.

Affect Regulation

Affect regulation is considered to be the keystone of social–emotional development during infancy characterising early childhood behaviour. The strategies infants develop to regulate emotion during the first year of life are theorised to underlie their ability to develop secure attachment relationships and achievement of autonomy in the second and third years of life.

Characteristic patterns of regulating state and organising experience are believed to develop from repeated interactions between infant and caregiver around the achievement of physical and later, emotional homeostasis (Sroufe, 1995). The establishment of such patterns early in life is now known to affect the development of neuronal pathways in the brain, encouraging the elaboration of those circuits that are activated repeatedly in infancy (Schore, 1994). The behaviour of caregivers is clearly central to this process, as it is the caregiver who provides strategies for state regulation, which are subsequently internalised by the developing child (Sroufe, 1995; Stern, 1985). These strategies generalise over time to include the regulation of affective states, arousal, attention, and the organisation of complex behaviours that include social interaction.

Infants born addicted to opiates have been described as extremely reactive to sensory stimulation, easily agitated and behaviourally disorganised (Freier, Griffith, & Chasnoff, 1991). It is reported that these infants spend most of their time in extreme states of sleep or agitation and crying. Their state changes tend to be abrupt and inappropriate for the level of stimulation encountered. Research using the Neonatal Behaviour Assessment Scale[3] shows infants exposed to opiates in utero display higher levels of arousal, poorer quieting, poorer motor control, higher muscle tone and poorer alertness/orientation (Hans, 1992).

Attachment

Research of methadone-exposed children who remain in the care of their drug-using mothers has shown they demonstrate higher levels of disorganised attachment behaviour, lower levels of contact maintenance, and higher levels of avoidance (Goodman, Hans, & Cox,1999) and extremely high rates of insecure-disorganised or insecure–avoidant attachments (Rodning et al.,1989).[4]

The research on attachment behaviour in opiate-exposed offspring only addresses those whose mothers are maintained on regulated doses of methadone. It does not address the supposedly higher-risk group of children whose mothers have continued unregulated and unsupervised heroin use, for whom the outcomes may be even more concerning.

Along with the impact of maternal characteristics and quality of interaction, which will be explored next, it is important to consider whether the teratological effects of the drug might leave the heroin-exposed infants with fewer strategies for organising their attachment experiences during periods of separation-anxiety. Indeed, Main and Solomon (1990) pointed out that 'some behaviours considered as indexes of disorganisation and disorientation (e.g., stereotypies) are not uncommon among children suffering neurological abnormalities' (p. 123).

Maternal and Environmental Characteristics

It is through ongoing emotional availability that a mother communicates she is aware of the infant's presence, is monitoring ongoing activity and is able to respond appropriately and empathetically. A mother makes her availability known through touching or holding, looking, listening and speaking with a soothing, responsive voice. A mother's state of mind, which Winnicott (1956) called *primary maternal preoccupation*, was regarded by him as closely related to the state of the newborn and as providing what the newborn needs. When things go well, the states of mind that the baby seems to engender in the mother become a basis for intense identification with, and sympathy for, the baby. Bion's model of the container-contained described earlier is also relevant here. With an emotionally available mother, the infant will explore to a greater extent and be more playful. However, when the mother is not affectively available, when she is depressed or drug-affected, the infant may experience a violation of expectancies and the *nameless dread* that Bion (1962) talks about and trauma is likely to ensue.

Women who use illicit drugs, alcohol or other drugs may have difficulty being emotionally available and responding to the demands of their infants (Carr, 1975; Luthar & Walshe, 1995; Nardi, 1994). The primacy of satisfying the addiction over the welfare of themselves and their children, the impairment from chronic drug use, and the consequent unavailability of mothers on a 'high' or coming down from a high, suggest the addicted mother's ability to be psychologically responsive may be greatly impaired, despite their often best intentions to parent well.

Substance-using women are more likely than other women to have chaotic lifestyles that are organised around addiction and drug seeking, which may place them in dangerous situations (Finnegan, Oehlberg, Regan, & Rudrauff, 1981). Their drug seeking can take them out of the home, distract them away from childrearing concerns and expose their infants/children to undesirable people and circumstances. These events could be experienced by the infant as threatening and impinging.

These mothers experience higher levels of comorbid psychopathology and longstanding personality problems such as passivity, a sense of worthlessness, a basic lack of trust (Hans, 1999). Characteristics that are frequently seen in drug-using mothers include impulsiveness, a low threshold for frustration, difficulty making decisions, anger, hostility, resentment, blaming and withdrawal (Luthar & Walshe, 1995).

Mother–Infant Interaction

What happens then when mothers who may have great difficulty regulating their own behaviour are paired with irritable, poorly responsive, easily over-stimulated, difficult to read, and distressed drug-exposed infants?

The importance of the infant–mother interaction for early child development has long been highlighted. Winnicott (1967) proposed that the infant looking at the mother's face during nursing gives the infant early experiences of positive self-esteem, the face like a 'mirror' that the infant looks into to see and feel positive, good, nurturing feelings. In order to develop a mutually fulfilling mother–infant relationship, each partner must have a repertoire of adaptive behavioural responses appropriate to the stimulation and cues provided by the other. The original work of Stern (1985) illustrated the interaction between mother and infant involved both self-regulation and a sensitivity to the state of the other, which has come to be known as *attunement*.[5] The mother initially regulates the infant's arousal by being aware of and sensitive to the infant's capacity to receive and use stimulation. Maternal interventions are important, in both timing and quality, to the baby's state, mood, and current interests. In response to the infant's cues, the mother provides stimulation when the infant is underaroused and reduces it when the infant is overexcited. With development, the children increasingly take more control of pacing themselves, internalising the regulation process. The emotional availability of the mother, the correct perception and interpretation of the baby's signals, appropriate timing, and affective attunement are the maternal characteristics that are considered to facilitate the 'good enough' interaction (Stern, 1985). More recently, researchers discuss the importance of maternal reflectiveness (Grienenberger et al., 2005). It is precisely all these things that have been found to be compromised in drug-abusing women (Burns, Chethik, Burns, & Clark, 1997).

The work of Tronick and Cohn (1989) has demonstrated the contingencies between infant and mother are not perfect and breakdown in attunement is inevitable. They suggest it is the microrepair of misaligned interaction that is probably at the heart of establishment of a good-enough viable human relationship. The infant's stressful experiences with a caregiver who poorly repairs intense and long-lasting dysregulated states are incorporated into right-brain long-term autobiographical memory as a pathological internal object relation — an interactive representation of a 'dysregulated-self-in-interaction-with-a-misattuning-object' — and become encoded as relational trauma (Schore, 1997).

Clinical and systematic observations suggest that maternal drug use (including methadone) negatively affects the quality of the mother–child interaction. Studies have found that drug-addicted mothers tend to exhibit deficits in parenting, with abnormalities in the quality of the interaction with their babies. Opiate-addicted mothers have been assessed as less emotionally involved than nondrug using controls; they seem to enjoy mothering less and gaze less into the infants' eyes, and are less responsive with their infants (Bernstein & Hans, 1994; Bernstein, Jeremy, Hans, & Marcus,1984; Fitzgerald, Kalkenbach, & Finnegan, 1990; Hans, 1992; Johnson & Rosen, 1990).

There are no studies assessing the impact of pharmacological factors, either drug intoxication or withdrawal, on a drug-using mother's capacity. Mothers who continue to use heroin and are themselves subjected to the highs and lows of the drug, are also likely to subject their infants to this inconsistency and unpredictability as they provide a fluctuating environment dictated by the addiction, rather than the baby's biological rhythms. Mothers affected by a drug that alters perception may provide interaction that is ill-attuned, and mothers who are abstaining may be irritable or disengaged while they are pre-occupied with the physiological and psychological symptoms of withdrawal.

Heroin addiction raises the spectre of an unresponsive mother, not only because of the pharmacological effects of the drug use but also because of the co-morbid depression, found in a large proportion of mothers with drug problems (Jacobson & Jacobson, 2001). If the mother becomes involved with herself, and loses her keen sense of identification with her baby, she may be impaired in her capacity to respond in a lively way. It is therefore clear that maternal depression and drug use collectively could be devastating in their consequences. From the baby's perspective the mother is no longer a lively and resonating other, either giving nothing back or emanating a feeling of lifeless-ness, and the growth of the baby's emotional self may become stunted. There has been significant research on the effects of maternal depression on infant development (Murray, 1988), demonstrating significant impairment of emo-tional and cognitive indices.

The drug-exposed infant's behavioural characteristics may also exert a detrimental influence on maternal mood and behaviour. Murray, Stanley and Hooper (1996) found a significant relationship between the infant's behaviour (assessed by the Neonatal Behavioural Assessment Scale[6]) and the mother's *subsequent* mental state. In cases where the infant's motor control had been rated as poor, the risk of maternal depression was increased almost fivefold. Irritability was the other neonatal characteristic that was found to predict later maternal depression.

Case Example: Timmy

Aged 2 years and 4 months old, Timmy was referred to the infant team of a Child and Adolescent Mental Health Service (CAMHS) by his father, Doug, who had recently been released from prison after serving 20 months in jail for drug trafficking. Doug reunited with Timmy's mother, Ellen, but quickly became concerned about Timmy's erratic and 'out of control' behaviour, the aggressive nature of his play and his disconnectedness within relationships. Doug was concerned that Timmy was only saying a couple of words and wanted to know whether Timmy had ADHD (Attention Deficit Hyperactivity Disorder).

Both parents come from backgrounds of hardship, deprivation and abuse, where their own primary attachment relationships were compromised by death of parents, violence, alcoholism and chaotic home environments. Both parents reported a lack of opportunity for identification with positive parental figures. Timmy's father had several episodes of incarceration for drug-related crime, although professed to not use drugs. Thirty-year-old Ellen began misusing substances from the age of 13 years, and had maintained a heroin habit from the age of 19 years through to the present.

Timmy was exposed to heroin, methadone and cannabis throughout the pregnancy. Hence he was born opiate-addicted and suffered neonatal withdrawal, being treated with morphine for 3 weeks postbirth. Ellen reported Timmy's withdrawal was painful to watch, manifesting in irritable and tremulous behaviour. Timmy's mother described these early weeks as unbearable as she was stricken with guilt and shame every time she looked at Timmy. The developing mother–infant relationship was further taxed by maternal unavailability along with unstable living arrangements, as Ellen maintained her heroin addiction and associated lifestyle; Doug was incarcerated when Timmy was 6 months old. Doug reported Timmy was exposed to traumatic scenes of drug use and prostitution and left in the care of known drug users. Ellen's reporting of Timmy's history became vague from the time Doug was incarcerated and she confusingly described Timmy as a difficult baby who cried persistently; but later reported he was quiet and didn't demand much. She was unable to comment on his developmental milestones. Ellen became distressed throughout the telling of Timmy's history and said she didn't think she had spent enough time with Timmy. At the time of referral, Timmy's routine was erratic, his parents were unsure of his bedtime; he was not sleeping during the day; his diet consisted of formula milk, crackers and hot chips; and they reported uncertainty about what a 2½-year-old should be saying, playing or doing. Both parents reported a wish to better understand and connect with Timmy and learn alternative ways of parenting than those they were exposed to themselves. Timmy's father was considered to be a protective factor in this less than ideal family situation. They were regular and reliable attendees during the assessment phase.

Initially, developmental guidance was provided regarding the emotional and social needs of a toddler and some practical suggestions were made regarding communication, play, structure, bedtimes and diet. Ellen frequently brought up her feelings of guilt and sense of shame she felt about Timmy's difficulties and spoke honestly about feeling she had been neglectful in her relationship with Timmy. Early on in the engagement phase, Ellen decided to try to 'detox' from heroin and began drug rehabilitation, which included methadone maintenance.

A family support agency was engaged to continue the developmental guidance and practical in-home work, and parent–infant play-based therapy sessions began at CAMHS.

The therapist worked with Timmy's parents, helping them to think about what was driving his hyperactivity and aggression and to look out for the subtle opportunities to connect with him. Finding a way to respond appropriately and meaningfully to Timmy's communications, underneath his defensive chaos and shambolic activity, meant he could feel 'held' and understood, responded and attuned to.

The notion of having an 'alive', available and consistent other to interact with was discussed with the parents. Ellen was able to think about the times Timmy may have experienced her as unavailable and emotionally absent.

Therapists working with infants and parents in such a high risk group need to be able to tolerate doubts, hostility and unpredictability projected onto them by both infant and parent patients. It seemed the therapist's task to receive fragments of Timmy's experience and attempt to assist the parents to process them, as Timmy could not. The therapist used countertransferential responses to talk about the feelings evoked in Timmy's play and attempted to provide a narrative. With the continued experience of having the therapist use countertransference to name Timmy's feelings, Timmy became more in touch with his own emotional experience and needed less to dart away. This manifested in more sustained interaction between Timmy and his parents, with symbolic play sequences emerging.

Timmy is now less disorganised in his interactions and attachment behaviour. He has demonstrated more frequent referencing towards his parents in the sessions, seeking them out when hurt and requesting their involvement in his play. He has shown a vastly improved capacity to communicate, explore and learn, utilising his parents as a secure base. Timmy has begun to use parents' gaze, positioning and voice to help him modulate his own affect and arousal. He is beginning to string two and three words together in meaningful communication.

Despite the obvious improvements in Timmy's development and his relationships, the therapeutic work with this family is still in its infancy and is anticipated to continue for some time. Doug has begun individual psychotherapy and Ellen is considering the same.

Implications for Clinical Practice

The literature indicates that under normal conditions prenatally drug-exposed children develop poorly. However, clinical experience suggests that the presence of particular socioenvironmental conditions and psychotherapeutic interventions can improve recovery from the infant trauma of substance exposure and positively impact the relationship between infant and substance-using mother. Intervention needs to focus on the infant–mother/father interaction, on important risk factors in the parents (such as depressive symptoms, ongoing illegal drug use, parent competence) and the social context (support, social stress).

Early problem identification enables the therapist to take advantage of the plasticity and recovery capacity of the nervous system during the infancy period, as well as the special window of opportunity to engage the mother in drug withdrawal treatment following the delivery of a newborn baby. There are benefits in screening infants/toddlers/children of known drug users to detect difficulties in the mother–child dyad and the child's emotional development at the earliest possible time, and focusing efforts on preventative intervention targeted toward both internal and external factors for the infant, mother and the dyadic relationship. Developmental guidance and demonstration can be good first steps towards building a functional relationship between drug-using mothers and their infants, fostering the relationship and informing the mother about her infant's competencies and needs. Mothers could be encouraged to learn comforting, positioning, and handling techniques that will enhance interaction and provide some positive feedback regarding the infants' capabilities and limitations, particularly during the withdrawal phase. The mother can be guided to learn early signals of distress, which will alert her regarding overstimulation of her infant. Giving the mother confidence in her maternal role will improve interaction and enhance development. These forms of intervention could help address those factors that are most likely to impede the development of drug-exposed infants.

With many of the mothers of drug-exposed infants identified as having associated psychopathology, infant–parent psychotherapy could be especially beneficial. This form of therapy can address the interaction between mother and child, as well as attempt to understand their internal worlds, with the aim being to help align the mother's perceptions and behaviours more closely with the baby's developmental and individual needs. The infant–parent psychotherapist takes careful note of both partners' contributions to the relationship, and the meaning of each of these contributions for the other. The irritable withdrawing infant may hold particular meaning for the vulnerable drug-using mother. Does she interpret her infant's attempts to shut out external stimuli as a personal rejection of her? Does this perceived rejection serve to confirm her feelings of being a 'bad mother', thereby increasing feelings of depression, guilt, and worthlessness she may experience? Do some mothers blame the baby for rejecting them and set in motion a pattern of ambivalent and hostile feelings towards their infants? What do these feelings about the infant tell us about the mother's own traumatic past? Infant–parent psychotherapy may serve to raise awareness and understanding about how the mother's current and past experiences are shaping perceptions, feelings and behaviours towards the infant and correct or prevent the possible dyadic dysfunction.

Summary

Children exposed to drugs in utero enter the world in a highly distressed state for which even the most 'perfect' mothers would have trouble compensating. The reality is that many of their drug-using mothers bring to the dyad their own severe problems in terms of their mental health, self-regulation, struggles with communication and attunement, and a paucity of social and environmental support. When these insecure, impulsive, distracted mothers are paired with irritable, easily overloaded, unresponsive infants, it is probable that a number of pathological maternal–infant relationships develop. During the period of early infancy these children are subjected to significant physiological and environmental impingements, occurring prior to a time when the psyche-soma is sophisticated enough to deal with them, and consequently trauma can ensue. These infants represent a population at extremely high risk.

An appropriate response to these children often requires the close collaboration of a number of agencies that include health, maternity services, adults and children's social care, adult treatment, courts, prisons and probation services.

Infant and child mental health clinicians will need to provide therapeutic treatment to the increasing numbers of infants suffering from psychopathology and developmental disorders induced by, or exacerbated as a result of in utero substance exposure, and the trauma within relationship with a substance-affected mother. Infant–parent psychotherapy, developmental guidance and later psychoanalytic child psychotherapy are suggested as possible interventions to improve an infant's chances of returning to a more normal developmental pathway, avert a vicious cycle of further trauma and damage, and help these severely compromised infants to overcome their early adversity.

Author Note

The case study is based on actual events, with names changed and identifying information removed.

Endnotes

1. Methadone is a legal heroin substitute used in treating opiate dependence. It is usually administered orally once a day.
2. All babies who are known to have been exposed to narcotics while in the womb are evaluated for signs of withdrawal. The scoring system covers the 21 most common symptoms of withdrawal and measures not only the signs but also the severity of the addiction (Davies, 1999).
3. Developed by Dr T. Berry Brazelton in 1973. Designed to assess the behavioural and emotional characteristics and individuality of newborns. This scale gives a profile of an infant's behaviour in response to a range of stimulation, as well as recording reflexes.
4. The anxious–avoidant pattern of attachment is characterised by the child rarely crying on separation and avoiding the mother on reunion (Ainsworth et al., 1978). The disorganised/disoriented pattern is characterised by fear of the attachment figure, contradictory attachment behaviours, and facial expressions that indicate the infant is dazed and disoriented (Main & Solomon, 1986).

5. Attunement describes taking the perspective of the baby, interpreting the baby's affective states, responding to the baby's needs, respecting the baby's interests and modulating emotional response to be appropriate (Stern, 1985).

References

Ainsworth, M.D.S., Blehar, M.C., Waters, E., & Wall, S. (1978). *Patterns of attachment: A psychological study of the Strange Situation.* Hillsdale, NH: Erlbaum.

Beckwith, L., Rodning, C., Norris, D., Phillipsen, L., Khandabi, P., & Howard, J. (1994). Spontaneous play in two-year-olds born to substance-abusing mothers. *Infant Mental Health Journal, 15,* 189.

Bernstein, V., Jeremy, R.J., Hans, S.L., & Marcus, J. (1984). A longitudinal study of offspring born to methadone-maintained women. II. Dyadic interaction and infant behaviour at 4 months. *American Journal of Drug and Alcohol Abuse, 10,* 161–193.

Bernstein, V.J., & Hans, S.L. (1994). Predicting the developmental outcome of two-year-old children born exposed to methadone: Impact of social–environmental risk factors. *Journal of Clinical Child Psychology, 23,* 349–359.

Bion, W. (1962). A theory of thinking. In *Second thoughts.* London: Maresfield.

Bowlby, J. (1973). *Attachment and Loss. Vol 2: Separation.* New York: Basic Books.

Brazelton, T.B. (1978) The Brazelton Neonatal Behavior Assessment Scale: introduction. *Monographs of the Society for Research in Child Development, 43* (5–6),1–13.

Burns, K.A., Chethik, L., Burns, W.J., & Clark, R. (1997). The early relationship of drug abusing mothers and their infants: an assessment at eight to twelve months of age. *Journal of Clinical Psychology, 53,* 279–287.

Carr, S. (1975). Drug patterns among addicted mothers. *Paediatric Annual, 66,* 409–17

Davies, J.A. (1999, March 6). Mother and child. *The Age.*

de Cubas, M.M., & Field, T. (1993). Children of methadone-dependent women: developmental outcomes. *American Journal of Orthopsychiatry, 63*(2), 266–276.

Finnegan, L.P., Oehlberg, S.M., Regan, D.O., & Rudrauff, M.E. (1981). Evaluation of parenting, depression, and violence profiles in methadone maintained women. *Child Abuse and Neglect, 5,* 267–273.

Fitzgerald, E., Kalkenbach, K., & Finnegan, L. (1990). Patterns of interaction among drug dependent women and their infants. *Paediatric Research, 27,* 10A.

Freier, M.C., Griffith, D.R., & Chasnoff, I.J. (1991). In utero drug exposure: Developmental follow-up and maternal-infant interaction. *Seminars in Perinatology, 15,* 310–316.

Goodman, G., Hans, S.L., & Cox, S.M. (1999). Attachment behaviour and its antecedents in offspring born to methadone-maintained women. *Journal of Clinical Child Psychology, 28,* 58–69.

Greenspan, S. (1990). Comprehensive clinical approaches to infants and their families: Psychodynamic and developmental perspective. In S. Meisels & J. Shonkoff, (Eds.), *Handbook of early childhood intervention* (pp. 150–171). Cambridge: Cambridge University Press.

Grienenberger, J., Kelly, K., & Slade, A. (2005). Maternal reflective functioning, mother-infant affective communication, and infant attachment: Exploring the link between mental states and observed caregiving behaviour in the intergenerational transmission of attachment. *Attachment and Human Development, 7,* 299–311.

Griffith, D.R., Azuma, S.D., & Chasnoff, I.J. (1994). Three-year outcome of children exposed prenatally to drugs. *Journal of the American Academy of Child and Adolescent Psychiatry, 33,* 20–27.

Hans, S.L. (1989). Developmental consequences of prenatal exposure to methadone. *Annals of the New York Academy of Sciences, 562,* 195–207.

Hans, S.L. (1992). Maternal opioid drug use and child development. In I.S. Zagon & T.A. Sotkin (Eds.), *Maternal substance abuse and the developing nervous system* (pp. 177–213). New York: Academic.

Hans, S.L. (1999). Demographic and psychosocial characteristics of substance abusing pregnant women. *Clinical Perinatology, 26,* 55–74.

Hans, S.L., & Jeremy, R.J. (2001). Postneonatal mental and motor development of infants exposed in utero to opioid drugs. *Infant Mental Health Journal, 22,* 300–315.

Householder, J., Hatcher, R., Burns, W., & Chasnoff, I. (1982). Infants born to narcotic-addicted mothers. *Psychological Bulletin, 92,* 453–468.

Jacobson, S.W., & Jacobson, J.L. (2001). Alcohol and drug-related effects on development: A new emphasis on contextual factors. *Infant Mental Health Journal, 22,* 416–430.

Johnson, H.L., & Rosen, T.S. (1990). Difficult mothers of difficult babies: Mother–infant interactions in a multi-risk population. *American Journal of Ortho-Psychiatry, 60,* 281–288.

Jordan, B. (2000). *The treatment of persistent irritability in infants.* Unpublished doctoral dissertation, The University of Melbourne, Melbourne, Australia.

Khoo, K. (2000). Methadone mothers: Affects on the unborn. *Drugs in Society, December,* 8–12.

Luthar, S. S., & Walshe, K. G. (1995). Treatment needs of drug-addicted mothers. Integrated parenting psychotherapy interventions. *Journal of Substance Abuse and Treatment, 12,* 341–348.

Mahler, M., Pine, F., & Bergman, A. (1975). *The psychological birth of the human infant: Symbiosis and individuation.* New York: Basic Books.

Main, M., & Solomon, J. (1986) Discovery of an insecure disorganized/disoriented attachment pattern. In T. Brazelton & M. Yogman (Eds.), *Affective development in infancy* (pp. 95–124). Westport: Ablex Publishing.

Main, M., & Solomon, J. (1990) Procedures for identifying infants as disorganised/disoriented during the Ainsworth Strange Situation. In M.T. Greenberg, D. Cicchetti,

& E.M. Cummings (Eds), *Attachment in the pre-school years* (pp. 121–160). Chicago: University of Chicago Press.

Marvin, R., Cooper, G., Hoffman, K., & Powell, B. (2002) The Circle of Security Project: Attachment-based interventions with caregiver-preschool child dyads. *Attachment and Human Development, 4,* 107–124

Metosky, P., & Vondra, J. (1995). Prenatal drug exposure and play and coping in toddlers: A comparison study. *Infant Behaviour and Development, 18,* 15–25.

Murray, L. (1988). Effect of post-natal depression on infant development: Direct studies of early mother-infant interaction. In I. Brockington & R. Kumar (Ed.), *Motherhood and mental illness* (Vol. 2; pp. 159–185). Bristol, England: John Wright.

Murray, L., Stanley, C., & Hooper, R. (1996). The role of infant factors in postnatal depression and mother–infant interactions. *Developmental Medicine and Child Neurology, 38,* 109–119.

Nardi, D.A. (1994). Parent–infant interaction during perinatal addiction treatment. *Issues in Comprehensive Paediatric Nursing, 17,* 161–175.

Pruitt, A.W., Jacobs, E.A., & Schydlower, M. (1990). Neonatal behaviour after drug dependent pregnancy. *Paediatrics, 86,* 639–642.

Rodning, C., Beckwith, L., & Howards, J. (1989). Characteristics of attachment organisation and play in prenatally drug-exposed toddlers. *Development and Psychopathology, 1,* 277–289.

Schore, A.N. (1994). *Affect regulation and the origins of the self.* Hillsdale, NJ: Erlbaum.

Schore, A.N. (1997). Early organisation of the nonlinear right brain and development of a predisposition to psychiatric disorders. *Development and Psychopathology, 9,* 595–631.

Sroufe, L.A. (1995). *Emotional development: The organisation of emotional life in the early years.* Cambridge: Cambridge University Press.

Stern, D.N. (1985). *The interpersonal world of the infant.* New York: Basic Books.

Tronick, E.Z., & Cohn, J.F. (1989). Infant–mother face-to-face interaction: Age and gender differences in coordination and the occurrence of mis-coordination. *Child Development, 60,* 85–92.

Winnicott, D.W. (1956). Primary maternal preoccupation. In D.W. Winnicott (Ed.), *Through paediatrics to psychoanalysis.* London: Hogarth Press and the Institute of Psycho-Analysis.

Winnicott, D.W. (1967). Mirror-role of mother and family in child development. In P. Lomas (Ed.), *The predicament of the family* (pp. 26–33). London: Hogarth Press.

Zagon, I.S., & McLaughlin, P.L. (1984). An overview of neurobehavioral sequelae of perinatal opioid exposure. In J. Yanai (Ed.) *Neurobehavioral teratology.* (pp. 197–233). Amsterdam: Elsevier.

Trauma and Ghosts in the Nursery

Parenting and Borderline Personality Disorder

Louise Newman

———

How can a woman parent well when she herself has been abused at the hands of her parents or other adult caregivers in her own formative years? Parents with a diagnosis of severe personality disturbance have usually themselves experienced early attachment-related trauma and maltreatment. Indeed, borderline personality disorder (BPD) may best be thought of as a trauma-related syndrome where significant abuse, typically at the hands of attachment figures, has disrupted personality development and interpersonal functioning. Traumatised individuals frequently experience core difficulties in understanding and responding to socioemotional information and interpersonal interaction and this may have a significant impact on parenting capacity, and child development.

This chapter has four main objectives:

- provide a description of BPD in terms of its characteristics, prevalence and causal factors, particularly considering BPD in mothers

- review the importance of mother–infant relationships on child development and the impact of disturbed early interactions
- demonstrate how BPD impacts on mother–infant interactions and perceptions of parenting
- consider approaches to early intervention for mothers with BPD and their infants.

Borderline Personality Disorder

Characteristics

BPD is a maladaptive form of personality development characterised by affective instability, impulsivity, identity distortions and relationship dysfunction (American Psychiatric Association [APA], 2000). Individuals diagnosed with BPD experience rapid mood changes and difficulty maintaining a positive mood, and are extremely sensitive to feelings of rejection in close relationships. They often have unrealistic expectations of relationships and are anxious about being abandoned. In an attempt to manage these anxious feelings, these individuals commonly engage in impulsive and self-soothing behaviours such as substance abuse, self-mutilation, reckless driving, binge eating and sexual promiscuity. Typically, individuals with BPD become easily involved with other people and enter into intense relationships in which they oscillate between idealisation and devaluation of the other. Diagnosis of BPD according to the DSM-IV (APA, 2000) requires the presence of five out of nine specified criteria, thus resulting in variations in the symptom profile. However, features found to distinguish BPD from other types of personality disorders are patterns of self-harming behaviours and repeated suicidal behaviours, abandonment fears as well as fears of being too close in relationships, an intolerance of being alone and a pattern of intense, volatile relationships.

The typical symptoms associated with BPD are likely therefore to impact on a mother's ability to cope with the everyday stresses involved in caring for a young child. Mothers with BPD may have core difficulties in establishing a secure attachment with their infants and also find it difficult to 'read' or understand their infants' emotional communication. They are at high risk of recreating, in their relationship with their infants, similar disturbed patterns of interaction such as they experienced in their own early lives, although many struggle to create a positive relationship. Maladaptive relationship patterns are argued to reflect an insecure, disorganised attachment system that impacts on the individual's ability to form stable relationships. These patterns are likely to be repeated or reenacted in the relationship with the child with a trans-generational transmission of relationship dysfunction and psychopathology. Despite the well-known risk of repetition of child abuse, mothers diagnosed with BPD have received little attention within the literature to date and there has been limited focus on the types of interventions which may be helpful.

Prevalence

BPD is the most commonly diagnosed Axis II disorder in clinical settings, and its prevalence is estimated to be at around 4% in the general population (APA, 2000). BPD has been connected to interpersonal and occupational impairment, suicide risk and high rates of medical and psychiatric treatment. This is a disorder that places a significant burden on mental health resources within the community and has proven difficult to treat. BPD is diagnosed primarily in females (75%) and symptoms tend to peak in young adulthood, corresponding with the prime childbearing years of these women (Swartz, Blazer, George, & Winfield, 1990). Although it has been found that women with BPD are less likely to have children than most other women (Stone, 1990), many will certainly become parents and it is expected that their parenting abilities will be impaired by features of the disorder.

Causal Factors

Hoffman and McGlashan (2003) have proposed an integrated developmental model of BPD in which genetic, biological and environmental factors interact to influence maladaptive personality development. According to this model the characteristic features of BPD, such as relationship problems and identity distur-bances, reflect a disorganised attachment system. BPD is argued to result from neurodevelopmental and environmental vulnerabilities, such as abuse and neglect, impacting on the attachment system. In support of this theory, early trauma is recognised as having a neurobiological effect on brain development that contributes to ongoing affective instability, impulsivity and poor affect control (Cicchetti & Rogosch, 2001). Evidence for a genetic influence on the development of BPD has come from a twin study, which found a heritability of .69 for BPD (Torgersen, 2000). Furthermore, the relatives of individuals diag-nosed with BPD have been found to demonstrate high rates of BPD, as well as affective disorders, antisocial personality disorder and alcoholism (Links, Steiner, Offord, & Eppel, 1988). However, genetic factors alone do not result in BPD, and considerable evidence exists to implicate environmental factors, particularly early abuse and maltreatment in childhood, in the aetiology of the disorder. An over-whelming majority of female inpatients with BPD report having been emotion-ally, physically or sexually abused (91%) and/or neglected (92%) during their childhood (Zanarini et al., 1997). Women with BPD who report more severe childhood abuse tend to display more severe BPD symptoms as adults (Silk, Lee, Hill, & Lohr, 1995), suggesting an environmental impact on the developmental outcome of the disorder. Other studies indicate that the families (of origin) of women diagnosed with BPD are characterised by neglect and underinvolvement (Gunderson & Phillips, 1991), emotional withdrawal and inadequate nurturing (Zanarini, Gunderson, Marino, Schwartz, & Frankenburg, 1989), low parental care combined with parental overprotection (Zweig-Frank & Paris, 1991), as well as parental mental illness and prolonged separations from caretakers. Therefore, it appears that environmental factors such as parental abuse, lack of family cohesion and negative parenting behaviours may be significant factors influencing the development of BPD, regardless of genetic vulnerability. In terms of relationships, mothers diagnosed with BPD are likely to experience difficulties in developing an appropriate secure attachment with their own children due to their own negative childhood experiences and are at risk of repeating patterns of relating from their own childhoods.

The Importance of Mother–Infant Interactions

As an infant's first exposure to the world is with her/his primary carer, it is through her that (s)he learns whether other people can be depended on to provide care. Therefore the early mother–infant relationship is considered important for the development of socially and emotionally well-adjusted children. While characteristics of the infant may impact on the mother–infant relationship, evidence suggests that in clinical samples the mother has more influence on the quality of the relationship (van IJzendoorn, Goldberg, Kroonenburg, & Frenkel, 1992). An extensive longitudinal study conducted by the National Institute of Child Health and Human Development (NICHD) demonstrated that parenting quality is related to the cognitive, language and socioemotional development of young children throughout the preschool years (NICHD, 2003). Furthermore, mothers who are more involved with their children and engage in more sensitive play interactions have children who are more compliant and self-controlled, and who display fewer behaviour problems.

As individuals diagnosed with BPD have enduring problems with relationships, it seems inevitable that their ability to form functional relationships with their children will be impaired. Bowlby (1982) argued that a mother's ability as a caregiver is dependent on both her natural capacity to cope with the demands of childrearing and her own 'history of interpersonal relations within her family of origin' (p. 342). Mothers diagnosed with BPD certainly have a reduced coping capacity due to their mental health problems, added to which many of these women have family histories of dysfunctional interpersonal relationships. Therefore, according to Bowlby's assertion, mothers diagnosed with BPD are likely to have reduced parenting abilities, which will in turn impact on the mother–infant relationship and child development.

The Influence of Attachment Theory

One of the most influential theories into the importance of mother–infant relationships is attachment theory (Ainsworth, Blehar, Waters, & Wall, 1978; Bowlby, 1973). According to attachment theory an enduring bond develops between the infant and mother as a result of the early care-giving experience (Bowlby, 1982). The development of these attachment bonds depends on the extent to which the mother provides her infant with a secure and dependable base from which to explore the world, and the extent to which she encourages and supports such exploration. Children internalise aspects of the care-giving relationship and this inner representation, or working model, is influential on their developing concept of self, others and relationships (Bowlby, 1982). Attachment is viewed as a primary need of all children, with the mother–infant relationship argued to influence safety, development, adaptive functioning, stress, coping skills and wellbeing across the lifespan (Bowlby, 1982). Bowlby states that 'patterns of interaction are transmitted, more or less faithfully, from one generation to another' (Bowlby, 1973, p. 323), further arguing that mental wellbeing or ill health is inherited predominantly through the early family environment. Therefore, attachment theory provides a developmental explanation for psychopathology and its transmission across generations.

Ainsworth and colleagues (1978) recognised that the quality of maternal care varies considerably between individuals and that these variations result in the development of differentiated attachment patterns in children. As a consequence, Ainsworth et al. (1978) developed an empirical measure of child attachment security, known as the Strange Situation Procedure. This procedure was designed to distinguish between different attachment patterns — secure, resistant and avoidant — on the basis of how children interact with their caregivers. These three categories were later elaborated on by Main and Solomon (1990) and a disorganised attachment system was included. So, while the consistent physical presence of a mother figure is enough to create attachment bonds (Bowlby, 1982), maternal sensitivity determines the security of the infant attachment (Ainsworth et al., 1978). Sensitivity, as conceptualised by Ainsworth (Ainsworth et al., 1978), refers to a mother's alertness to her infant's signals, correct interpretation of these signals and her prompt and appropriate response. Appropriate timing of the sensitive response is crucial to allow the infant the opportunity to develop self-regulation of emotions and coping strategies, without allowing the infant to get too distressed (Thompson, Easterbrooks, & Padilla-Walker, 2003).

A mother's ability to provide sensitive care is influenced by many features of her life experience, such as amount and type of social stress, the mother's personality and her own childhood care-giving experiences (Fonagy, Steele, & Steele, 1991). Mothers with histories of early abuse will have specific difficulties in developing a representation, or model, of themselves as safe and caring parent and may have wishes and needs that they hope an infant will fulfil. For example, a mother who has been neglected and emotionally deprived may hope that her child will care for her and meet all her emotional needs. In high-risk parenting relationships the mother may be anxious that she will repeat dysfunctional patterns of relating with her child or she may even see negative characteristics that her own abusive parents attributed to her in her child. This is an example of the child being the object of projections from the past of the parent. Current understanding indicates that a diagnosis of BPD will impact on maternal sensitivity and mother–infant relationships, with the possibility of various patterns of relational disturbance ranging from parental anxiety and overprotection of the child, to parental hostility and rejection. The majority of parents with a history of abuse however, struggle not to repeat these patterns with their own child and often seek support and intervention.

Recent Influences on Understanding Mother–Infant Interactions

Since Ainsworth's initial conceptualisation, there has been a change in the operational definition of maternal sensitivity. According to Stern (1985) the ideal mother–infant interaction should resemble a 'dance' in which the dancers can fluidly follow each other's lead and interact in an effortless and enjoyable manner. It is conceivable that a mother may be behaviourally performing all the specific actions that demonstrate engagement, yet fails to show any emotional involvement when interacting with her child. Therefore, both theorists and researchers have begun to move the emphasis away from appropriate behavioural responses and towards emotional warmth and acceptance in mother–infant relationships.

Mahler, Pine and Bergman (1975) coined the term 'emotional availability' to describe the mother's ability to provide a secure base and an emotionally supportive presence for her infant. Emde and Easterbrooks (1985) later conceptualised emotional availability as how emotionally expressive and receptive a mother is to her infant. Mothers who are attuned to their infants' signals and needs, and who respond in a sensitive manner, encourage the development of affective expressivity and regulation in their infants (Emde, 1980). Furthermore, the emotional atmosphere within which infants' interactive encounters take place is believed to underlie the development of secure attachment relationships (Aviezer, Sagi, Joels, & Ziv, 1999).

An important recent advance in the area of emotional availability is the development of psychometrically supported measures of parenting ability, one of which is the Emotional Availability Scale (EAS; Biringen, Robinson, & Emde, 2000).

An important feature of the EAS is that emotional availability is no longer viewed as an intrinsic quality of the mother, but as a relational construct incorporating features of both mother and infant interactive behaviour: '[E]motional availability is a complex, dynamic characterization, in which the behaviour of one partner becomes interdependent with that of the other' (Biringen & Robinson, 1991, p. 264). In an emotionally available relationship the mother displays sensitivity and age-appropriate responsiveness, as well as a supportive and nonintrusive presence (Kogan & Carter, 1996). Therefore, maternal sensitivity is one specific aspect of an emotionally available relationship. Studies using the EAS have found emotional availability, more specifically maternal sensitivity and structuring, to be related to infant attachment security (Aviezer et al., 1999; Ziv, Aviezer, Gini, Sagi, & Karie, 2000). Therefore, the early emotional atmosphere of mother–infant interactions appears to be an important aspect of the dyadic relationship and of secure attachment relationships.

An important study conducted by van den Boom (1994) experimentally manipulated maternal sensitivity by 'improving the mother's ability to monitor infant signals attentively, perceive infant signals accurately and respond appropriately and contingently' (p. 1458) over a 3-month period. This study was conducted with 100 mother–infant dyads from lower socioeconomic status families with normal but irritable 6-month-old infants. Postintervention observations, conducted when the infants were 9 months old, found that mothers in the intervention group were rated higher in sensitivity and that their infants were more sociable, more able to soothe themselves and demonstrated more cognitively sophisticated exploratory behaviour as compared to the control group. Furthermore, when attachment security was assessed at 12 months, more of the intervention group infants were found to be securely attached than the control group infants. This study provides convincing evidence for a causal, not just correlational, role of maternal sensitivity on infant emotional regulation, behaviour and attachment security. Another relevant study found the socioemotional and cognitive development of adopted children, not biologically related to their adoptive parents, to be predicted by early mother–infant interactions with their adoptive mothers (Stams, Juffer, & van Ijzendoorn, 2002). This provides further evidence for environmental influences on children's development, independent of genetic relationships. These two studies support the argument that maternal sensitivity has a predictive role in the later social and emotional functioning of infants. It appears that assessing emotional availability in mothers of young infants will provide useful information about the quality of the mother–infant relationship independent of measures of attachment.

Self-Perceptions of Parenting Competence and Stress

It is not just observable behaviour that provides insight into the complexities of mother–infant relationships. Information can also be gained by assessing cognitive representations of the self as a parent through self-report measures. Such self-report questionnaires aim to establish how mothers perceive themselves as parents. Recent theoretical and empirical work has recognised the need to expand on descriptions of mother–infant interactions and to address the issue of what role maternal cognitions play in the development and maintenance of mother–infant relationships (Bugental & Johnston, 2000).

Research into parental cognitions has been influenced by both social learning theory (Bandura, 1989) and attachment theory (Bowlby, 1982). Bowlby's notion of working models emphasises how cognitive representations developed during the early mother–infant relationship can influence future self-esteem and social functioning. Bandura, by contrast, argues that an individual's perception of how competent she is impacts on the amount of sustained effort she is willing to invest in a role. This suggests that perceptions of parenting abilities influence an individual's sense of self as well as their actual parenting skills, thereby impacting on child development (Goodnow & Collins, 1990).

Self-Efficacy

Bandura defines self-efficacy as a belief in a person's ability to successfully perform a particular behaviour. People who lack confidence in their own abilities tend to give up easily due to expectations of failure and to quickly lose faith in themselves when failure does ensue (Bandura, 1989). As applied to parenting, self-efficacy refers to an individual's concept of how capable (Coleman & Karraker, 1997), competent and effective she is as a parent. This suggests that mothers who feel more competent as parents are likely to experience greater satisfaction and to persevere, despite the inevitable setbacks involved in child-rearing. It is argued that more negative parental self-efficacy beliefs impact on the quality of the mother–infant relationship by reducing parental enjoyment, detrimentally influencing dyadic interactions and thereby increasing the likelihood of insecure attachments in children (Coleman & Karraker, 1997; Teti & Gelfand, 1991). Recent empirical research with self-efficacy indicates that the construct may prove useful in enhancing understanding of the subjective satisfaction involved in parenting, as well as overt parenting behaviour (Coleman & Karraker, 1997). The review of self-efficacy by Johnston and Mash (1989) found negative correlations with maternal depression, maternal stress levels and behaviour problems in children.

Furthermore, self-efficacy has been positively associated with parenting behaviour in both natural (Teti & Gelfand, 1991) and laboratory-based environments (Donovan & Leavitt, 1989). Teti and Gelfand (1991) found that maternal self-efficacy beliefs were significantly related to maternal behavioural competence, and that self-efficacy explained the relationship between several predictor variables such as infant temperament, socioeconomic status, depression and parenting quality. Furthermore, Cutrona and Troutman (1986) demonstrated that self-efficacy in new mothers mediated the effects of infant temperament and social support on postpartum depression, thus providing evidence that other variables impair parental functioning only through their influence on perceptions of self-efficacy. These findings suggest that it is parental self-efficacy that needs to be targeted in intervention programs, as an increased sense of competency may negate the impact of nonmanipulable variables, such as poverty. As mothering a young infant is a very demanding role requiring high levels of effort and commitment, a tendency to lose faith in oneself and give up easily is likely to impair the adequate functioning of the mother–infant relationship and impact on child outcomes (Coleman & Karraker, 1997). Self-efficacy beliefs in mothers diagnosed with BPD may be influenced by characteristics of the disorder itself such as mood reactivity, therefore this construct may prove useful in assessing parenting cognitions in this population.

Parenting Stress

Stress experienced in the parenting role is believed to have an adverse affect on mother–infant relationships by impairing the mother's capacity to parent optimally. Several authors argue that stress is related to adverse outcomes for parents, children and families. Abidin (1992) argues that higher levels of parental stress result in a negative authoritarian style of parenting which, in turn, has a detrimental impact on the child's behaviour. Stress affects parents' ability to tolerate and manage children's dependency needs and may also impair parents' ability to accurately interpret their children's needs. It has even been suggested that the psychological and emotional separation resulting from parenting stress may be more detrimental on parent–child relationships than actual physical separation. Empirical research has supported these claims, finding associations between parenting stress and both parent and child behaviour (Abidin, 1992; Vondra & Belsky, 1993), particularly in terms of insecure attachment relationship, child abuse and harsh, authoritarian parenting (Emery & Tuer, 1993).

Therefore from an attachment theory perspective, stressed parents are unable to develop emotionally available relationships with their infants, which then results in insecure attachments and a variety of negative outcomes. Mothers diagnosed with BPD are likely to experience high levels of stress as they attempt to raise a child while simultaneously coping with their own psychopathology.

Summary

This review has demonstrated that maternal emotional availability, self-perceptions of parenting competence and parenting stress are all highly influential on the quality of mother–infant relationships. It has further demonstrated that women diagnosed with BPD are likely to have a reduced capacity to provide optimal care for their infants, due to their impaired mental health. As dysfunctional mother–infant relationships are recognised as impacting on the later social and emotional development of the child, it is important to understand how mothers diagnosed with BPD interact with their children, especially during the critical early years of the developing mother–infant attachment relationship.

How BPD Impacts on Mother–Infant Interactions and Perceptions of Parenting

Impact on Mother–Infant Interactions

The ability of mothers diagnosed with BPD to relate to their children is likely to be affected by specific features of the disorder such as mood instability, impulsivity and difficulty controlling anger. They will have particular difficulty in developing a self-concept as a parent, and sense of their own capacity to nurture and protect a child. In addition, borderline parents will have ongoing anxiety in all relationships resulting in a fear of involvement with others and an intense neediness from all interpersonal relationships (Hoffman & McGlashan, 2003). Overall, women with BPD are likely to find childrearing challenging, and may not be capable of understanding and responding appropriately to their infant's emotional needs. Furthermore, as the majority of these women have experienced backgrounds of abuse and neglect, they are unlikely to have been exposed to appropriate role models on which to base their own interactive behaviour. These factors increase the likelihood of continuing the cycle of abuse with their own children. Mothers with a history of abuse may be painfully aware of their limitations and well motivated to change, but may have significant limitations in parenting skills and in empathic understanding of their infants' needs. They are often overwhelmed by the emotional demands of parenting and have difficulty managing the dependency of a young child. Studies conducted into the families (of procreation) of mothers diagnosed with BPD have found them to be unstable and low on cohesion, with children exposed to high levels of parental substance abuse and suicide attempts (Weiss et al., 1996). Research also indicates that up to 40% of children with mothers diagnosed with BPD are living apart from their mothers (Feldman et al., 1995), probably as a result of maternal mental health issues impacting on the mother's ability to adequately support and raise a child. This suggests that the family environments of children with mothers diagnosed with BPD are very unstable. Consequently, it is not surprising to find that the children of mothers diagnosed with BPD are at risk of developing childhood BPD, attention deficit hyperactivity disorder and other disruptive behaviour disorders (Weiss et al., 1996).

In conclusion, preliminary evidence certainly suggests that mothers suffering from BPD fail to provide their children with the stable nurturing environments necessary for normal child development. Given the potential impact of inadequate mother–infant interactions on the social and emotional development of the children, it is essential for more research to be conducted into the parenting experience of mothers diagnosed with BPD.

Two studies have examined the mother–infant interactions of mothers diagnosed with BPD and compared them to mothers with no psychiatric disorder. Eight mothers were video recorded interacting with their two-month-old infants using the 'still face' procedure (Crandell, Patrick, & Hobson, 2003). The still face procedure involves the mother maintaining a still, neutral facial expression and refraining from interacting with her child for a specified period of time. Following this, the mother then re-engages with the infant and returns to natural interactions. Results of this study indicate that mothers with BPD interact with their children in an intrusively insensitive manner and that their infants respond with dazed facial expressions. Therefore, the study by Crandell et al. (2003) provides preliminary evidence for dysfunctional mother–infant interactions from a very early age. However, the still face procedure requires the mother to perform atypical blank facial expressions and consequently the results may not be representative of the true mother–infant interaction. Furthermore, the infants who participated in the study were very young (two months old) and the number of mother–infant dyads was small ($N = 8$) as there were difficulties in recruiting mothers diagnosed with BPD.

A more recent study (Newman, Stevenson, Bergman, & Boyce, 2007) systematically examined mother–infant interactions and perceptions of parenting ability in mothers diagnosed with BPD. It was hypothesised that, when compared to mothers from the community, mothers diagnosed with BPD would (1) be observed to be less emotionally available in their mother–infant interactions, (2) report a lower sense of parenting competence, in terms of satisfaction, efficacy and parenting self-esteem, and (3) experience higher levels of parenting stress. All hypotheses were supported except for parenting perceptions of efficacy, on which no significant differences were found between mothers diagnosed with BPD and community mothers. A secondary hypothesis was that a relationship would be found between observed mother–infant interactions and parenting perceptions of competence within the group of community mothers. Results did not support this hypothesis. However, a significant negative relationship was found between self-perceptions of parenting stress and parenting competence within the community group. Overall, this suggests that mothers diagnosed with BPD are less emotionally available, less satisfied, lower on parenting self-esteem and more stressed than mothers from the general community. Furthermore, the more stressed a mother perceives herself to be, the less satisfied and competent she feels as parent. Despite the small sample size of mothers diagnosed with BPD ($N = 6$) this study provides overwhelming evidence of maladaptive parenting within this group.

Mothers diagnosed with BPD were considerably less sensitive, less capable at structuring play and more hostile in their mother–infant interactions than mothers from the community group. Furthermore, the children of mothers diagnosed with BPD were less responsive and less involved with their mothers than community children indicating that the mother–infant interactions of mothers diagnosed with BPD are highly dysfunctional. These findings are consistent with the findings of Crandell and colleagues (2003) described above.

Working With Mothers With BPD and Their Infants

Overall, recent research has provided considerable evidence for maladaptive mother–infant interactions and parenting cognitions in mothers diagnosed with BPD. The consequences of this are considerable in terms of the developmental outcomes of their children. According to the integrated developmental model proposed by Hoffman and McGlashan (2003), psychopathology results from the interaction of genetic, biological and environmental influences. The children of mothers diagnosed with BPD are certainly likely to have a genetic predisposition towards personality disturbances, and the results of this study indicate that these children are exposed to potentially pathological environmental influences in the form of dysfunctional mother–infant interactions. Therefore, these children are at high risk of developing social and emotional problems of their own. Research supports these conclusions with evidence indicating that children of mothers with BPD have a higher prevalence of childhood BPD, ADHD and disruptive behaviour disorders (Feldman et al., 1995). Furthermore, it is recognised that a lack of emotional availability in mother–infant relationships has a deleterious impact on several developmental processes including the development of secure attachment and later parenting capacity, resulting in a risk of replicating abuse with their own children. The transmission of emotional disturbance and parenting difficulties are significant public health problems and a major challenge for health and welfare services (see Chapter 4 and Chapter 5).

There are significant implications for service provision and models of intervention, suggesting that an early intervention approach to this group should focus on improving emotional interaction and quality of the child's attachment experience. Specifically, research attention should be given to the modification of parenting programs and infant–parent psychotherapy approaches for high-risk parents who may be less easily engaged and less responsive to traditional approaches. A parent's history of unresolved trauma may need to be a focus of intervention where that is intruding into the relationship with the child and there is a risk of ongoing relationship disturbance. Effective interventions help the traumatised parent understand the ways in which their own early experience impacts on their feelings about, and interactions with, their infant. Supporting the parent to see the infant as a separate individual with his own developmental agenda and emotional needs involves making connections between the past and the present, and reflecting on the way in which trauma intrudes in the parenting role (Newman & Stevenson, 2005).

Working with traumatised parents requires a focus on the parents' needs for support and consistency as well as attention to the infant. Dyadic approaches need to consider the high anxiety a parent may feel in the presence of her child and her underlying fear that she may harm the child. For some parents there is a risk that they may become envious of the attention paid to the children unless their own needs are addressed. Clinicians also need to be aware of child protection issues and the degree of risk to which the child is exposed. Effective engagement with parents with personality disorder requires a clear discussion of the child protection framework and the role of clinicians as reporters of concerns.

A central clinical dilemma is the question of the time period available for interventions in situations where an infant may be experiencing trauma and is thought to be at developmental risk. Some features of personality disorder are unlikely to change in a brief intervention and some parents require individual and longer-term therapies. For the infant, a period of several months is highly significant in terms of development and potential negative impacts of disturbed and confusing parenting (see Chapter 4). These are common clinical concerns and require close monitoring. There are clear benefits, however, of working dyadically and focusing at the level of the relationship. First, the infant will have new experiences of his carer as responsive and available. Second, the parent may have some positive experience of being competent and of her infant responding to her with joy and interest. Third, positive change may occur rapidly in terms of the infant's experience of being contained and regulated. It remains a question for future research as to the possible benefits of using both individual and dyadic therapies for high-risk parenting situations.

References

Abidin, R.R. (1992). The determinants of parenting behavior. *Journal of Clinical Child Psychology, 21*, 407–412.

Ainsworth, M.D.S., Blehar, M.C., Waters, E., & Wall, S. (1978). *Patterns of attachment: A psychological study of the Strange Situation.* Hillsdale: NJ, Erlbaum.

American Psychiatric Association. (2000). *Diagnostic and Statistical Manual of Mental Disorders* (4th ed.). Arlington, VA: American Psychiatric Association.

Aviezer, O., Sagi, A., Joels, T., & Ziv, Y. (1999). Emotional availability and attachment representations in kibbutz infants and their mothers. *Developmental Psychology, 35*, 811–821.

Bandura, A. (1989). Regulation of cognitive processes through perceived self-efficacy. *Developmental Psychology, 25*, 729–735.

Biringen, Z., & Robinson, J. (1991). Emotional availability in mother-child interactions: A reconceptualization for research. *American Journal of Orthopsychiatry, 61*, 258–271.

Biringen, Z., Robinson, J.L., & Emde, R.N. (2000). Appendix B: The emotional availability scales: an abridged infancy/early childhood version (3rd ed.). *Attachment and Human Development, 2*, 256–270.

Bowlby, J. (1973). *Attachment and Loss: Vol 2. Separation.* New York: Basic Books.

Bowlby, J. (1982). *Attachment and loss: Vol 1. Attachment* (2nd ed.). New York: Basic Books.

Bugental, D., & Johnston, C. (2000). Parental and child cognitions in the context of the family. *Annual Review of Psychology, 51*, 315–341.

Cicchetti, D., & Rogosch, F.A. (2001). Diverse patterns of neuroendocrine activity in maltreated children. *Developmental Psychopathology, 13*, 677–693.

Coleman, P.K., & Karraker, K.H. (1997). Self-efficacy and parenting quality: Findings and future applications. *Developmental Review, 18*, 47–85.

Crandell, L.E., Patrick, M.P.H., & Hobson, R.P. (2003). Still-face interactions between mothers with borderline personality disorder and their 2-month-old infants. *British Journal of Psychiatry, 183*, 239–247.

Cutrona, C.E., & Troutman, B.R. (1986). Social support, infant temperament, and parenting self-efficacy: A mediational model of postpartum depression. *Child Development, 57*, 1507–1518.

Donovan, W.L., & Leavitt, L.A. (1989). Maternal self-efficacy and infant attachment: Integrating physiology, perceptions, and behavior. *Child Development, 60*, 460–472.

Emde, R.N. (1980). Emotional availability: A reciprocal reward system for infants and parents with implications for the prevention of psychosocial disorders. In P.M. Taylor (Ed.), *Parent–infant relationships* (pp. 87–115). New York: Pergamon Press.

Emde, R.N., & Easterbrooks, M.A. (1985). Assessing emotional availability in early development. In W.K. Frankenburg, R.N. Emde, & J. Sullivan (Eds.), *Early identification of children at risk: An international perspective* (pp. 79–101). New York: Plenum.

Emery, R.E., & Tuer, M. (1993). Parenting and the marital relationship. In T. Luster & L. Okagaki (Eds.), *Parenting: An ecological perspective* (pp. 121–148). Hillsdale NJ: Erlbaum.

Feldman, R.B., Zelkowitz, P., Weiss, M., Vogel, J., Heyman, M., & Paris, J. (1995). A comparison of the families of mothers with borderline personality disorder and nonborderline personality disorder. *Comprehensive Psychiatry, 36*, 157–163.

Fonagy, P., Steele, H., & Steele, M. (1991). Maternal representations of attachment during pregnancy predict the organization of infant–mother attachment at one year of age. *Child Development, 62*, 891–905.

Goodnow, J.J., & Collins, W.A. (1990). *Development according to parents: The nature, sources and consequences of parent's ideas.* North Ryde, New South Wales: Macquarie University.

Gunderson, J.G., & Phillips, K.A. (1991). A current view on the interface between borderline personality disorder and depression. *American Journal of Psychiatry, 148*, 967–975.

Hoffman, P., & McGlashan, T. (2003). *A developmental model of Borderline Personality Disorder.* Washington DC: American Psychiatric Publishing.

Johnston, C., & Mash, E.J. (1989). A measure of parenting satisfaction and efficacy. *Journal of Clinical Child Psychology, 18*, 167–175.

Kogan, N., & Carter, A.S. (1996) Mother-infant re-engagement following the still-face: The role of maternal emotional availability in infant affect regulation. *Infant Behavior and Development, 19*(3), 359–370.

Links, P.S., Steiner, B., Offord, D.R., & Eppel, A. (1988). Characteristics of borderline personality disorder: A Canadian study. *Canadian Journal of Psychiatry, 33*, 336–340.

Mahler, M.S., Pine, F., & Bergman, A. (1975). *The psychological birth of the human infant: Symbiosis and individuation.* New York: Basic Books.

Main, M., & Solomon, (1990). Procedures for identifying infants as disorganized/disoriented during the Ainsworth Strange Situation. In M.T. Greenberg, D. Cicchetti, & E. M. Cummings (Eds.), *Attachment in the pre-school years* (pp. 121–160). Chicago: University Press of Chicago.

NICHD (National Institute for Child Health and Human Development), 2003. Does quality of childcare affect child outcomes at 4½ years. *Developmental Psychology, 39*, 457–469.

Newman, L.K., Stevenson, C.S., Bergman, L.R., Boyce, P. (2007). Borderline personality disorder, mother–infant interactions and parenting perceptions. *Australian and New Zealand Journal of Psychiatry, 41*, 598–605.

Newman L.K., & Stevenson, C.S. (2005). Ghosts in the nursery: Parenting and borderline personality disorder. *Clinical Child Psychiatry and Psychology, 10*, 385–394.

Silk, K.R., Lee, S., Hill, E.M., & Lohr, N.E. (1995). Borderline personality disorder and severity of sexual abuse. *American Journal of Psychiatry, 152*, 1059–1065.

Stams, G.J.M., Juffer, F., & van IJzendoorn, M.H. (2002). Maternal sensitivity, infant attachment, and temperament in early childhood predict adjustment in middle childhood: The case of adopted children and their biologically unrelated parents. *Developmental Psychology, 38,* 806–821.

Stern, A.N. (1985). *The interpersonal world of the infant.* New York: Basic Books.

Stone, M.H. (1990). *The fate of borderline patients.* New York: Guilford.

Swartz, M., Blazer, D., George, L., & Winfield, I (1990). Estimating the prevalence of borderline personality disorder in the community. *Journal of Personality Disorders, 4,* 257–272.

Teti, A., & Gelfand, D. (1991). Behavioral competence among mothers of infants in the first year: The meditational role of maternal self-efficacy. *Child Development, 62,* 918–929.

Thompson, R.A., Easterbrooks, M.A., & Padilla-Walker, L.M. (2003). Socio-emotional development in infancy. In R. M. Learner, & M.A. Easterbrooks (Eds.), *Handbook of psychology: Developmental psychology, Vol 4.* (pp. 91–112). New York: John Wiley and Sons.

Torgersen, S. (2000). Genetics of patients with borderline personality disorder. *Psychiatric Clinics of North America, 23,* 1–9.

Van den Boom, D.C. (1994). The influence of temperament and mothering on attachment and exploration: An experimental manipulation of sensitive responsiveness among lower-class mothers of irritable infants. *Child Development, 65,* 1457–1477.

van IJzendoorn, M.H., Goldberg, S., Kroonenberg, P.M., & Frenkel, O.J. (1992). The relative effects of maternal and child problems on the quality of attachment: A meta-analysis of attachment in clinical samples. *Child Development, 63,* 840–858.

Vondra, J., & Belsky, J. (1993). Developmental origins of parenting: Personality and relationship factors. In T. Luster & L. Okagaki (Eds.), *Parenting: An ecological perspective* (pp. 1–34). Hillsdale, NJ: Erlbaum.

Weiss, M., Zelkowitz, P., Feldman, R., Vogel, J., Heyman, M., & Paris, J. (1996). Psychopathology in offspring of mothers with borderline personality disorder: A pilot study. *Canadian Journal of Psychiatry, 41,* 285–290.

Zanarini, M.C., Gunderson, J.G., Marino, M.F., Schwartz, E.O., & Frankenburg, F.R. (1989). Childhood experiences of borderline patients. *Comprehensive Psychiatry, 30,* 18–25.

Zanarini, M.C., Williams, A.A., Lewis, R.E., Reich, R., Vera, S., Marino, M., et al. (1997). Reported pathological childhood experiences associated with the development of borderline personality disorder. *American Journal of Psychiatry, 154,* 1101–1106.

Ziv, Y., Aviezer, O., Gini, M., Sagi, A., & Karie, N.K. (2000). Emotional availability in the mother–infant dyad as related to the quality of infant–mother attachment relationship. *Attachment and Human Development, 2,* 149–169.

Zweig-Frank, H., & Paris, J. (1991). Recollections of emotional neglect and overprotection in borderline patients. *American Journal of Psychiatry, 148,* 648–651.

Working With Infants and Their Families in Particular Settings

Sick Babies and Troubled Parents

Therapeutic Work With Parents and Infants in a Paediatric Hospital Setting: The Baby is The Subject

Campbell Paul

—◦—

Becoming a parent is to be met with some of life's most profound responsibilities. Not surprisingly, therefore, when parents already have emotional problems and their infant appears physically sick, or parent–infant issues exist, there are likely to be significant interactions with a paediatric hospital. These issues are the subject matter of this chapter.

The baby in her family is an essential and integral part of a dynamic and constantly changing system of human beings. The parent does not exist without the baby and the baby cannot exist without a mother and father (Winnicott, 1973). The baby and his mother and father form the core of an expanding and complex human system. Bound together like this, emotional experiences and physical illnesses for any one of this triad will have implications for the emotional life of each of the others.

The individual's world of emotional meaning or *internal representations* is communicated necessarily through behaviour. Daniel Stern (1995) in *The*

Motherhood Constellation has developed a systems model which posits that *maternal representation* drive *maternal actions* which impinge upon the *baby's actions* and then influence the *baby's internal representations*. This is a reciprocal equation: it is equally important to understand how the baby's internal representations influence her behaviour, and, through this, her parent's behaviour, and then the parent's own internal representations or mental state.

When a baby is sick or troubled, his parents are worried and often take the baby to hospital. The hospital is usually seen as a place of safety and relief, and parents may not always differentiate between physical and emotional difficulties, so there are many infant presenting symptoms. Similarly, the range of emotional problems with which a baby's parents can present in the paediatric hospital context is very wide. We see:

- parents whose severe pre-existing mental health disorders further decompensate in the face of their child's illness
- babies who present with physical symptoms which constitute the harbinger for their parent's unrecognised inner conflicts.

Previously healthy parents of a sick child may seem pushed to the precipice of psychological disintegration, and yet we also see very vulnerable parents whose strong identification with, and commitment to their infant means that they can become *extra-ordinarily devoted parents* as they meet the emotional needs of their sick child.

I believe it is essential to keep the baby's mind at the forefront of our thinking as we work with troubled parents and their sick infants.

The experience of *premature infants and their families* in the neonatal intensive care unit may be especially stressful and traumatising, and has been the subject of a number of studies (Affleck, Tennan, & Rowe, 1991; Browne, 2003; Furman & O'Riordan, 2006; Keren, Feldman, & Tyano, 2003; Minde, 2000; Tracey, 2000). Living through this extremely traumatic and crisis-ridden period, families may have to confront additional problems, which will not be explored further in this chapter.

The Context of Mental Health Work with Hospitalised Infants and Parents

The Royal Children's Hospital in Melbourne, Victoria, has an established infant mental health service, Royal Children's Hospital Infant Mental Health Group (RCHIMHG), which is embedded in the broader paediatric hospital and a community-based child and adolescent Mental Health Service.

As an interdepartmental and cross-disciplinary service, the RCHIMHG provides primary and secondary consultations for infants and families referred by the broader paediatric hospital staff. Some infants and parents are specifically referred to the infant mental health service and others to infant mental health specialists within the collaborating departments of Social Work, Nursing, Speech Pathology and Paediatrics. In 2006, 80 infants were referred to RCHIMHG and another 38 referred to Speech Pathology and Social Work (Scheffer & Paul, 2007). The maternal and child health nurse in the group assessed a similar number of infants and families.

There have been few published descriptions of infant mental health services in a children's hospital (Kaukonen & Tamminen, 1998), with most reports of infant mental health programs describing community-based clinics (Frankel, Boyum, & Harmon, 2004; Keren, Feldman, & Tyano, 2003; Lieberman, van Horn, Grandison, & Pekarsky, 1997). The types of problems referred to hospital-based infant mental health program are very varied and, as an audit showed, differ from the community-based clinics in that the infants tend to be of younger age (average age at referral 6.7 months) and have more medically-based presenting problems. Seventy-five per cent of the cohort were inpatients at the time of referral, with the reasons for referral shown in Table 1.

The preponderance of emotional or relationship-based difficulties is striking, but there was, nevertheless, a wide range of problems. For some it was primarily a disturbed parent whose distress may have led to sleep difficulties for the baby, whereas for some other infants the medical problem may have led to death. Our role was to support the infant, his parents and the staff during this painful process. Children's hospitals are generally seen as places for cure, but inevitably there are those children whose illness or disability is so severe that they do not survive. Six of the 80 infants seen by our service in 2006 died. The complex needs of modern medicine require parents at times to make many urgent decisions and deal with multiple hospital staff, often with minimal

Table 1

Reasons for Referral

Reason for referral	%
Assessment of parental mental state	46
Assessment of parent–infant relationship problems	19
Infant regulatory problems	18
Infant's reaction to illness	9
Emotional problems	8
Behavioural problems	1

support from extended family. These demands are time-consuming and can lead to very distressed parents missing out on the opportunity to build relationships with their child. Therapeutic work with the baby before death can contribute significantly to the parents' ability to have a real relationship with their child and accomplish a better later adjustment themselves.

Infant referrals to the RCHIMHG over a 6-month period included three infants for liver transplantation, two with congenital heart disease, four with ventilator dependence, five with multiple problems (e.g., tracheo-oesophageal fistula with complications, complex congenital abnormalities), and four infants on the artificial heart lung machine (ECMO). Many other infants were discussed with unit staff without formal referral.

The referral pattern at The Royal Children's Hospital has been clearly influenced by the manner in which the RCHIMHG has developed its relationship with hospital units and staff. There is a strong liaison component, involving regular meetings with general paediatric and subspecialty units and with the neonatal intensive care unit (NICU). Many of the hospital medical staff have spent a period of their paediatric training working within the mental health service. We have endeavoured to encourage those caring for sick infants to consider:

- the baby's experience of her illness
- an understanding of the way that parents are impacted upon by having an ill infant
- how parents' own problems may contribute to an infant's psychosomatic development.

Modes of Presentation

1. The Physically Sick Baby as Subject and Catalyst for Parental Mental Health Problem

Amy, aged 5 weeks, and her mother Mandy were referred in crisis to the infant mental health service because Mandy felt she could no longer 'take it any more'. She wanted to leave Amy in hospital while she returned alone to her home in the country. She had become convinced that she could not be mother to Amy and that she would 'go crazy' if she stayed visiting Amy in the intensive care unit. She had strong thoughts of ending her own life as well.

Amy was born with a major congenital respiratory anomaly; she had already had an open chest operation and was still dependent on the ventilator and the multiple tubes into her body. She was now stable, but likely to remain in hospital for several months. Mandy spoke readily about her current feelings and of her past experiences. Amy's father had been violent and abusive in his relationship with Mandy. He had no contact with her since the middle of the pregnancy. Mandy had an older son from a previous relationship, and as she talked about him she said she felt destined to have disastrous relationships with men. This seemed so from her earliest memories, as she had been physically and sexually abused as a child by a stranger. In fact, the whole pregnancy and birth process took her back in time to vividly re-experience that set of traumas. She had a troubled adolescence and early adulthood with a number of hospital admissions for self-harm and frequent suicidal preoccupations. While sitting by her daughter in the intensive care unit and seeing her in pain and distress, Mandy felt those states of mind returning, and began to relive her own childhood trauma. She had hoped these memories had long gone from her mind. Thoughts of suicide, feelings of worthlessness and a bitter anger drove her to distraction. She could not see Amy as an individual there before her: all that she could see was her own self as a young terrified girl. She knew it would be wrong to abandon Amy, as she had felt abandoned by her mother, but she could see no other choice.

We spoke at length about her past, but then drew Amy into our conversation. We talked about the moment during the pregnancy when Mandy was told of Amy's heart problem and of her overwhelming feeling of panic. Mandy gave a very accurate account of her baby's treatment in hospital, but returned to the impact of her traumatic memories, her sleeplessness and her periods of disconnectedness. She felt detached from Amy, as if Amy were not her child. However, we were able to look directly at Amy and speak to her, and to touch her forehead. Mandy said that Amy would withdraw her hand if that was touched.

We met a number of times by the cot in intensive care, gradually increasing interaction with Amy. Amy became more responsive to Mandy and we reflected together on the exquisite way that her gaze would turn to meet her mother's gaze as she spoke or softly touched her. A real relationship developed as Amy emerged as a curious, engaging person. Mandy continued to visit Amy regularly, and she reconnected with distant relatives who were able to provide her with practical and ongoing support away from the realm of the trauma of hospital.

All babies need an attuned responsive adult to develop their own sense of self (Stern, 1995). Such a person was described by Winnicott (1988) as the 'good enough mother' or the 'ordinary devoted parent'. The very sick baby, however, needs an 'extra-ordinary devoted parent' to manage the trauma of facing danger and death and despair so often. Amy's capacity to be engaged was crucial in enabling Mandy to become that extra-ordinary devoted parent.

Mandy initially presented as a troubled young woman with a history of depressive illness and an acute exacerbation of a complex posttraumatic stress disorder, with some of the characteristics of borderline personality organisation. With this mother–infant work, Mandy's functioning improved significantly.

Mandy and Amy typify much of what confronts very sick infants and parents within the paediatric setting. Mandy was overwhelmed by the gravity of her baby's problems. She felt she could not cope, and had to hand her to someone to care for her. Therapy with Mandy enabled her to disentangle some of the painful memories and embroiled affect.

There are a number of effective ways of intervening with traumatised mothers and their infants. Daniel Schechter and his team (2006) have demonstrated how the use of video feedback of interaction between the traumatised mother and her symptomatic infant can lead to significant change in the mother's relationship with the baby and her own *internal representations* of her infant. The capacity for *reflective functioning* in mothers improved significantly when guided through a video tape of herself and her baby interacting.

> Sitting with her beside Amy in the intensive care unit, we seemed to give Mandy a safe space — some time to get to know Amy as a real person and not as the sum of her ancient fears from previous relationships and her projected anxieties.

Identification

Having such a sick infant in hospital exposed Mandy to both her strengths and vulnerabilities. Initially, she appeared to be disintegrating, with intrusive powerful images from the past of abuse and abandonment. After time and with intervention, however, she was able to *identify* with that part of Amy which represented survival. Mandy could recognise at least two aspects of herself in her daughter. Amy personified the pain of the violent, abusive relationship which led to her unexpected conception. She also represented that hopeful part of Mandy which had struggled to survive, recalling the positive attachment relationship she had had with several of her aunts. Working at the cot-side with both Amy and Mandy together, we could begin to put words and affects to these current and past identifications and experiences.

What Was Our Role?

Although Amy required extensive medical intervention and nursing care, it was still possible to engage her: initially with gaze and facial expression and for Mandy also with her voice and gentle touch. Mandy could *see* then that Amy recognised her and responded to her, even if ever so subtly. At once she could see Amy as a frightened, but fighting, separate, *autonomous* person and she could see *herself*, Mandy, reflected in her daughter.

Although it was a very long and slow process during 4 months in hospital, several cardiac surgical procedures and many medical setbacks, Mandy could begin to conceptualise Amy's ongoing survival — both physical and emotional.

2. The Dying Infant as Subject and as Catalyst For Parental Mental Health Difficulty

> John, an overwhelmed father, was sitting beside his 3-month-old baby who was attached to the artificial heart–lung system. He felt unable to touch, talk to or look at his child. He experienced severe and disabling anxiety symptoms and a recurrence of an earlier conversion symptom that had accompanied a severe anxiety disorder as a young man. He felt angry with himself that he could not help his daughter and, despite her being a desperately wanted baby, he felt resentful of her continued existence. She caused him so much pain. With exploration of his past mental health problems, it was possible for him to see that he did have profound things he could give his gravely ill daughter before she died. He was able to become a supportive father as he gently touched her, spoke with her and saw how she calmed and settled as he did so.

For John, developing a real relationship with his extremely sick infant enabled his release from the mental anguish and conversion disorder from which he suffered — he could fill his role as a father, albeit briefly. When parents realise that the mind of their baby is being 'held', it can be easier to approach the hidden conflicts, fears and remembrances that have driven the psychological crises they confront.

Eric Clapton eloquently describes the agonising sense of loss a father has in grieving for his son, 'Would you know my name if I saw you in heaven?' (Clapton & Jennings, 1992). His son died in an accident when he was 4 years old. In his song Eric Clapton emphasises the importance of the real relationship that had developed between him and his very young child. His son had become a powerful presence and very meaningful for him despite their relatively short relationship.

Kazak et al.'s (2006) three-phase model for understanding the trauma experienced by very sick children and their families has been an excellent guide to understanding some of the issues these families are experiencing and for planning intervention.

3. The Parent's Mental Illness Presenting Through the Physically Well Infant

Parental Mental Health

The review of referrals at RCHIMHG revealed that the majority of infants (75%) had at least one parent with a significant mental health problem. The full spectrum of mental health problems was represented — with parents experiencing mild anxiety or depressive symptoms through to posttraumatic stress disorder and to major psychotic illnesses. The relationship between the parent's own psychological state and her response to her infant's hospitalisation is complex. Influences include the parental couple's previous relationship and mental health, the process of the pregnancy and child's birth, the infant's own medical problem and the relationship of the family with the health care system itself.

A parent's mental health may be severely compromised although the infant appears physically well. When a parent has decompensated the hospital may still have a major role in intervening in such a family crisis. The paediatric hospital is a place where troubled parents will bring their child when they fear for their health.

> Three-month-old Carl was brought to a hospital emergency department by his mother Joan, who was in a very distressed and agitated state. Carl was admitted to a general paediatric ward. Joan talked directly and intently to the medical and nursing staff, insisting that there were tests to be done: she was horrified at the sight of insects emerging from his skin through his scalp and his arms. Suddenly she would point to a minuscule blemish on his otherwise pristine skin, exclaiming in horror that the baby was infected, perhaps to die, with these apparent insects. Her husband, thin and wiry and rather hostile to the staff, agreed with her observations and demanded immediate action. His son needed some blood tests he said, and maybe X-rays to see how they had managed to track from his throat to the top of his scalp.
>
> Carl's body seemed very passive, lying there languidly across his mother's lap as she pushed his head sideways and prised open his tight mouth to demonstrate the creatures. His gaze was frozen: he looked fixedly on the nurse as the infant mental health consultant tried to commence an assessment of the situation. His eyes spoke.

His body seemed to have given up, it was limp and passive, and he responded to the handling by his parents as if he were a rag doll.

His mother's concern was clearly for him, but she seemed so agitated she could not see him as a person. There was no attunement between Joan and her infant son; it was as if all that his mother could see were the insects, which no one else could see. She could not see the distressed intensity and fear in his gaze.

Despite attempts by the medical staff to reassure her that all would be done for her son's welfare, Joan and her husband picked up their children and tried to flee when there was a suggestion that Carl's sister also needed to be examined. They feared that their children would be removed from them. Both children became even more fearful as their parents' agitation increased. The adult mental health crisis team and police were called to try and contain the situation and Joan was taken to an adult mental health assessment unit. Her agitation and paranoid ideation intensified over the subsequent 24 hours but then she slept and calmed when given a moderate dose of a major tranquilliser. Joan revealed that she had been using amphetamines, and that this was a long-term habit. Her need had spiralled desperately in recent times as she strived to keep herself awake sufficiently to care for her children.

Joan was experiencing an acute paranoid psychotic illness secondary to her drug misuse. Her husband was also using 'speed', and he became uncontactable for some weeks following Joan's transfer to the acute psychiatric unit.

As Joan was recovering from her acute psychotic illness she seemed reassured that her baby was at the hospital, even as she began to realise that he was not infested with insects. It seemed that for Joan the distress of becoming a parent again was a significant precipitant for her intensified dependence upon stimulant drugs and her psychotic break.

Amy's mother was able to modify the disorganising threat of the trauma she experienced. Carl's mother was unable to do so. The care of mothers with a psychotic illness requires close collaboration between specialist perinatal psychiatric services and the mother's ongoing mental health team and psychiatrist. This close collaboration is especially important because in the busy caseload of an adult mental health clinician the needs of the infant may not be apparent to the treating team. The gravity of the parent's illness may make it very hard to see the emotional and developmental needs of her young infant.

There is an increasing literature describing the mental health needs of parents and their infants (Stone, Chapter 14 this volume; Sved Williams, 2004).

A national initiative, Children of Parents with Mental Illness (COPMI)[1] has produced some extremely useful resources and publications to assist those caring for mothers with chronic or severe mental illness in order to coordinate the care of the infant and the infant parent relationships. Grunebaum, Weissman, Cohler, Hartman and Gallant (1982) followed a cohort of such families for many years in Chicago and demonstrated how hard it can be for mentally ill parents who strive to continue to provide care and love for their children in the face of the pervasively disruptive impact of serious mental illness. They emphasised the need for active links between mental health, family support, child health and child protective services.

Infant–Parent Interactional Problems Manifesting With Feeding Problems

Feeding difficulties were the most common infant problem, present in 28% of our case series. Infant feeding involves two people and is generally sited in an ongoing relationship. Successful feeding requires very close, reciprocal attunement between baby and carer. The 'good enough' mother allows for the young baby to develop awareness of self through the mother's capacity to 'understand what the baby is feeling, because she is alive and has an imagination' (Winnicott, 1973, p. 47).

Because of this relationship basis, infant feeding can be the vehicle for the presentation of a wide range of parent mental health problems. Where either the mother or the infant is depressed or disturbed, then it is likely that the feeding experience for the baby is also distorted (Murray, Cooper, & Hipwell, 2003). The presenting symptom of poor feeding or poor growth may represent the final common pathway for a broad range of causative processes.

Failure to thrive as a syndrome in infancy has been the subject of much research and debate over recent decades, with the traditional dichotomy of 'organic' and 'nonorganic' failure to thrive proving simplistic and not clinically useful. It is now seen as a complex multifactorial problem that encompasses a wide range of primary causes and associated biological, familial and social vulnerability factors.

Chatoor (2004) describes a classification system for feeding problems in infancy, which clinicians may find useful. Conflicting data exists about the nature of the infant–carer feeding behaviours associated with poor growth velocity where there is no obvious medical cause (Benoit, 2000).

Feeding is a major issue for many children with chronic illness. For example, interventions in the infant–carer relationship for babies with severe congenital heart abnormality may significantly contribute to improvement in feeding and weight gain. Simmons, Goldberg, Washington, Fischer-Fay and Maclusky (1995) followed 30 children diagnosed with cystic fibrosis in their first year of life and found that those infant–mother dyads where there was an *insecure avoidant form of attachment* had significantly more problems with feeding, nutrition and growth. Disentangling the many interacting factors in families when infants present with poor feeding and growth velocity can be challenging, as the following vignettes reveal.

1. Feeding Disorder as a Presentation of Maternal Schizophrenic Illness

Alicia, aged 11 months, was referred from a medical ward, where she had been admitted for investigation of poor growth, nutritional deficiencies and a fracture associated with rickets. Her mother concerned the nursing staff because of her unusually withdrawn behaviour. They could not follow her speech, which appeared illogical, nonsequential and not consistent with her apparent mood. When seen by the mental health team it was clear that Alicia's mother was suffering from a chronic paranoid psychotic illness. Although she had previously been a patient of the local adult community mental heath team, her family had not noticed her deteriorating mental state or her incapacity to read Alicia's signals about hunger. Alicia herself was flat and withdrawn, but responded well to responsive care on the ward and moved back quickly to a normal growth velocity in hospital. An extensive community treatment plan was drawn up, and this included a referral to child protective services, and Alicia had a transitional period in foster care.

2. Feeding Disorder as a Presentation of Possible Factitious Disorder by Proxy

Jane, aged 8 months, was transferred from a rural hospital with profound failure to grow despite intensive assessment and intervention. Her weight was only a few grams above her birth weight. No specific genetic or metabolic disorder was found. A cautious but prolonged mental health assessment revealed parents who had worked in the education professions and had experienced severe childhood and recent traumata themselves. Eventually, Jane's mother was able to tell us that she had been suffering from anorexia and bulimia nervosa and she found feeding Jane very stressful. She could not read her cues of hunger and there was significant improvement in Jane's growth and development when both parents were able to share their intense ambivalence about Jane's birth and its impact upon their own careers. Her father temporarily took over more of her feeding regime and her mother was able to engage in psychotherapy locally. She gradually felt more able to safely feed Jane.

It can be very difficult to ascertain the conscious motives behind parent's actions in the care of children. Factitious disorder by proxy, or Munchausen's syndrome by proxy, is a serious, complex and contentious disorder whereby the carer of a child deliberately fabricates medical symptoms in order to obtain medical attention. There is a broad spectrum of problems considered in this diagnostic group ranging from extensive seeking of medical opinions to deliberately fabricating serious symptoms in the child that require at times life-threatening treatment. Lyons-Ruth, Kaufman, Masters and Mu (2006) discuss the issues in identification and management of such problems within a clinical infant mental health service. They emphasise the difficulty in obtaining a balance between developing a long-term treatment relationship with the family, limiting harmful behaviour and preventing a flight away from treatment.

3. Feeding Disorder as a Presentation of Infant Response to Persistent Peri-Oral Trauma

Catrina was aged 11 months when referred because of her refusal to swallow any food with texture other than water. She had been born with congenital tracheo-oesophageal fistula and spent 7 months in hospital. She was a hypervigilant and engaging girl who cried at the sight of the bottle, which she pushed away vigorously with her hands. She had had multiple intrusive corrective surgical procedures around her mouth and nose including repeated dilations of strictures in her oesophagus. Catrina knew when she was approaching the hospital and became agitated and distressed. We presumed she had a clear memory of the trauma experienced. Her parents had become very distressed about the ongoing nature of her nasogastric tube feeding and wished the tube would be removed. Their anxiety was intensified by the past history of an aunt and great-uncle, each of whom had died because of other conditions that were inoperable.

Catrina's formal diagnosis was one of posttraumatic feeding refusal. She was admitted to hospital and a collaborative approach between parents, grandparents, nursing staff, surgeon, speech pathology and infant mental health clinician assisted Catrina in feeling confident to take water and then milk in the bottle from her mother. An integrated team approach was necessary in order for both Catrina and her mother to feel held and safe during the critical time when the nasogastric tube was removed.

4. Feeding Disorder as a Presentation of Maternal Depressive Illness

Lia's mother, Sarah, had been admitted to a mother–baby psychiatric unit because of Sarah's depression and fears of self-harm. Sarah was very ambivalent about her care of Lia. When Lia, aged 6 months, became difficult to feed and cried at night, she was weaned from the breast. However, Lia refused to take bottled milk offered to her and she lost weight and became listless, avoidant and very flat in mood. She was transferred to the paediatric hospital and seen by the infant team. Her mother was very anxious about Lia's weight, now below the third percentile. We met Lia with her parents. Sarah talked about her hostile feelings towards Lia, which reflected her anger with her own mother, Margaret. Sarah blamed Margaret for 'poisoning her about the whole business of motherhood' because of Margaret's multiple adverse life experiences. As a consequence, Sarah felt she had no positive mother role or ideal. When Lia refused the bottle, she felt bitter and disillusioned about being a mother and believed her baby hated her. She seemed to enact this in the way they were with each other — Sarah held Lia facing away from her, could not talk softly with her or engage her and Lia, for her part, became increasingly gaze avoidant, floppy and cried in a mournful way. It seemed they were moving further and further away.

In the course of infant mental health assessment, we were able to pick up on a small playful response of Lia to a finger-tapping game I initiated when I unconsciously responded to a movement in her hand. We established a game that developed into a finger-touching game, then a smiling and grimacing game as we exchanged expressions one after the other. Her parents observed this playful game, and believed they could do it themselves. Tension diminished as Lia and her mother enacted similar play in the session and again back in the ward. Using facial expression and voice in a similarly playful manner, Sarah was able to help Lia overcome her fear of the bottle and reduce the apparent anger directed towards her mother. Lia began and continued to feed well.

Sarah's depressive illness was demonstrably a two-person illness. Lia experienced it also. It was as if when Lia looked to her mother she saw someone who was not there.

The Mirror Role

Babies need the attuned responsiveness of their carers to begin to know who they are. Winnicott (1971, p. 131) built upon a key paper of French psychoanalyst Jacques Lacan to describe the

> mirror role of the mother and family in child development. 'What does the baby see when he looks into his mothers face? … he sees himself: the expression on the mother's face reflects what she sees in her baby. When the mother is depressed, her face is a mirror to be looked at, not into.'

This concept is a critical one in infant mental health. The baby's sense of self is dependent upon the responses he gets to his curious excursions into the world outside. Recent important neurobiological research has identified a range of neurons in primates that mirror the physical action of an observed other and, as more recent research demonstrates, also mirror the emotional state of the observed other. How the baby's brain develops depends on the way his own emotional state is mirrored — reflected back in a tangible way — by those caring for him (Gallese, Fadiga, Fogassi, & Rizzolati, 1996; Thomson-Salo, 2007; Trevarthen, 2001).

This has implications for therapeutic interventions: if we can facilitate a new mode in the interaction between a depressed, avoidant mother and her emotionally flat infant we can build up a positive therapeutic process between them. The relationship is very much a *mutual* one. The baby can be the therapist for the parent as well.

Lia was able to assist in changing her own mother's capacity for *reflective functioning*. Fonagy and his colleagues (1991) have developed the concept of reflective functioning: the parents' capacity to hold the child's mental states in mind. Slade (2005) describes how this capacity can be quantified in clinical practice.

Personalisation

The communications from the baby — her gaze, the smallest of movements … of a finger, or changes in breathing, rhythm — are part of the process of the baby beginning to know about her own body. Winnicott (1972) discusses 'ordinary' parental care, which promotes the development of a working relationship between the baby's *psyche* and *soma*. Through their '*handling*' and '*holding*' (at once both psychological and physical processes) of their sick infant, a parent can help the baby learn about his own body — his own sense of self. To do this the parent needs to be aware or free of his own sadness or fear — to allow for curiosity about his child. The baby only knows the body she has, so the extra-ordinary parent in hospital is constantly introducing and reintroducing the baby to her own body. The parent 'personalises' the infant's body.

Treatment: Direct Therapeutic Engagement With the Baby

The therapeutic intervention with Lia and her mother illustrates the particular model of infant–parent psychotherapy that the RCHIMHG has developed. It is based on Winnicott's notions of mirroring, playfulness and a systemic understanding of the total environment for the infant and family.

The therapeutic principles include:

- directly engaging the infant as a participant
- understanding the *emotional* meaning of the situation for infant and parents
- determining the need for immediate intervention
- selectively using psychoanalytic, attachment, family systems and psycho-physiological regulation theories
- appropriately using other intervention models, such as developmental guidance, interaction coaching, brief serial treatment, long-term psychotherapy
- sharing our hypotheses and liaising with other hospital/community staff: working with the whole system.

Specificity of the Infant-Directed Psychotherapy

We aim to make an emotional connection with the infant through gaze, touch, talking and playfulness and to provide mutual play that helps the infant 'symbolise'. We also help the parents understand the baby's mind/body, through 'holding' and 'containing' of projective identification, unhooking projections, making links, and making space for ambivalence (Thomson-Salo, 2007).

This model of working is also applicable to premature and very sick babies. Although some very sick infants have recourse to a useful protective withdrawal, if this state of withdrawal is too deep or persistent, it can leave the sick child isolated and suspend development, with consequences for his ongoing neurodevelopment. Thus our work may be critical for parents and nursing staff to interpret the emotional communications of the very sick infant.

Conclusion

Infants who have serious illness or are hospitalised,generally have concerned and stressed parents. Babies exist only in a relationship, usually with their parents. Stress and distress can be communicated in both directions between infant and parent. Some parents of ill babies present to the paediatric hospital with severe psychiatric decompensation or disorder and yet other parents, despite having an extremely sick child, may present with minimal evident distress or psychological symptoms.

It is important to implement preventive mental health principles for all sick babies, and a critical role for the infant mental health clinician is to support all health care professionals working with babies to consider the baby's state of mind and the nature of the relationship between baby and parent.

Endnote

1   http://www.copmi.net.au

Acknowledgments

I wish to thank the families with whom I have been privileged to work, and I acknowledge that I have changed many of the details in order to protect their identities. I also wish to thank my colleagues Ann Morgan, Brigid Jordan and Frances Thompson Salo who have been so constantly supportive of this work.

References

Affleck, G., Tennan, H., & Rowe, J. (1991). *Infants in crisis: How parents cope with newborn intensive care and its aftermath.* New York: Springer-Verlag.

Benoit, D. (2000). Feeding disorders, failure to thrive and obesity. In C.H. Zeanah (Ed.), *Handbook of infant mental health* (2nd ed.; pp. 339–352). New York: Guilford Press.

Browne, J.V. (2003). New perspectives on premature infants and their parents. *Zero to Three, November,* 4–12.

Chatoor, I. (2004). Feeding and eating disorders of infancy and early childhood. In J.M. Wiener & M.K. Dulcan, (Eds.), *Textbook of Child and Adolescent Psychiatry* (3rd ed.) (pp. 639–657). Washington, DC: American Psychiatric Publishing.

Clapton, E., & Jennings, W. (1992). *Tears in heaven.* Music and lyrics by Eric Clapton and Will Jennings. WEA/Warner Bros.

Fonagy, P., Steele, M., Steele, N., Moran, G.S., & Higgitt, A.C. (1991). The capacity of understanding mental states: The reflective self in parent and child and its significance for security of attachment. *Infant Mental Health Journal, 12,* 201–218.

Frankel, K.A., Boyum, L.A. & Harmon, R.J. (2004). Diagnoses and presenting symptoms in an infant psychiatry clinic: Comparison of two diagnostic systems. *Journal of American Academy of Child and Adolescent Psychiatry, 43,* 578–587.

Furman, L., & O'Riordan, M.A. (2006). How do mothers feel about their very low birth weight infants? Development of a new measure. *Infant Mental Health Journal, 27,* 152–172.

Gallese, V., Fadiga, L., Fogassi, L., & Rizzolati, G. (1996). Action recognition in the premotor cortex. *Brain, 119,* 593–609.

Grunebaum, N., Weiss, J.L., Cohler, B.J., Hartman, C.R., & Gallant, D.H. (1982). *Mentally ill mothers and their children.* Chicago: University of Chicago Press.

Kaukonen, P., & Tamminem, T. (1998) The psychiatric infant–family ward at Tampere University Hospital. *Infant Mental Health Journal, 19,* 168–179.

Kazak, A.E., Kassam-Adams, N., Schneider, S., Zelikowsky, N., Alderfer, M.A., & Rourke, M. (2006). An integrative model of pediatric medical traumatic stress. *Journal of Pediatric Psychology, 31,* 343–355.

Keren, M., Feldman, R., & Tyano, S. (2003). A five-year Israeli experience with the DC: 0–3 classification system. *Infant Mental Health Journal, 24,* 337–348.

Lieberman, A.F., van Horn, P., Grandison, C.M., & Pekarsky, J.H. (1997). Mental health assessment of infants, toddlers, and preschoolers in a service program and a treatment outcome research program. *Infant Mental Health Journal, 18,* 158–170.

Lyons-Ruth, K., Kaufman, M., Masters, N., & Mu, J. (2006). Issues in the identification and long-term management of Munchausen by proxy syndrome within a clinical infant service. *Infant Mental Health Journal, 12,* 309–320.

Minde, K. (2000). Prematurity and serious medical conditions in infancy: Implications for development, behaviour, and intervention. In C.H. Zeanah, (Ed.), *Handbook of infant mental health* (pp. 176–194). New York: Guilford Press.

Murray, L., Cooper, P., & Hipwell, A. (2003). Mental health of parents caring for infants. *Archives of Women's Mental Health, 6,* s71-s77.

Schechter, D.S., Myers, M.M., Brunelli, S.A., Coates, S.W., Jnr, C.H.Z., Davies, M., Grienenberger, J.F. et al. (2006). Traumatized mothers can change their minds about their toddlers: Understanding how a novel use of videofeedback supports positive change of maternal attributions. *Infant Mental Health Journal, 27,* 429–447.

Scheffer, H., & Paul, C (2007). [Infant referrals to a specialised infant mental health service]. Unpublished data.

Simmons, R.J., Goldberg, S., Washington, J., Fischer-Fay, A., & Maclusky, I. (1995). Infant-mother attachment and nutrition in children with cystic fibrosis. *Developmental and Behavioral Pediatrics, 16,* 183–186.

Slade, A. (2005). Parental reflective functioning: An introduction. *Attachment and Human Development, 7,* 269–281.

Stern, D.N. (1995). *The Motherhood Constellation: A unified view of parent–infant psychotherapy.* New York: Basic Books.

Sved Williams, A. (2004). Infants of mothers with mental illness. In V. Cowling (Ed.), *Children of parents with mental illness 2: Personal and clinical perspectives* (pp. 17–40). Melbourne, Australia: ACER Press.

Thomson-Salo, F. (2007). Recognizing the infant as subject in infant–parent psycho-therapy. *International Journal of Psychoanalysis, 88,* 961–980.

Tracey, N. (2000). *Parents of premature infants: Their emotional world.* London: Whurr Publishers.

Trevarthen, C. (2001). Intrinsic motives for companionship in understanding: Their origin, development, and significance for infant mental health. *Infant Mental Health Journal, 22,* 95–131.

Winnicott, D.W. (1971). The mirror role of mother and family in child development. In D.W. Winnicott (Ed.), *Playing and reality.* London: Tavistock.

Winnicott, D.W. (1972). *On the basis of self in body. Psychoanalytic explorations.* Cambridge, MA: Harvard University Press.

Winnicott, D.W. (1973). *The child, the family and the outside world.* London: Pelican Books.

Winnicott, D.W. (1988). *Babies and their mothers.* London: Free Association Books.

Childcare

A 'Holding Environment' Supporting Infants and Their Parents With Mental Illness and Emotional Difficulties

Robyn Dolby, Cecilia Ebert and Sally Watson

B owlby (1988) described parenting as hard labour and said that parents need as much support as possible to carry out their crucial role. Childcare can be a major source of this support and this can be particularly important for families where a parent has a mental illness. Parental mental illness is a recognised risk factor for children, particularly when combined with other psychosocial risks that can compromise the development of a secure attachment (Sameroff, 1998). As a nonstigmatising community service, child-care can play a significant role in the lives of these children, as well as providing an additional community support for parents with emotional difficulties.

Early relationships have a profound impact on children's social, emotional, and health-related developmental outcomes (Ainsworth, Blehar, Waters, & Wall, 1978; Shapiro & Applegate, 2002; Siegel, 2001). Childcare can provide an opportunity for the child to form relationships with others in a way that fosters trust, consistency, and predictability. These relationships are of utmost impor-tance for social and emotional development. Childcare can also connect with the child's family and so support the child at home as well as at childcare

(Virmani, 2002). However, if childcare practitioners are to provide emotional support for parents and children, they must be well supported themselves.

This chapter will present some models of childcare support for parents with a mental illness and for parents who are likely to have some compromise in their attachment relationships, which potentially impact on their children's emotional health and wellbeing. We describe what this support can look like for the children, the parents and the childcare staff themselves and show how changing childcare practices and supervision can provide excellent outcomes for families and staff.

Gerhardt (2004) states that the qualities of good parenting are essentially regulatory:

> ... the capacity to listen, to notice, to shape (organise) behavior and to be able to restore good feelings through some kind of physical, emotional or mental contact, through a touch or a smile, a way of putting feelings and thoughts into words. (p. 214)

These qualities apply also to good quality childcare practice, where staff can lend regulatory support to the parent as well as the child.

For the children, childcare providers can become alternative attachment figures (Cassidy & Shaver, 1999). For a vulnerable child, such as one whose mother has a mental illness, childcare can provide a space where the child can develop a model of how relationships work that will help to sustain a relationship with his/her mother. At the same time, the relationship that the childcare provider develops with the mother can support her, helping her to focus on her child's needs, and coming to feel less alone.

Childcare staff are in a unique situation to develop close relationships with parents. They greet parents at the beginning of the day, they hear from them about how the morning has gone and hear their joys and tribulations. When childcare staff talk about the children and share experiences with the parents, they show that they really care about the children. This encourages the parents to talk, not because this is expected of them but because they want to. The childcare worker gains an intimacy with the family that very few other professionals achieve. S/he is seen as caring for the child and enjoying her company, not making an assessment or providing treatment. The relationship is built on their shared concern for the child. This unique relationship allows childcare to become a 'holding environment' for both the child and the mother (Winnicott, 1986): a place where they feel safe, where the staff are on their side and attuned to their emotional experiences.

Thus, when childcare staff have additional training from infant mental health workers who are based at times in the centre, the potential exists for normalising relationships for mother and child, and building stronger emotional wellbeing for the child and potentially also for the mother.

Two models that add special elements to a childcare setting are a program developed at the Lady Gowrie Child Care Centre, Adelaide, called Through the Looking Glass, and a Sydney program called the Attachment Matters Project — from relationships to learning at preschool (Dolby & Swan, 2003) developed from a collaboration between the Benevolent Society and KU Children's services. Before these are described in detail, the concepts of primary care-giving, based in the principles derived from the attachment theory of Bowlby (1988), and providing a holding environment are discussed.

Primary Care-Giving

All parents and children benefit from the primary care-giving model, because it runs through the whole centre (when centres decide to work in this way), regardless of whether children have special needs or join additional programs. It is a relationship-based system of care where every child has a special staff member who is her/his 'primary caregiver' (Lieberman, 1993). Each childcare professional is allocated to a small group of children, with the responsibility of knowing the child, forming a strong relationship and becoming a 'secure base' for the child and the child's family.

To be able to develop secure and healthy relationships with the children, the childcare professional needs to have an understanding of attachment theory, a sufficient capacity for reflection and an ability to be emotionally available for the children. This means being able to accept and validate children's emotional needs. During the daily routine in childcare, the primary caregiver helps the child to manage and 'organise' their feelings, friendships and relationship with peers and adults (Marvin, Cooper, Hoffman, & Powell, 2002).

This is essential for children's development. Young children internalise the 'sense' and overall style of their interactions with their parents and other care-givers. The positive or negative characteristics of these relationships have a profound impact on children's confidence in human relationships and influence their trust in themselves, others and the world. Speltz (1990, p. 40) refers to 'how the child's observable relationship with the caregiver serves as the basis for developing cognitive and emotional responses in early relationships and potentially bring strong effects on behaviour'.

Primary care-giving systems provide the parent with a familiar, consistent, supportive relationship with a professional in a nonstigmatising community service. As the relationship grows it becomes a journey of little steps, focusing on the child and engaging with the parent around the child's needs and strengths. This partnership becomes a place where the parent can work through his/her relationship with their child, and the child's need for a secure base and safe haven can be illustrated with examples from the experience of the child in childcare.

In a primary care-giving setting, therefore, each childcare worker becomes a secure base for particular infants with evident benefits for each infant. From this beginning, there is a natural flow to providing close ongoing relationships with family members and a basis for other programs that meet the family's emotional needs.

Providing a Holding Environment for Parents

Stern (2004) highlights the importance of a positive atmosphere where the 'mother is supported and validated rather than criticised, (and) where legitimate fears are construed as evidence of caring and involvement' (p. 39). Childcare is well placed to provide this. It is a universal, nonstigmatising setting, used by a wide range of parents and for all kinds of reasons: because they work, or study, or need some form of respite. It is child-focused, and provides an opportunity to have contact with other families, and to enter into the social world of parenthood, sharing stories, experiences and just being around other families.

Stern describes how a parent can benefit from having someone as a benign 'grandmotherly figure' to 'hold' her psychologically as she explores her relationship with her child. While the primary caregivers or therapists may not be 'grandmotherly', they can be seen as benign figures (genial and kindly: *Oxford English Dictionary*, 2008) who help the mother explore her new role, by talking with her about her child, sharing what they observe with each other, and enjoying the child together.

Program One: Through the Looking Glass

Through the Looking Glass is an attachment-based parenting program in a childcare setting, which has been developed with funding from the Australian government. The program has a number of components, most relevant to this chapter are childcare that uses the primary care-giving model, and a therapeutic intervention with the mothers consisting of a group program and individual work. Therapy is provided by a trained therapist with an understanding of infant mental health working with one of the childcare workers, and with support of the centre's staff.

Parents with mental illness are referred from a wide range of agencies who have noticed both mental health difficulties and compromised parent–child interactions. Each child attends the childcare centre up to twice a week and, on one of these days, the parent(s) attend a group run by the two co-workers. The group provides a safe place for parents to focus on their relationship with their infants, using an attachment-based intervention that relies heavily in the use of video feedback, and frames of reference from ideas provided through the Circle of Security model (Marvin et al., 2002).

A very important component of this program is the childcare staff's understanding of the particular difficulties facing a parent. For instance, some parents sometimes find it difficult to separate from their child at the start of the childcare day. The primary caregiver can support the parent, helping her deal with her sadness and explaining what separation means for the child. Together they can consider the child's 'fear of losing the parent' and his/her fantasy that the parent is leaving because of something he/she has done. The primary caregiver can help the parent to recognise and validate the child's distress, and explain the importance of 'being there' for the child without trying to deny the child's sadness.

For many parents, the relationships they have with their child's primary caregiver and the group/individual therapist in the Through the Looking Glass program is their first experience of a sustainable adult relationship, where they have been supported, not judged. As well as helping women to understand what is happening between themselves and their infants, they may learn to better understand other attachment relationships to other adults — their difficulties with their infants are often reflective of a range of compromised adult relationships. Some find it hard to negotiate 'repair' of a relationship when things go off the rails — an ability to repair or rejoin after distress is believed to be a seminal quality of 'good-enough' parenting (Winnicott, 1951).

Two quite different examples illustrate this point. In one group program, a member felt that her experience had not been valued by another participant. Previously, she had made private comments about finding the participant annoying and on this occasion she expressed her feelings in the group. This was taken up and talked about, in keeping with the agreement that any conflict/rupture would be worked through in the group. While this was difficult, participants were able to stay with the discomfort, talk about it and repair the relationships. These repaired relationships have continued after the completion of the group, and those involved have found that when issues arise, they are now able to talk about them and resolve them.

A second example occurred when a 'child at risk' notification was made to the statutory child protection agency. Following usual practice in the project, the participant was informed that the notification would be made. While she was clearly upset about the notification, the social worker and mother were able to talk through the situation and identify concern for the child as common ground between them. This led to a very positive ongoing relationship, based on openness, honesty and trust. Importantly, the mother had experienced a significant rupture in the relationship, but had experienced being able to repair, as the value placed on the relationship overcame the rupture.

Many parents have talked about how they see the childcare centre as their secure base. For mothers who have a mental illness this secure base is essential to their recovery and enables them to become responsive to their child's needs. A secure base enables the parent to explore her role, just as a child's secure base enables him/her to go out and explore the world (Guedeney, 2005). As Winnicott (1986) states 'We need to provide an opportunity for the patient to have experiences that properly belong to infancy under conditions of extreme dependence. We see that such conditions may be found apart from organised psychotherapy' (p. 106). Through the Looking Glass shows how childcare can provide this, particularly through a system of primary care-giving.

Winnicott quotes John Rickman as saying 'Insanity is not being able to find anyone to stand you' (1986, p. 109). The childcare worker who is nonjudgmental with a parent with mental illness, enjoys moments talking with her about her child and values her perspectives shows that someone *can* stand her, and so contributes to rebuilding her mental health.

Program evaluation (Aylward & O'Neil, 2007) provides clear evidence of the value of this program for attendees, with clear improvements in ratings for depression and stress over the period of the program. These changes were sustained at follow-up. In addition, 92% of parents reported feeling closer to their child, with improvements in child behaviour. Many reported increased confidence in parenting and general improvements in family functioning. These changes were also noted by staff.

At the beginning of their involvement in Through the Looking Glass, it is not uncommon for mothers to express very high levels of hostility and resentment towards their infants and young children. Comments such as 'he is so demanding', 'She just won't leave me alone', and 'He just wants me to get angry at him' are not uncommon. However, it is equally common at the end of the group for these mothers to say 'Being involved in this group, has meant I have been able to start a new relationship with my child', 'I am able to enjoy the moment with my child now', 'I can be there now for him' or 'I feel less angry towards my child'.

Program 2: The Attachment Matters Project: From Relationships to Learning at Preschool

The 'Attachment Matters Project—from relationships to learning at preschool' (Dolby & Swan, 2003) has been running for seven years at an inner city preschool in Sydney and is currently funded by the Robert Christie Foundation. The philosophy of the program is that each person in the pre-school community (child, family, staff) has someone to turn to if they are unsure about what the children need or feels overwhelmed when trying to help the children to regulate their feelings.

Just as parents need to avoid becoming overwhelmed by their infants' emotions as they try to regulate them, so it is important that the childcare worker does not become overwhelmed by the parent's or child's distress. We have found the image of 'the hands within the hands' (Hoffman, Cooper, & Powell, 2007) extremely useful in thinking this. If the childcare worker is to provide a 'holding environment', s/he also needs someone to provide a holding environment for him or her, to help manage the unregulated affect arising from the children's needs or the parents' anxieties about their parenting and their lives more generally. This holding environment comes, in part, when the childcare worker feels truly valued in the work s/he does. As Gerhardt (2004) states, 'To bring about conditions where every baby has the kind of responsive care she or he needs to develop well, means that the adults who do this work must be valued and supported in their task' (p. 217). This applies to both parent and childcare worker.

In the Attachment Matters Project, a child and family worker (this could be a psychologist, social worker, or infant mental health professional) works alongside the staff four mornings a week. She provides a 'secure base' for the

Figure 1
Hands within hands (Hoffman, Cooper, & Powell, 2007).
Reproduced with permission.

staff, to help them think about the relationship support the children need to settle in and enjoy their day, and she is available for similar conversations with parents. This is done informally, through having an 'empty chair' for parents beside her in the playground. Parents in distressed relationships are more comfortable making contact with the child and family worker in this informal way, rather than through a formal appointment. Although it is informal, it is predictable: the worker is in the same space each morning when the parents arrive, and the empty chair is always there. The parents use the chair to make contact with her when they feel ready.

The same idea guides the way in which staff facilitate contact with the children. The structure at the start of the day has been changed to make the reunion with staff very predictable. Before the children arrive, the staff sit down in individual 'play spaces'. Each brings an activity to her play space that she can share with the children. She waits for the children and parents to come to them, observing how each child approaches and trying to get her welcome 'just right'. Children find it easier to get to staff when they are in play spaces and to start to play with other children once there. This is best described as 'active waiting' (Aarts, 2002), and through it the staff pick up information as to how each child is starting the day (emotionally ready or not ready) and how they can start with them.

Mentoring is provided through video review, giving childcare staff the opportunity to 'see themselves in action' with the children and talk about what they see with a mentor (the child and family worker and her own clinical supervisor). These video review meetings are made possible by the relationship of trust and support between the staff and the child and family worker. In this atmosphere of trust, video review becomes another way for staff to explore what the children need, to reflect on their own feelings about the children's behaviour, and to reflect on how they can use certain interactive moments to support the children.

The ideas they use in these discussions come from the Circle of Security framework (Marvin, et al., 2002; Powell, Cooper, Hoffman, & Marvin, 2007) and in their conversations they use 'Seeing and Guessing' (Cooper, Hoffman, Powell, & Marvin, 2005). Workers and mentors say what they see the children do and guess what they need, using the Circle of Security map as a guide. Ideas also come from the Marte Meo program (Aarts, 2002), which enable staff to see how effective they are at a procedural level: they see on video moments where they are or can be naturally supportive of the children. These moments are often not immediately visible to them.

In the Attachment Matters project, special emphasis is given to how the parents and children and staff come together. The start of the childcare day is a good opportunity for building connections with parents and children. For the children, drop-offs in the morning represent both a separation from parents and *a reunion* with staff. A successful reunion with staff at arrival can create for the child a strong foundation for how to appropriately connect with staff and peers for the rest of the day. What can the staff do when children and parents first arrive to bring them into relationship with them? This will be particularly important for parents and children who are vulnerable to stress and distress.

An Example:

> Mickie was 3 years old. His mother Tina described him as a 'handful'. When they first arrived at childcare in the morning, Tina would off-load with staff, recounting the difficulties of the previous night (e.g., Mickie's late bedtime) or the fraught start to their morning. As she talked, Mickie would run back and forth between her and the door and pull her by the arm saying, 'Come on. Let's go!' Tina was unsure about how and when she should leave. Usually she would ask Mickie, 'Can I go now?', and Mickie would become very upset, clinging to her and refusing the arms of his teacher. When they got to the gate, Mickie would try to go through. After returning his mother's kiss he would run quickly back into the playground, leaving his teacher Julie uncertain of how to support him. He would look around to check that Julie was following but run off each time she came closer. She found it difficult to break this cycle and connect with Mickie.

Mickie's drop-off in the morning was filmed and staff, the family worker and clinical supervisor watched it together. It was immediately apparent that Mickie needed 'hands' (as drawn on the Circle of Security) — someone 'bigger, stronger, wiser and kind' who could make the transition to childcare feel safe. Although the way he ran between his mum and the door seemed demanding, they could see that it might have a very different meaning: perhaps 'Please take charge, I know you can do it. I believe that you can take charge and help me feel safe and that's why I keep coming back to you'. This contained a very respectful message to his mother: 'I really believe in you, in your capacity to help me'.

This opened up a different approach to supporting Mickie and his mum, through addressing his relationship need. Showing Mickie how the important 'big people' at childcare (his mother and teacher) could work together to take charge over the transition would leave him feeling he was in safe hands. The child and family worker watched the video clip with Mickie's mother. They discussed what they saw and made guesses about Mickie's underlying emotional needs (using the Circle of Security map as a guide). Mickie's mother began to see his behaviour differently, suggesting that the real question behind his demands was, 'Is anyone in charge here?' She tearfully confided that she often felt uncomfortable 'taking charge' for fear of 'squelching Mickie', as she had experienced when she was growing up. The conversation turned to how to take charge so that Mickie felt *safe*.

Mickie's teacher and mother then worked together to show Mickie that they could focus on him when he first came in and provide more structure for him, by telling him what was going to happen and so making themselves more predictable to him. Now Julie was ready and waiting to welcome Mickie when he first arrived. The conversation went something like this:

> **Mother (Tina) to Mickie:** 'Let's go and see Julie.'
>
> **Mother to Julie:** 'Mickie has brought his favourite book to read.'
>
> The three sat together. Tina introduced the book and sat close, listening as Julie read. When Mickie began to point out the pictures and look up at her and smile, Julie indicated to his mother that this would be a good moment to say goodbye, now that Mickie was settling in with Julie.
>
> **Mother said to Julie:** 'Julie, I'm leaving now, I want you to look after Mickie' and to Mickie, 'Julie will look after you'.
>
> **Julie to Mickie:** 'I'm glad you're with me Mickie, I will take care of you. I'm here to keep you safe and to play with you'. To Tina, she added, 'We'll see you when you get back'.

In this new arrangement, Mickie hears about the care that is being passed from his mother to his teacher. Hearing the negotiation helps him feel that he is safe: he is in the minds of two big people who care for him and want to help him. He says goodbye to his mother from the secure base of his teacher. Instead of feeling 'lost' and relying on himself for support (running off quickly after kissing his mum goodbye), he can draw on the connection that Julie has made with him. He may think, 'You have noticed me and got interested in what I am interested in (my book). I can anticipate us going on together'. Mickie's mother also enjoys Julie's support, 'This is something important that we can work at together'.

The reunion with Julie at the start of the day had other advantages. It meant that Julie could be on hand to support Mickie when he invited peers to play with him or responded to their invitations. She supported these interactions by noticing his bids. Specifically, Julie highlighted the social aspect of the situation (Aarts, 2002) so that Mickie felt seen and could see the contributions of the other children: 'Oh look Mickie, Jesse is pushing his truck. After that he will be able to look at your car'; 'Oh Jesse, look Mickie has a car he wants to show you'.

The child and family worker showed Julie and Mickie's mother some recent video segments to confirm Mickie's progress. At childcare he began to link in with Julie and then go out to explore, coming back to share discoveries or seek comfort when something went wrong (a contact–explore rhythm). Julie and Tina saw how they themselves also came in to him before asking him to do anything (a contact–action rhythm). For example, Julie came in close and put her arms around Mickie before telling him that he must wait for his turn on the trampoline. The close contact helped Mickie to wait and then he celebrated his turn with Julie.

Now 6 months later, Mickie has a reliable start to his preschool day with Julie. He is comfortable to relinquish control and let her set limits when needed. Anxiety about keeping himself safe has been replaced by an enthusiasm for learning and sharing with staff and joining in with his peers (e.g., he takes Julie's hand in the playground and says, 'Come on Julie, let's get a front row seat' when it is time to go indoors for group time run by one of the other staff; 'Make the crocodile burp *again*' he says in a delighted way to the teacher who is leading group time). His mother is reassured when she arrives early and sees how he gives and receives kindnesses with his peers. She is more confident about being firm with him and realises that she can do this by holding Mickie in her arms so that he feels safe and can relax. They now do this when they meet at the end of his childcare day.

This approach is similar to a preschool program (Goldsmith, 2007) where the staff members address the children's internal working models, or expectations of them. When they are with the children, the staff emphasise that they want to help them and they demonstrate how they can keep them in mind, just as would an ideal grandmother.

An evaluation of the Attachment Matters project with the staff (Dolby & Swan, 2003) shows that children have become more settled, with lower levels of emotional and behavioural difficulties, and staff have a different view of their relationship with the children — protective rather than focused on control. They have also reported that they enjoy the children more and that the intervention has had a positive impact on staff retention.

Summary

Childcare settings are important environments for children's development, wellbeing and mental health. High quality childcare is beneficial for most children and in particular can provide a holding environment for children and families who find it difficult to make connections and build relationships with each other. When the childcare philosophy is relationship-based, it can provide a 'space' for the child and parent to feel safe, supported and secure. The childcare becomes a secure base and safe haven (Bowlby, 1988). This gives children confidence that someone will be there when they need them, physically and emotionally, and the sense of security for the explorations through which learning can occur.

For parents, the childcare centre can also act as a secure base and safe haven by supporting them in a nonjudgmental manner. This enables them to explore and resolve the struggles they may be having in their lives and so feel more able to provide a secure base and safe haven for their children, and be 'bigger, wiser, stronger and kind'. Once a secure base is established, parents will be ready to allow staff to link them with other organisations and services in the wider community. For parents recovering from mental illness, a childcare-based program provides a safe holding space for parent and child, promoting recovery and teaching new skills. Their infants are observed to benefit from a better and more confident understanding of their needs, in a system which supports the whole family.

References

Aarts, M. (2002). *Marte Meo basic manual.* Harderwijk, Netherlands: Aarts Productions.

Ainsworth, M.D.S., Blehar, M.C., Waters, E., & Wall, S. (1978). *Patterns of attachment: A psychological study of the strange situation.* Hillsdale, N.J.: Erlbaum.

Aylward, P., & O'Neill, M. (2007). *Invest to grow local evaluation report: Through the Looking glass – A community partnbership in parenting.* Retrieved June 16, 2008, from http://www.adelaide.edu.au/health/gp/publications/Interim_Report_ItG_PA.pdf

Bowlby, J. (1988) *A secure base.* London: Routledge.

Cassidy, J., & Shaver, P.R. (1999). *Handbook of attachment: Theory, research & clinical application.* New York: Guilford Press.

Cooper, G., Hoffman, K., Powell, B., & Marvin, R. (2005). The Circle of Security intervention: Differential diagnosis and differential treatment. In L. Berlin, Y. Ziiv, L. Amaya-Jackson & M. Greenberg (Eds.), *Enhancing early attachments: Theory, research, intervention and policy* (pp. 127–151). New York: Guilford Press.

Dolby, R., & Swan, B. (2003). Strengthening relationships between early childhood staff, high needs children and their families in the preschool setting. Developing practice. *The Child, Youth and Family Work Journal,* 6(Autumn) 18–23.

Gerhardt, S. (2004). *Why love matters: How affection shapes a baby's brain.* London: Routledge.

Goldsmith, D.F. (2007). Challenging children's negative internal working models: Utilising attachment-based treatment strategies in a therapeutic preschool. In D. Oppenheim & D.F. Goldsmith, *Attachment theory in clinical work with children: Bridging the gap between resoearch and practice.* New York: Guildford Press.

Guedeney, N. (2005, July). *Listening to a difficult past.* Paper presented at the Clinical Applications of Attachment Conference, Paris.

Hoffman, K., Cooper G., & Powell, B. (2007, August). *The unregulated affect icon and supporting hands illustrations. Building on attachment theory: Developing greater insight into relationships.* Australian Association of Infant Mental Health South Australian Branch workshop, Adelaide, Australia.

Lieberman, A. (1993). *The emotional life of the toddler.* New York: The Free Press.

Marvin, R., Cooper, G., Hoffman, K., & Powell, B. (2002). The Circle of Security Project: Attachment-based intervention with caregiver–preschool dyads. *Attachment and Human Development, 4,* 107–124.

Oxford English Dictionary. (2008). Oxford University Press. Available at 22.askoxford.com/results

Powell, B., Cooper, G., Hoffman, K., & Marvin, R. (2007). The Circle of Security Project. A case study — 'It hurts to give that which you did not receive' In D. Oppenheim & D. Goldsmith, (Eds.), *Attachment theory in clinical work with children* (pp. 172–202). New York: Guilford Press.

Sameroff, A, (1998), Management of clinical problems and emotional care: Environmental risk factors in infancy. *Pediatrics, 102*(5), Suppl., 1287–1292.

Shapiro, J., & Applegate, J. (2002). Child care as a relational context for early development in neurobiology and emerging roles for social work. *Child and Adolescent Social Work Journal, 19,* 97–114.

Siegel, D. (2001). Toward an interpersonal neurobiology of the developing mind: Attachment relationships, 'mindsight', and neural integration. *Infant Mental Health Journal, 22*(1–2), 67–94.

Speltz, M. (1990). The treatment of preschool conduct problems: An integration of behavioural and attachment concepts. In M.T. Greenberg, D. Cicchetti, & E.M. Cummings (Eds.), *Attachment in the preschool years* (pp. 399–426). Chicago: University of Chicago Press.

Stern, D. (2004). The Motherhood Constellation: Therapeutic approaches to early relational problems. In A.J. Sameroff, S.C. McDonough, & K.L. Rosenblum (Eds.), *Treating parent-infant relationship problems: Strategies for intervention* (pp. 29–42). New York: Guilford Press.

Virmani, E.F. (2002). *Supervision and training in child care settings: A comparative study of reflective and traditional methods and their effect on caregivers insightfulness.* Unpublished master's thesis, University of California, Davis, California.

Winnicott, D.W. (1951). Transitional objects and transitional phenomena. *International Journal of Psychoanalysis, 34,* 89–97.

Winnicott, D.W. (1986). *Home is where we start from: Essays by a psychoanalyst.* London: W.W. Norton.

Contributors

Amy (pseudonym) has been a consumer of mental health services for the last 12 years. Prior to being diagnosed with a mental illness she was a qualified nurse working in the aged care sector, and also worked as a therapist for riding for the disabled. More recently she has contributed to professional education and training programs for mental health workers, child protection workers, and other professionals, as well as tertiary students. Amy has a Certificate for Mental Health Support work, and has worked in a community outreach program for some time. She is presently completing a Certificate for Allied Health Assistant. But far and beyond anything else, her best accomplishment is my beautiful, loving, 10-year-old daughter.

Peter Ballard completed social work training both in the United Kingdom and Australia. He has worked for 13 years as Senior Social Worker, Helen Mayo House, Adelaide, where he has a special interest in working with male partners of women with a serious mental illness.

Professor Bryanne Barnett is a child and family psychiatrist and Conjoint Professor at the School of Psychiatry, University of New South Wales, where she completed a doctoral thesis on Maternal Anxiety and Attachment. She is Senior Perinatal and Infant Psychiatrist, Sydney South West Area Health Service, Chairman of the Board at Karitane Early Parenting Centres, and current President of the International Marcé Society. She has been involved in the Perinatal Mental Health Program of the beyondblue national depression initiative since 2001, with a particular interest in cultural aspects, including Aboriginal and Torres Strait Islander Peoples.

Nichola Coombs is an occupational therapist and child psychotherapist. Nichola has worked with infants, children and parents within mental health in the UK, Romania, Bangladesh and Australia. She works at the Alfred Child and Adolescent Mental Health Service in Victoria, and is a Committee Member of the Victorian Branch of the Australian Association of Infant Mental Health.

Vicki Cowling, OAM, is an advocate for children of parents with a mental illness and their families, and has contributed to research, service development, professional education, and publications including editing two books concerning children of parents with mental illness (1999, 2004). Partnerships with consumers, carers and family members are integral to this work. Vicki is a member of the Reference Group for the National Children of Parents with a Mental Illness (COPMI) Initiative.

Dr Robyn Dolby is a psychologist who has worked in the field of Infant Mental Health for thirty years. She works as Senior Research Fellow at the Benevolent Society, coordinates a relationship-based intervention that supports staff, parents and children at preschool, and she runs child observation seminars for child psychiatry trainees at the New South Wales Institute of Psychiatry, a unique collaboration between child psychiatry and early childhood.

Cecilia Ebert works at the Lady Gowrie Child Centre Adelaide Inc. as team leader in the toddler room and part of the Centre's Management team. She also is part of the Gowrie training team delivering training to the Early Childhood Community within Australia. Cecilia was trained as a teacher in Colombia South America. In Australia she completed a Masters Degree in Infant Mental Health with the NSW Institute of Psychiatry.

Sue Ellershaw has qualifications in nursing, midwifery, mental health, health counselling and health service management and has worked as Nursing Unit Head, Perinatal and Infant Mental Health Services of the Children, Youth and Women's Health Service in South Australia for 23 years. She has a passionate interest in the needs of women with mental illness, infant mental health/attachment issues, particularly the need for preventive and early intervention work and in teaching others about postnatal depression, puerperal psychosis and attachment.

Jennifer* (Grandmother of Sam)
* pseudonym

Jennifer has raised two families, and has four children, aged 43, 40, 30 and 28. In the 13 years prior to the events described in this book, she moved to Adelaide and gained two degrees: BA Prof Writing and Comms (Uni SA), and BScEnvSc (Flinders). The intention was to write books for children about the environment.

Lynly Mader is an Infant Mental Health Therapist and Senior Occupational Therapist within the Perinatal and Infant Mental Health Service of the Child, Youth and Women's Health Service in Adelaide. She has worked within mental health services for over 20 years, the majority of this time within Helen Mayo House services, and holds a commitment to working with parents facing multiple stressors and social inequalities.

Dr Sarah Mares is a child and family psychiatrist with interests in the psychiatry of infancy and early childhood, transgenerational issues in parenting and assessment of parenting and risk. She is currently the Head of Infant and Early Childhood Studies at the NSW Institute of Psychiatry. She is coauthor with Professor Louise Newman and Beulah Warren of Clinical Skills in Infant Mental Health (ACER Press 2005), and coeditor with Professor Newman of Acting from the Heart: Australian Advocates for Asylum Seekers Tell Their Stories (Finch, 2007).

Paola Mason is an Adult Child who cares for a Parent with a Mental Illness. Her parent became unwell when she was 6 years of age. Paola is now 48. She is Co-Convenor COMIC (Children of Mentally Ill Consumers) www.howstat. com/comic and Project Officer at the COPMI (Children of Parents with a Mental Illness) National Initiative www.copmi.net.au. Paola lobbies and advocates for better services for children and their parents within her role as Co-Convenor. Her work with the COPMI National Initiative entails mental health community liaison.

Dr Jennifer McIntosh is Director, Family Transitions, and Adjunct Associate Professor, School of Public Health, La Trobe University. Jenn is a clinical psychologist and family therapist. She trained at the University of Melbourne and the Tavistock Clinic, London. Her research interests include foster care, the impacts on children of attachment disturbance and divorce trauma.

Anne Mercovich is Assistant Manager Child Protection, Eastern Metropolitan Region, Department of Human Services Victoria. Anne is a social worker who has worked with the Department of Human Services since 1979. Her major work has been in the field of operational child protection work and service planning. She has managed a regional High Risk Infant program and, more recently, Intake and Response Units that receive and investigate reports of child abuse and neglect. During 2006 Anne was a panel member for a group analysis titled 'Tackling SIDS — A Community Responsibility', which reported to the Victorian Child Death Review Committee examining sudden infant death (SIDS) risk factors in the child protection population and strategies to minimise the risk of SIDS among high-risk and hard-to-reach families.

Associate Professor Helen Milroy is a descendant of the Palyku people of the Pilbara region of Western Australia, born and educated in Perth. Helen worked as a general practitioner and consultant in childhood sexual abuse before completing specialist training in child and adolescent psychiatry. Helen is a member of the Royal Australian and New Zealand College of Psychiatry committee for Aboriginal and Torres Strait Islander Mental Health through which she has contributed to the development of position statements, guidelines and curriculum on Indigenous mental health. Helen works as a consultant child and adolescent psychiatrist and is Director for the Centre for Aboriginal Medical and Dental Health (CAMDH) at University of Western Australia

Professor Louise Newman is the Chair of Perinatal and Infant Psychiatry at the University of Newcastle and the previous Director of the New South Wales Institute of Psychiatry. Professor Newman is a practicing infant psychiatrist with expertise in the area of disorders of early parenting and attachment difficulties in infants. She has undertaken research into the issues confronting parents with borderline personality disorder and histories of early trauma and the impact on infant development. Her current research is focusing on the evaluation of infant–parent interventions in high-risk populations.

Associate Professor Campbell Paul is Coordinator, Infant Mental Health Group, Royal Children's Hospital Mental Health Service, Melbourne and Honorary Principal Fellow, Department of Psychiatry, University of Melbourne. As a consultant infant psychiatrist, he has been involved in establishing the hospital-based clinical infant mental program, the University of Melbourne postgraduate training courses in infant mental health, and a consultative program in Victoria for those working with parents with major metal illness who have a young infant. He has been a Regional Vice President of the World Association for Infant Mental Health, and was also involved in setting up the Koori Kids Mental Health Network in Melbourne.

Dr Ros Powrie is a child and adolescent psychiatrist who has a special interest in perinatal and infant psychiatry, trauma and transcultural psychiatry and is Head of the Perinatal and Infant Mental Health Team at Womens and Children's Hospital, Children, Youth and Women's Health Service in South Australia.

Dr Susan Priest is a practising clinical psychologist and researcher specialising in perinatal mental health issues (maternal and infant mental health; fertility/infertility and ART; reproductive health; services development) and consulting in Sydney and in Coffs Harbour, New South Wales. She is also engaged in perinatal research projects and research student supervision and holds positions as Conjoint Senior Lecturer in the School of Medicine and Public Health at The University of Newcastle (Australia) in the new Perinatal Psychiatry Program, and as Visiting Fellow in the School of Public Health and Community Medicine at The University of New South Wales.

Mandy Seyfang is an infant mental health therapist, Helen Mayo House Services and Psychiatry, Women's and Babies Division, Children, Youth and Women's Health Service, Adelaide. This role includes supporting workers in the community who work with vulnerable families, and working to enhance the attachment relationship between mothers and babies where mothers struggle with significant mental health issues. As a lecturer at the University of South Australia she teaches health workers at the undergraduate level.

Dr Julie Stone is a child and family psychiatrist whose clinical passion is working with very young children and their families. She has a special interest in supporting colleagues working with distressed children and families involved with the child protection system. Julie is an alumni fellow of Zero to Three.

Sally Watson has worked as a social worker for nearly 25 years in a variety of settings, including child protection, community health, hospitals and child and adolescent mental health. Sally has been in her current position for 6 years, with the Through the Looking Glass project, at Lady Gowrie Child Centre in Adelaide. Sally has reliability rating status in the Adult Attachment Interview, and has participated in a significant amount of other attachment related training. Sally is married with three children aged 13, 10 and 8.

Dr Anne Sved Williams is the Director, Perinatal and Infant Mental Health Services, Children, Youth and Women's Health Services, South Australia and Clinical Senior Lecturer in Psychiatry, University of Adelaide. Anne trained in family therapy at the Ackerman Institute in New York, and in psychiatry. Her major work foci have included perinatal and infant psychiatry particularly as a trainer, general practitioner training and support systems in psychiatry.

Nichole Whiting is a 39-year-old mother of two boys aged 15 and 11. Nichole has a diagnosis of bipolar affective disorder and has had admissions to psychiatric hospitals since she was 17. For the past 3 years Nichole has worked as a consumer advocate at the James Fletcher, Maitland and Morisset Hospitals, in New South Wales, supporting the emotional wellbeing and the rights of people with a mental illness.

Kevin Williams is a 32-year-old air force engineer. He and his partner, Maureen, have a 4-year-old boy, Gabrial, and a 1-year-old girl, Estelle. Maureen is 35 and formerly worked as a banking manager and trainer.

Index